C000192970

Illuminati Hunter

III

ISBN 978-1-914195-80-8
Illuminati Hunter.com

'Truly amazing adventure. Exciting, intriguing, funny, addictive, this stella trilogy has it all!'

Al Wardle, Area Manager West Holts Jazz World Stage Glastonbury Festival 2009-2014.

Original book photographed 2012.

ISBN 978-1-914195-80-8

Book layout and design by Ethan Harrison. Production management by UKBookPublishing.Com.

Foreword

After the successful republication of Illuminati Hunter, the original of which I found in a secondhand book shop, I was contacted by the great granddaughter of the owner of Necromancer, the English publishers that first printed it in 1913. To my surprise she told me that she had come across the two subsequent volumes planned for serialisation which never saw the light of day and, after a quick negotiation, they came into my hands. As with the first book, after this brief introduction, the following text, aside from the addition of the footnotes and the rear appendix, is an exact reprint of the last episode of these extraordinary and previously unreleased volumes.

There are many reasons which inspired me to republish this book. Mainly because, like the first two, it is a marvellous read written in a surprisingly modern style that I am sure readers will appreciate. But also, as with its predecessors, when I checked the details of the story on the internet I found that many of the claims, however unbelievable, were backed up by existing records or so close that it is impossible to believe they could all be coincidence. Hence the footnotes so you can see for yourself.

If the story contained within these volumes is true then it would throw an entirely new light on what is already an enthralling period of history. I am sure that you will find it fascinating, especially if you explore the E Book links or the website addresses in the paperback's appendix. I hope that you enjoy researching the background of this exciting adventure as much as I have and, of course, that you are thrilled by the incredible story itself.

E. Harrison 2021

ILLUMINATI
HUNTER
III

Count Bassus & The Statue of Baphomet

By Sebastian P. Drechsler

Published in Great Britain by Necromancer Press 1913.

Introduction

This volume is formed from a collection of memoirs discovered in 1898 at the University of Munich in Bavaria. Sebastian Pierre Drechsler was a student and eventually lecturer at Ingolstadt University between 1783 – 1800, before the faculty was closed down. He later went on to become Professor and then Director of History at Munich University until he retired in 1833. It is understood that the original memoirs were dictated by the scholar on his deathbed (circa 1852) and that he had not wanted them to come to the public's attention for 'some time' after he died so as not to besmirch his fine reputation achieved after many years working within academe. He was on record to have made claim that they would be valuable 'To those in the future who are already illuminated, or are ready to come into the light.' It should also be noted that the transcript was dictated to an Englishman, a court stenographer by trade, who was not fluent in the Bavarian tongue but the far-sighted Professor had understood that his scribe's natural dialect was fast becoming the international language of the world and so by means of this translation would secure the text's widest readership when it eventually saw the light of day. This detail and the fact that it is a vocal record would explain the sound effects, British measurements, occasional vernacular and the constant personal observations of a humorous nature.

A. Jones, Editor Necromancer Press. 1913

From a loving Father to a brilliant Son

'Know Thyself'

'Gnothi Seauton'

I, Sebastian Drechsler, write these memoirs in the year 1853 from the bed in which I shall die. I write them as testimony to my actions and those of others, so that these efforts are not wasted in the abyss of unrecorded time. I swear to my almighty God that, though at times they may sound unbelievable, the story I tell is the truth, the whole truth and nothing but the truth. I pray that the text has survived as long as I have intended before coming to the public's attention and that the incredible tale you are about to read no longer contains a very necessary warning for the world. But if that is the case then may God Almighty have mercy on your souls.

No great story is without great sorrow or great joy. For, only by possessing both these elemental opposites can it be truly great. I believe our best hope as mortals and, as such, the authors of the stories of our own lives, is that, in the end, these two conflicting states become, at least, equal. If only in as much that we finally learn, though it is often hard to truly understand why, one cannot exist without the other. I truly believe that the next part of my awesome tale is one such story. I do not say this in vanity or with an overly-inflated view of my own opinions, I simply know that because it contains both these aspects, in such depth and equal measure then, in some way, it must be great.

Chapter 1

Celebrations and Tribulations

A wise man once told me that as we age our sweetest memories become like fine meals upon which we can always feast. With this adage in mind, I will begin the next chapter of my tale on a night exactly such as this: New Year's Eve 1786. Though it was almost seventy years ago, I still see it as clear as through crystal glass. For that night, as the last few minutes of that momentous year ticked away, it was the best of times. Oh yes, it was the best of times.

Being but a simple student, soon to be twenty-two, recently sent from a simple village by loving but deeply superstitious parents to be educated at the distinguished University of Ingolstadt during the transformational Age of Reason, I had expected to be educated, yes, to be intrigued, hopefully, and to be worked hard but made better by the experience, eventually. More importantly, like any other Bavarian buck, whilst maintaining the pretence of great courtesy and observing strict social protocol with typical Teutonic precision, highly amused and thoroughly debauched in the process, most definitely. But nothing on God's green Earth could have prepared me for the transformation to my fates that my journey had brought about.

For, a little more than two years later, I was on top of the world. How could I have come to any other conclusion? There I was, perched on top a wind-ravaged, snow-capped peak some twenty miles from Ingolstadt, ensconced within the walls of a mighty castle: The Castle Landfried no less (the finest building that I had ever seen) where I was celebrating Christmas in the finery of the grand banqueting hall along with the cheerful staff and the extraordinary new companions who had helped me on my way.

To top it all I was sitting upon a throne. Though, admittedly, this last detail was due to the household's tradition of Roman Saturnalia practised at this time of year where masters become servants and vice versa. I watched the happy souls exchanging gifts around the fire from my lavish pew and took stock of the many adventures that had led me to this wonderful place. Christmas has always been my favourite time of year: the goodwill, the songs, the holidays, as little religion as possible and, of course, all the copious drinking and eating. That Christmas, in particular, I had every reason for celebration and to be truly thankful.

For I was alive. This may seem a strange thing for an ordinary student to expect at Christmas but, by this stage, I was far from an ordinary student. Somehow, and only God really knew, I had survived a series of incredible ordeals to eventually come out the victor in a seemingly never-ending fight to the death against the sinister and powerful Illuminati and played my part in foiling their diabolical plans to rule the world. To achieve these most heroic accomplishments, I first had to escape the clutches of my old lecturer at Ingolstadt University, chief Illuminati instigator Adam Weishaupt, more times than I could count, before ensuring his eventual downfall and the sect's banishment from Bavaria. After performing this miracle, through several twists and turns, I had ended up slaying the man who first indoctrinated Weishaupt into the Order; the merchant, Franz Kolmer. I drowned that fiend with my bare hands in a freezing river halfway to Russia.

During this short but turbulent period, I had also survived encounters with an indestructible zombie General, a monstrous dog from Hell, fiendish traps, terrifying rituals, lightning strikes, countless Illuminati hooded sentinels, numerous assassination attempts, several death-defying coach chases, phantasmal ghouls including 'The Eye of Horus,' deadly duels, sword fights, court cases, torture machines, faulty weaponry, rigged exams, poisonings, orgies, hours of gruelling training in the dark arts of the Illuminati Hunter, the constant jibes of my beloved and, of course, all the usual homework, bills, rent and sundries of your average eighteenth century student. Crucially, I had also outlived many of my contemporaries; some innocent, some not so, and witnessing the destruction of many, many lives, guilty or not, had had the most earnest effect on me. *[1]

Though in equal measure with the bad, these profound experiences had brought me great joy and personal satisfaction and, along with a growing sense of worthiness on my way to graduating and, hopefully, becoming a gentleman, a strong orientation of what was right and wrong. They had also allowed me to amass a small fortune far greater than I had ever imagined accruing in my life, let alone by the age of twenty one, and far greater than that of even my hard working parents.

And, all this in the service of my master and his life's work: to rid the earth of the evil Order. As these thoughts coalesced my eyes naturally fell upon him: my master. My tutor, employer, friend, sometime saviour, sometime agitator but always my beguiling guide through the many layers of understanding to true Illumination, the truly awesome Professor Van Halestrom.

---

1. **Adam Weishaupt & The Bavarian Illuminati.** Widely regarded as the Grandfather of modern conspiracy, Adam Weishaupt was the founder member of the Bavarian Illuminati in 1776. He was Dean of Faculty of Canon Law at influential Ingolstadt University, (the romantic setting for Mary Shelley's *Frankenstein*), but was sacked in February 1785 under new laws banning secret societies throughout Bavaria and he subsequently fled to nearby Regensburg after incriminating Illuminati documents revealing the society's plans for power were seized by the authorities when messenger Jakob Lanz was struck by lightning and killed. The Merchant Kolmer was a mysterious German merchant from Jutland who spent many years in Egypt studying and trading ancient artefacts and was commonly believed to have initiated Weishaupt into the darker hermetic mystery school religions.

The one man, without whom, none of my remarkable story would ever have happened. For it was he, some two and a half years before, in his office at the University, who had first initiated me into this twilight world. His eagle eyes spotted me watching him on his stool and he chuckled from behind his greying beard and a cloud of pipe smoke, "Having fun, Sebastian? It's your turn next I think. Now Bacon has a surprise for *you*."

His ancient but learned servant, originally of English stock but who had adopted Bavaria as his own and now spoke our dialect fluently (as well as many, many others), rose from his dining chair and condescendingly sniffed his master's smoke, "If I may venture my humble opinion, sir. As everyone else has already received a gift and there is only one left, it will hardly come as a surprise, even to Master Drechsler, that it is for him?"

"Granted, old friend," humoured Van Halestrom, nursing his outstretched, bandaged leg, "But what is it eh?"

There had been a time when I had not understood the Professor's indulgence of his servant's grating sarcasm. But that was before I knew the servant was, in reality, the master. Not only of the house, but of our entire clandestine organisation and that his servitude was mere pretence. Now I understood that these enigmatic gentlemen were never more at ease than when mocking convention - and each other - in this way and revelled in such role reversal. A habit which also extended to the evening's festivities.

Bacon picked up the small wooden box from the table and cleared his throat as if about to address King Ludwig himself. His solemn stare fell upon me and he portentously announced, "As you know, sir, in accordance with our Saturnalian tradition, the master of the house should naturally be giving you this." He cast a withering eye over the Professor's injured leg and his walking stick and ungraciously sighed, "But as we all know he has chosen to cripple himself on his two-wheeled death trap."

"*Bi rota*. I keep telling you *bi rota*: Two wheels, two wheels" protested Van Halestrom and assured us all, "The invention will revolutionise the world. Once I fix the steering. You wait and see."

"I know what I said, sir," continued the confounding old rascal, "So, once again, on my only day off of the year, I suppose the burden of its safe and punctual delivery falls upon me."

Much to the children's delight, and his master's exasperation, Bacon exaggerated his usual plodding walk as he had done giving everyone their presents and eventually gave me the gift along with his usual derisive sniff before slowly returning to his chair in the same humorous but painstaking fashion.

I foolishly asked, "What is it then?"

"As you will, no doubt, have noticed, sir, the inclusion of the lid on the top renders its contents a secret to the uninitiated, hence the term; *surprise*. Yet do not fear, sir" he ground on, "This seemingly insurmountable obstacle can be overcome by simply unfastening the clasp holding it in place."

Such was the length of his tedious admonishment that he had already sat down by the time he had finished but, as such, had not seen me pulling my most facetious face behind his back. (Please gentle reader do not be troubled by these apparently harsh exchanges: It was simply the way we spoke to each other.)

"Don't be silly, Sebastian. Open it," coaxed the sweet voice beside me, it's provocative French accent stirring the deepest embers of my soul. I stared into the big brown eyes of the last, and best, of my new companions: my love, my muse, my queen, the only one who ever truly won my heart, from Russian nobility no less, but educated in France, courageous fellow Illuminati Hunter and soon-to-be-mother of my child. The dearest, tantalizing, sometimes infuriating but always delectable, Lady Francesca Nicola Kropotkin.

My senses soared as they always did when I beheld her wondrous beauty. A beauty further intensified by the glowing flush of impending motherhood. Our thrones were close enough together for me to gently lay a hand on her growing belly and, as I revelled in her unfathomable gorgeousness, I mused that even if the box contained the keys to the Bank of England and all the other banks in the world and all the palaces and all the treasure locked within them it would not be as valuable to me as her.

"Open it silly. Everyone is waiting."

This was true. Her eyes flashed around at the expectant faces and even Van Halestrom flustered, "Come on, come on, Sebastian. I've been putting off giving everyone their gifts for days now. It is a tradition I do not like to break." He waggled his pipe, "Well? Cook has her pots and new knives. The maids have their hair clasps and thick gloves and stockings. Klaus has a barrow for the garden and a stout hat to keep his head warm. Willy has a new bridle for Jutta as her old one has worn out. I have my walking cane, Francesca has her wonderful earrings, Bacon his glasses and the children all have their toys. So..? What do you have?"

I looked down at the box and he blustered, "Mighty Socrates would lose his patience. Open it!"

Well they had said it was a surprise and surprise it was. For when I did open it I found, laying upon a fitted black velvet cushion, an exquisite silver pocket watch. This incredible object was worth a fortune in itself: enough to buy not only one house but a row of houses, even a small village. Such was the novelty of the technologies that fifty years before only kings or popes could attain such wonders. I carefully lifted it up on its chain and held my other hand underneath just in case - God forbid - I dropped the treasure. There was a hushed gasp from all the staff and the children and even some excited cooing from the maids.

"There is an inscription on the back," prompted Van Halestrom, pointing his pipe at the timepiece and blowing out a loop of smoke. I turned it over and read out the engraving in the candlelight, "'Tempus est semper.' There... is...always... time..." I trailed off, utterly overwhelmed by the gesture.

"As usual your Latin is faultless, Herr Drechsler," smiled Van Halestrom, "Which just goes to show that an expensive education is never wasted on a true scholar. Now, before you get carried away, it is not new but belonged to Bacon before I had it and, now, *we* feel that it's time for *you* to have it." He nodded at the grand old clock at the end of the room. "It should be spot on. All the clocks in this house are precisely on time. Which is one tradition I refuse to break." He flicked his eyebrows and grinned, "Now you have no excuse for being late eh?"

"I do not know what to say, sir," I mumbled.

Francesca nudged me fiercely in the ribs and quipped, "I believe *thank you* is traditional at times such as these. Even in Russia. No?" She said this last part in a faux Russian accent to intensify my humiliation. It worked like a charm and brought me to my senses.

"Thank you, Professor, and... to you too... Bacon. Happy Christmas." I opened the wonder like an oyster and thrilled at the extraordinary craftsmanship. The face was fittingly laced with mother of pearl and it even had a calendar displaying the date!

"It is... incredible, sir," I gasped in dumbstruck awe.

"For once I have to agree with you, darling," hummed Francesca, shifting around next to me to get a better view and pouted at the Professor, "I have to admit, I am a little envious."

"My dear, I'm sure, being a countess yourself, you have no end of expensive clocks, timepieces, sundials, hourglasses and all manner of expensive chronological paraphernalia scattered around one palace or another. One more would make no difference but your earrings, on the other hand, are an exception." He blew out another ring of rolling smoke, leant forward on his stool and like a storyteller of old weaved the tale for us. "One ruby originates from the mines of distant California where the Pacific Ocean laps at the edges of the known world. The other is a matching gem from the deepest, darkest jungles of Sumatra where no European soul has yet set foot. No woman, in either the West or the East since the days of forgotten Atlantis, has ever possessed jewellery from such far-flung corners of the earth."

We all cooed as Francesca turned her swan-like neck first one way then the other to show off the exotic jewels. She seemed satisfied so he turned the subject of his banter onto me.

"Honestly, Sebastian, you looked at that box as though there was a bomb inside and it was going to blow your head clean off. Boom!" he roared at the children even scaring some of the little ones. Though everyone laughed they had no idea that it was a secret joke and that he *had* given me exactly such a box during one of my training exercises only a few short months before that had, indeed, almost blown my 'head clean off.'

He threw me a sly wink turning my frown to a smile and everyone joined in with the laughter as though we were all one big, happy family: old and young, masters and servants, great and small, rich and poor, all in loving union under a single roof.

It was typical of the charmed spirit that pervaded the castle. A spirit which showed scant regard for the normal social standards of the day, of which there were countless and all completely unnecessary. And on that night it was a spirit which I appreciated with great tenderness and much sincere heartfelt affection. I regarded the happy faces around the fireside and sighed with perfect contentment then decided there on the spot, with all considerations complete, all was well. Yes indeed! All was well.

And this is the sweet memory that I still savour to this day. That particular moment: New Year's Eve 1786, a point in time made even more lustrous in retrospect for I now realise that it was the very last final shimmering hurrah of the mighty renaisance, sitting there with Francesca on our grand chairs with everyone happily gathered round the fireplace at the Castle Landfried and watching the hands of my superb new timepiece matching those of the grand old clock in the banqueting hall, counting down the last minutes before 1787. How lucky I felt to be alive and to have all my nightmare experiences behind me. I was safe, happy, loved, even healthy and wealthy and, though perhaps not completely wise, secure in what flimsy knowledge I did possess that if I had died at that very moment, at least once in my life, I had been perfectly satisfied.

I raised the wonderful gift to my ear and heard its ingenious mechanism tick softly just once, before the merriment in the room was broken by the pounding of approaching hooves.

Chapter 2

Who Goes There?

An even wiser old man once told me that you should never refuse a meal, fine or otherwise, because you never know when you might eat again. That is why one magical, bright memory ends here and a darker one begins. Unless you're being rescued, the pounding of approaching hooves can only mean one thing: trouble. A great deal of experience in this field had instantly led me to the conclusion that this particular set fell squarely into this most singular category. Not many souls ventured to this isolated place, not even on New Year's Eve, but I could already hear the unmistakable clatter of coach wheels rattling up the heavily snowbound track to the castle, convincing me that the driver, or whoever was inside, was either extremely determined or slightly deranged. As the sound grew louder the light-heartedness in the room disappeared and in a flurry of activity the maids and servants collected their children and gifts and hastily departed to their quarters.

"Open the gates!" called Van Halestrom and faithful Willy the groundsman, pelted from the room to release the vital lever operating the machinery to open the gate. Van Halestrom, Bacon, Francesca and myself came together by the fire and I questioned, "Why open the gates? We don't know who it is. It could be an enemy."

"Do you really think an enemy would mount an attack tonight? Now? One carriage? In the dark? Charging up the road and announcing their presence to everyone inside?"

"No, no, no," I huffed, annoyed at not having thought this through.

"No. In this particular case," he pondered, "Intuition tells me someone is in need of our help."

"Who could it be, Professor?" wondered Francesca as we heard the carriage roar through the opened gates and the driver urge the horses up the short road leading to the courtyard.

"There is but one way to find out," he concluded and set off with his usual haste only to have to limp awkwardly and lean heavily on his cane. Francesca came to his aid, supporting his arm and old Bacon brought up the rear so I grabbed the biggest candlestick I could find and led the charge.

Willy was ready by the front door when I arrived and I gave him a nod to withdraw the bolts. A flurry of snow blew inside as he swung back the door and I tugged my dining jacket around me and held the spluttering candlestick into the doorway. Sure enough, in the shadows at the base of the stone stairs, a team of eight horses stood panting in front of a large dark carriage.

"Who goes there?" I called out to the silhouetted driver.

There was an unsettling pause before he shouted back amidst the whining wind, "My master will be with you shortly!"

At that moment the door on the far side of the carriage banged open followed by a rumble of curses crude enough to make a pirate blush before and an agitated figure emerged from the shadows appearing to have a problem with his trousers. He noticed me watching him from the door and stopped to finish whatever he was doing, swore profusely, refastened his cloak, rubbed his hands together and made his way up the stairs.

"Hello there, Christian," he halloed breathlessly as he came up out of the gloom.

For some reason I answered without thinking, "How do you know I am Christian, sir?"

Whoever it was sounded most indignant to hear this and pompously rumbled, "Are we not all Christian?" before appearing in front of me in a flurry of snowflakes.

Well, I did not recognise the man from the town butcher.

He was clearly a gentleman of some standing and perhaps even handsome back in his day, but now a more haggard and dishevelled man I had rarely seen. He was big, as tall as me but slovenly portly and, though I guessed he was around fifty, looked more like sixty. He had greasy unkempt hair and four days of stubble covering a face which displayed all the telltale marks of heavy drinking and possessed perhaps the most untrustworthy pair of eyes that I had ever seen. There was obviously something deeply questionable going on behind them and I knew right there and then that I was in the presence of a rogue.

He was also agitated and impatiently observed, "You, I think, are not the master of the house," and peered rudely over my shoulder presumably searching for Van Halestrom.

Disregarding my usual politeness, especially when answering the door of another man's house, I was about to tell the rogue to go to the next castle down the road when he noticed my displeasure and, realising propriety probably his best approach given the present circumstances, promptly excused himself, "Ah. Yes. Of course. Forgive me, Christian," he coughed and tried to arrange his messy hair, "Let me introduce myself. I am Canon Priest Jacob Danzer."

Gadzooks! He was a canon priest? Even Jesus of Nazareth would have been horrified, especially had he heard him curse. Though it explained his dismay upon hearing me blaspheme. Seeing that I was still not fully convinced he unclasped his cloak to reveal a grubby set of robes, a crucifix and a tangled rosary.

Damn it. He must have left his filthy hat in the carriage. Mortified to have insulted a man of the cloth I ushered him over the threshold and awkwardly offered my excuses, "So sorry, so sorry, Canon Danzer. I had no idea." Then I did what any young man would who had suffered years of church attendance at the hands of over pious parents; like a fool, I made the sign of the cross and took his hand to kiss.

"No, no, no. That won't be necessary," he balked and yanked away his hand which I was horrified to see him sniff. Willy shared my bewilderment and offered a half-hearted bow but the Canon urged him away too, "Not necessary, not necessary," before giving his fingers another furtive sniff and flinching in disgust.

Well this *man of the church* was a character for sure. I had known a few odd clerics before, but this one was definitely the most eccentric. He was clearly drunk. He reeked of brandy and some other pungent substances the origins of which I was less sure. Though, one thing was certain: they were not from any church that I had visited recently. Not that I had visited a church recently.

In the nick of time the Professor welcomed from the hallway, "Ah, Canon Danzer!".

"Ah ha. Now comes the master of the house," crowed Danzer and edged past my candlestick, fawning, "Please, Professor, you must call me Joseph." At last the rogue shook someone's hand but I made a mental note to tell Van Halestrom to wash his afterwards.

"Sebastian is the master of the house now," insisted the Professor, "At least while it takes me this long to answer the door."

I brimmed with pride at being awarded this new badge of honour and obediently closed the door as the Professor attended to the social niceties, "Bacon you have already met Canon Priest Joseph Jacob Danzer: Dean of the faculty of Salzburg University, lecturer on Catholic morality and most trusted friend of our organisation."

"*Catholic morality*?" I mumbled to myself as Danzer bowed to Bacon. I reflected that it would take all sorts to fight the Illuminati and tried to reserve judgement for another day.

I was pondering whether I would ever get to meet all our strange band of allies when the Canon's beady eyes lit up as they fell on Francesca and he hungrily enquired, "Have we met before, my dear? You seem... vaguely familiar."

"Yes," responded Francesca as cold as the draft coming under the door and rudely crossed her arms.

"I see," flinched Danzer, seemingly incriminated and withdrawing his hand.

'What's this?' I wondered, 'These two are acquainted?'

The Professor broke the tension. "Tell us, my friend, what brings you here? You know you can always confide in us."

Willy knowingly made himself scarce and Danzer watched him go before eyeing us all and quizzing the Professor, "Are they safe?"

"Yes. They are safe," patiently confirmed Van Halestrom.

The priest seemed satisfied with this coded answer but now, instead of telling us why he was there, closed his eyes and began drumming his fingers on his lips. He slipped into a deep rumination in which his fingers became a blur before he suddenly opened his eyes, stared straight at the Professor and ominously stated, "I have found The Book of Servants."

"Where?" Exclaimed Van Halestrom with such ferocity that I almost dropped my candlestick.

Francesca sprang to the Professor's side and excitedly rallied, "With The Book of Servants in our hands we can smash this barrel of vipers once and for all."

"This is indeed excellent news," chimed Bacon. "It is the last missing piece of the puzzle."

I held up the candlestick to scan their intense faces for any clue as to what The Book of Servants might be. Alas there was none and a blob of wax fell on my hand causing me to loudly suppress a curse.

Ignoring my vexations Danzer kept his eyes firmly fixed on Van Halestrom and said. "It is in a place but ten miles away. But I cannot get it alone. So you must accompany me there now."

I am sure he would have left that very moment had the Professor not cautioned, "Unfortunately, my friend, I feel it may be impossible for me to go anywhere tonight. Though I am willing my leg is not."

In his haste Danzer had not noticed the Professor's injuries and an awkward silence reigned while he regarded the bandage and walking stick. When it finally sank in he raised his hands to his face as if going to pray then without warning spun on his heel, crouched down and furiously yelled, "Bugger the Saints!"

Even Van Halestrom was shocked by this outburst and offered, "Please calm yourself, Joseph. We will find a solution."

Danzer's mind was already elsewhere and now his eyes dwelt on me like an undertaker measuring a corpse for a coffin. A sly smirk spread across his fevered face as he quibbled, "Then pray, does not the *master of the house* have two willing legs?"

Damn this unwelcome, untrustworthy priest. I wished to slip into the shadows like a ghost but this is impossible when holding a huge candlestick and slowly, one by one, all eyes fell on me.

Loyal Francesca attempted to come to my rescue and declared, "I will do it, Monsieur. Where do I have to go?" She stepped forward punching her fist into her hand for good measure. But I knew it was useless. She was clearly pregnant and even a screaming coward like me would rather go than let her do it.

The Professor spoke on the side of rationality. "No, Francesca. This is no job for a woman, especially a woman who is to be a mother." He put out a protective arm in front of her.

Danzer agreed, "That's right, my dear. No place for a lady of your..." his eyes swivelled before he carefully chose, "... Disposition."

"I knew it!" spat Francesca lashing out like a cornered cat. "If it is no place for a lady of my *disposition* then it is no place for a man: especially a-man-who-is-going-to-be-a-father."

She defiantly put her fists on her hips while we all traded glances until I foolishly spoke, "Perhaps she's right?" All eyes fell back on me and I wished that I had remained silent.

Van Halestrom attempted to break the stalemate and ventured, "You understand the importance of The Book of Servants, my dear."

She looked forlornly at him then back at me and before I could say anything else, to either defend or incriminate myself, Bacon nodded in solemn accord, "It would be a great coup for us, sir. I truly believe it could mean the Order's final destruction in Bavaria."

I raised a finger to air a contrary opinion but this time Danzer beat me to it. "It is only a simple errand, good Christian. No harm will come to you... I promise," he stumbled. This unconvincing afterthought seemed unnecessary as he was already certain that he had secured my unwilling help and grinned like a frog that had swallowed a fly.

"Mon Dieu! I'm not happy about this. Not at all," complained Francesca and turned to Danzer, demanding, "Where are you taking him?"

"Taking me?" I fretted, feeling like a pig off to the abattoir. For I too shared my Lady's displeasure at the idea of going anywhere on this cold, dark night further than fetching a couple of logs from the woodpile. But as I looked between their serious expressions my heart sank as I realised that it was already too late. They had made up their minds. It had to be me. Curses.

"All right, I will go. I will go," I conceded, "But for the love of God will someone please tell me what is The Book of Servants?"

Danzer had no time to explain and lurched back by the door to boom orders at his driver.

Van Halestrom shook his head and said, "I am disappointed, Sebastian. What do you think *The Book of Servants* could be?"

He searched my eyes for any sign of understanding. Unfortunately, there was none and I rattled, "How would I know? That's why I asked." I flustered momentarily before arranging my thoughts aloud, "I guess it's... a book?"

I knew this part had to be right but quickly continued before anyone could sarcastically comment and managed to manifest, "Containing... the names of... Illuminati *servants*?"

Van Halestrom nodded promisingly and made a circle with his finger prompting me to continue.

"So... if we have the book we can find out who they are and... expose them all?"

"Bravo, sir, bravo," concluded Bacon, "However, there is one critical factor you did not deduce, sir. The book also contains the agent's codenames which will allow us to properly decipher their messages and finally identify them all." He put his hand on my shoulder and added with some sincerity, "Well done, sir. I have never witnessed your bravery at first hand but, I must say, I found it quite inspirational."

Worryingly, he said this with no hint of sarcasm whatsoever.

Before I could tell him how much this troubled me Danzer impatiently warned us, "Hurry, hurry. Time is not on our side," and hovered by the door, chomping at the bit to get going.

The Professor's leg may have been half broken but there was nothing wrong with his lungs and he hollered, "Willy! Bring some warm clothes for, Sebastian!" with such vigour that I was almost deafened. In a flash the indispensable Willy returned with a thick fur coat, some boots and a hat and Francesca helped me to get dressed like a mother readying her son to go to war, while all the time demanding Danzer tell her, once and for all, where we were going. After he brushed her off for the umpteenth time suggesting that it was somewhere 'a lady of her high station would prefer not to visit' she finally lost her patience with him.

"A brothel! You're taking the father of my unborn child to a brothel aren't you? Why don't you just say so you pathetic man? I knew it. Damn you, Danzer. Damn you to Hell and back!"

And so began my first day of 1787. After a storm of advice about how to get home if an accident befell us, and how to read the stars if this awful situation transpired, and how, if I even as much as looked at any of the harlots, not to bother, before I knew it I was being pushed down the stone stairway into the courtyard clutching my hat and fur coat.

With the love of my life passionately remonstrating behind me, "How dare you try to justify letting that despicable *priest* take the father of my unborn child to a brothel!" Danzer bundled me into the waiting carriage. His driver cracked the whip, skilfully brought the team of horses round in the icy courtyard then charged them down the short road toward the castle's open gate. *²

---

2. **Illuminati Codenames & Secret Documents.** The Bavarian Illuminati, being a secret society, used codes and codenames for much of its correspondence and for all clandestine messages. Agents adopted codenames usually taken from Roman or Greek antiquity especially those associated with antipathy toward Rome. Illuminati leader Adam Weishaupt famously chose the codename Spartacus, the Spartan general and ex-gladiator who led the slave mutiny against Rome in 270 B.C. Inevitably, the Illuminati was compromised by the seizure of incriminating documents. Notably, in 1784, when Illuminati messenger, Jakob Lanz, was killed by a lightning strike while delivering secret papers which were then found by the authorities and in 1786, when the residence of chief government lawyer and fellow Illuminati agent Xavier Zwack, codename Cato, was raided by police who seized many documents copies of which were later circulated by the authorities in an attempt to alert the public and other governments to the secret society's conspiracy.

Chapter 3

Madame Zukkerburg's

I am sure, because I have met such fellows, that many men thrill at the thought of visiting a brothel. However, I would like to assure women everywhere that there will always be many of us, who do not. I am unequivocally of this second persuasion. For, to tell the truth, I find it one of the most vulgar and embarrassing experiences on earth and would always rather spend an unhappy hour visiting the dentist. That is merely visiting a brothel mind, not actually indulging myself in one which is an act too gross to even consider and I would honestly rather be buried alive.

Though I had known mad-eyed Danzer for only half of one hour, I strongly suspected him to be of the first persuasion. Accordingly, with our dissolute quest underway, his spirits had lifted somewhat, though he was still obviously possessed by an overriding obsession to get the book. His driver seemed to share his eagerness and drove the team of horses down the twisty, snow-bound track from the castle at such breakneck speed that it was impossible to keep my balance and I was being fairly thrown across my seat.

"Drink, Christian?" shouted my host over the roaring of the wheels as I frighteningly slid towards the window. "Maybe it will calm your nerves!"

Apart from erratically muttering and swearing under his breath it was the first thing I had heard him say since we had left. I decided to humour him, finding myself a little ill at ease after being so rudely plucked from the comfort of the fireside and thrown into this chaotic errand. After all, it was impossible to forget that we were not collecting any old book, we were collecting a top secret Illuminati book. I tried to remain calm and urged myself, 'Remember Seb: All is well. All is well.'

He produced a sizeable leather keg from a cubby hole in the seat next to him and unplugged the stopper. After taking a long swig he passed it over then regarded me balefully and scorned, "No need to be coy now, Christian! You know where we're going?"

"Let me assure you, sir, I have no idea!" I yelled back and took a gulp then tried to compose myself as the raw brandy burned its way down my gullet.

"Of course not! Of course not!" he scoffed then boomed, "Everyone knows Madame Zukkerburg's!"

Well, of course, I had heard of the place. Half the rakes at university went there on a regular basis, but I had no time for their tales of depravity or frightening diseases.

"I have merely heard of it in passing, sir!" I called but spilled the brandy over my fur coat as we bounced over a jarring pothole.

"Pah ha!" he laughed like a schoolboy, obviously unconvinced, "Of course, Christian! Only heard of it in passing! That's right, that's right." He grabbed the keg back and teased, "Do not fear, Christian, I won't tell your wife."

"She's not my wife!" I shouted, trying to clean up the mess.

He took another greedy quaff and wiped his mouth with his sleve. "So, no wife and no knowledge of Madame Zukkerburg's? I see. Pa' ha! You best have another drink then eh, Christian? Even a lonely student should have, at least, *one* vice!"

I was already beginning to tire of Canon Danzer. My mother had always wanted her only son to become a priest but I was sure that she would have changed her mind in less time than it took to perform a hasty Hail Mary the moment she had met this 'Man of God.' I retrieved the keg from him and took another slug, making sure not to spill any this time as we surged around another rutted bend.

Something else crossed my mind so, after a few more crashing potholes, I called out, "Surely, sir, I am not here to merely consume your brandy! So please tell me, why *am* I here?"

His expression stiffened as he took back the keg and shouted, "You will aid our entry, Christian! Once inside, I get the book! Then we return to the castle. Understood?"

"Understood!" I yelled, still completely non-the-wiser about what I was supposed to do which did little to ease my growing apprehension. He helped himself to another long guzzle then settled back in his seat muttering to himself and sniffing his smelly fingers. So I spent the rest of the journey calming myself with his brandy and trying not to get turned on my head by his unruly driver.

After an hour or so there was a thump on the roof and I saw through the trees that we were fast approaching what looked like a large house with seductively glowing crimson windows. To my great surprise Danzer suddenly threw me his filthy hat, flung himself between my knees, pulled the bottom of my fur coat over his head and hissed like a snake, "Pretend youre a priest from Salzberg and youve come to see Frisky Fifi the French Maid. Understood?".

"Understood," I spat, although the words, 'May God forgive your fetid soul?' would have been more appropriate. I shook my head, thanked God that my mother could not see me and pulled on his crumpled hat. The carriage turned off the road, rolled along a short driveway and pulled up at some snow-covered railings. A lantern flickered outside and presently there was a knock at the door. 'Here we go Seb,' I said to myself and lowered the window.

A rough looking man with a huge frosted nose regarded me curiously for a few seconds before grunting, "Evening, squire." Unaware of the protocol upon entering such a house of ill repute, I waited for him to continue but instead he leant closer and spied into the carriage.

Quickly realising that some response was expected I warbled in my best feigned baritone, "I am Canon Drechsler from Salzburg. I have come to see Frisky Fifi."

An uneasy handful of seconds passed before he muttered, "Have fun, Your Grace," and signalled our driver to enter.

I closed the window much relieved that the first part of the ordeal was over only to have Danzer pop up between my knees and wheeze, "Well done, Christian, well done. Old big nose swore that he would cut off my testicles if he ever saw me here again."

The old lush struggled back into his seat as we drew up next to a row of carriages parked outside a looming, timbered-framed house covered with snow. While Danzer cautiously peeked outside I was sure that I saw a shadow move across the red light falling from an upstairs window. When he was satisfied that the coast was clear he opened the door and whispered, "Do as I do, Christian."

'When Hell freezes over you dirty dog,' I thought and stepped out after him into the cold night air. We crunched across the frozen driveway past piles of snow shovelled against the walls of the house as high as the front door and Danzer whispered over his shoulder to his driver, "Prepare yourself, Heinz."

This did nothing to quell my jangling nerves and as we came up to the door it occurred to me, "Before we go any further, sir, why is The Book of Servants here at all?"

He sealed his lips tighter than a miser's purse and boggled his eyes with such untrustworthiness that I resolved never to waste my time asking again and, after one final wild boggle, he opened the door and shuffled inside. I cursed unreservedly under my breath and followed him into the house.

We crept up a dim hallway leading into a brighter, larger room overlooked by a mezzanine balcony along which ran a

row of coloured doors - the boudoirs I guessed. On the ground
floor a dozen or so men were lounging around, mostly the worse
for wear and, amongst them, six or so girls in various states of
undress - the whores I presumed. In the far corner a shabby
quartet played an old polka on battered instruments with a lack
of enthusiasm that suggested they had played it many, many
hundreds of times before.

'Well done Seb.' I congratulated myself as I looked around.
Along with the cracked ceiling and stained wallpaper, the seedy
atmosphere was exactly as I had imagined. Danzer gestured for
me to wait on a lonely chaise longue at the end of the hallway
and I gratefully obliged. He sidled over to a table where an older,
haggard woman - the infamous Madame Zukkerburg I assumed
- sat gossiping with one of the girls. Her eyes froze with anger
as she saw him coming but he was instantly fawning by her side
and after he slipped her a purse and whispered something in her
ear she thawed and pointed to a purple door up on the balcony.

He did not need telling twice and scampered up the stairs like
a starving rat up a table leg. After impatiently knocking he was
immediately invited inside and before you could say 'knife' the
door closed behind him.

'Well that's that,' I told myself. 'With any luck we'll be back
in front of the fire at the castle drinking schnapps and reading
the book in an hour with me the returning hero who has saved
the day yet again.'

The girl - and she was only a girl – who had been gossiping
with old Zukkerburg blew me a kiss. I hurriedly looked away
and prayed that Francesca would bear me a son.

At that moment the front door barged open and four menacing
characters trooped inside wearing black hats and greatcoats.
They were obviously fresh from the road; plastered in mud and
accompanied by the telltale tinkle of spurs. I did not like the
look of them one bit and when the hefty moustachioed brute

leading the squadron glared at me, I instinctively turned away and cowered on the chaise longue. He went to speak with the madame while one of his men blocked the hallway and the other two strayed over in my direction making me sufficiently nervous to get up and wander into the larger room towards the bottom of the stairs as nonchalantly as I could. My heart raced as I imagined who this bunch could be and when the old dragon nervously pointed back to the purple door and the men strode towards me it began to pound like thunder. I bolted up the stairs as fast as my clumsy fur coat would allow me with my mind in turmoil. If we were here to get this damned book and these brutes were here for the same reason surely that could only mean one thing.

"You there! Stop!" barked a voice behind me and the nightmare began again and the all-too-familiar feeling of terror ripped through my being once more. I flung myself along the balcony and crashed through the purple door, screaming at the top of my voice, "Illuminati!"

Whatever I had expected to find it was not Danzer strangling a whore in a skimpy basque and bellowing, "Burn in Hell bitch!"

He threw her on the bed and I went to scream again but he roared, "I heard you, Christian! I have it!" He brandished a little black book then turned around and yanked at the window, yelling, "Come on! Help me! It's stuck!"

I ran over to him but the whore flew at me from the bed and lashed at me with her fingernails. I threw her over my shoulder sending her flailing towards the open door but in a flurry of black overcoats she landed right in the arms of the moustachioed brute. She seemed to recognise him and stroked his cheek as he steadied her and his three confederates piled into the room behind him.

"Help!" panicked Danzer, straining with all his might.

I tried to but saw that the window frame had been nailed shut and wailed, "Nails!"

"Bugger the Virgin Mary!" roared Danzer, "They weren't here last week!"

I turned to see the moustachioed brute draw a long dagger but instead of coming at us he looked the whore right in the eyes and, in one truly terrifying instant, slit her throat. I almost vomited as she clutched at her neck and stared at him with abject horror as he dropped her to the floor.

"What are we going to do, Danzer?" I yelled as bile flooded my gullet but saw that he was transfixed with fear beside me reciting the Lord's Prayer. The brute's eyes fell back on us and he motioned to one of his men who swung out a huge blunderbuss from under his coat. It was time to do or die. I took one step back, flung myself into Danzer's midriff and smashed us both through the window.

We burst outside in a cloud of flying glass and splinters as the blunderbuss thundered behind us, sending burning shot thudding into my fur coat. I could not see anything from behind Danzer's shoulders but as I had hoped, we landed with a heavy thud in a deep snowdrift piled up against the rear of the house and pulled ourselves apart before scrabbling off towards a small woodshed.

'Boom!' Another massive shot scattered over our heads forcing us to duck down as we waded through the snow and the shouts of our pursuers echoed amongst the trees. At the woodshed Danzer grabbed a pair of snow shovels leaning against the wall and thrust one into my hand.

"Now - do as I do!" he puffed and, much to my amazement, hopped a few steps then jumped aboard the shovel with its handle between his legs and slid off down the sloping, snowy ground at a fair pace.

'Bang!' Another shot zipped over my head removing any remaining reservations that I may have had and I ran a few steps then jumped aboard my shovel and slid after him. Fortunately, the hill dropped away steeply and we quickly picked up speed as the cries began to fade and another distant shot rang out. Sensing that we had somehow escaped with our lives, I yelled out in delight and even began to enjoy the ride. I hit a bump and spun around making it impossible to see where I was going then after a few more violent bumps and another disorientating rotation, I slid past Danzer who had safely come to a halt by a bush and was being helped up by his driver.

"Stop, Christian! You go too far!" he bellowed.

What the blazes did that mean? I did not have time to ask and accelerated at a frightening pace over the crisp moonlit snow then as I came around again saw, to my horror, that I was inevitably slithering toward the edge of a ravine over which was a sheer drop. "No!" I screamed, desperately trying to slow myself down with my feet and hands. At the last moment, more by luck than good judgement, I managed to grab an exposed tree root as the shovel slipped from under my arse and flew off into the dark. "Help!" I yelped and held on for dear life as my feet dangled over the edge and I listened to the shovel clang down, down, down ever further into the ravine. At last it came to a rest and all was quiet. All I could hear was the wind whistling over the snow and my heart pounding in my ears. I tried to pull myself up on the root but it immediately gave way under my weight and I slipped another heart-stopping foot over the side.

"No! I don't want to die like this!" I raged into the night. I had been so happy two short hours ago, sitting contently around the fire with my loving friends and sweet Francesca next to me. Now I was going to fall to my death in this freezing ravine where no one would ever find my shattered body. Shit! Think Sebastian! Think!

I fumbled around with my free hand frantically looking for something else to hold other than the pathetic, flimsy root. But there was nothing. Nothing at all. Nothing but wet, sloppy snow and crumbling soil. Damn it! While I hung there cursing and helplessly flapping about the root suddenly gave way again and I slipped another terrifying six inches lower. No! If that happened once more I was a dead man for sure.

Chapter 4

Cliffhanger

I could tell that the root was about to give way and send me plummeting to my death. It was no good. Surely this was the end. With the root inexorably inching out of the snow and all hope gone I began to pray to God when from nowhere, a powerful hand grabbed my wrist and yanked me from the jaws of disaster. Though it was not God but Danzer's trusty driver with Danzer, in turn, pulling him from behind and roaring like a cannon, "Come on, Christian! Help us here!"

After a huge heave from all three of us, I managed to get a foothold and, at last, scramble back over the edge and onto my feet. I scampered uphill behind them through some low frozen brambles to the carriage which I was overjoyed to see parked on the road leading from the brothel. But my stomach clenched with fear when we leapt aboard and the shouts of our pursuers and the muffled thump of hooves drifted down the hill. We were not out of this yet. Danzer's driver quickly lashed the horses into action and we were soon tearing down the hill at great speed, careering round the corners and smashing through the snowdrifts like a Roman charioteer. I estimated that if he kept up this speed without killing us then we might actually get away, but as the road levelled out our pace slackened dramatically and my blood turned to ice when out of the rear window I saw three galloping horsemen catching us up.

"Come on!" I roared, banging my fist on the back seat and willing our horses to go faster. 'Boom!' I ducked down in fright when a mighty shot thundered from overhead as Danzer's driver fired off a round and I watched in shock and awe as one of the riders went down in a flailing heap of mangled flesh and mortal agony.

"Send 'em all to Hell Heinz!" roared Danzer next to me but the two remaining horsemen relentlessly closed in and came level with the windows, daringly, one on each side. I panicked when I saw the nearest preparing to fire a blunderbuss into the cabin, "We need guns too! Now!"

"Here. Take this!" yelled Danzer, cowardly flattening himself against the back seat and jiggling from his sleeve a pathetic 'lady's pistol,' not more than six inches long.

"Thunder and lightning!" I fumed and snatched it off him only to see the second rider aiming a pistol at me through the opposite window. There was no time to think and I pointed the gun at him and fired. The glass smashed to pieces but the measly shot whined harmlessly off into the night.

"Damn this toy!" I raged and flung the useless thing at the rider. The carriage swerved violently round a bend throwing us to the floor in a sprawling heap and I watched aghast as the book slid across the back seat and ended up precariously lodged against the last shard of glass still rattling in the window frame. I tried to push Danzer off but the old drunk was too heavy and, as we crashed over another bevvy of potholes, the riders reappeared at the windows getting ready to fire and I could only watch helplessly as the book's pages fluttered in the wind and the fragment shuddered out of the frame.

"The book!" I yelled and, with one last gigantic heave, managed to wrestle free and fling myself across the cabin to grab it as it fell away and both the riders simultaneously fired. 'Baboom!' The cabin imploded in a cloud of shattered glass and flying coachwork, but by a miraculous twist of fate the shots missed us and dealt both the riders a fatal blow. For one instantly fell from his steed, being horrifically dragged behind by his stirrups whilst the other slumped in his saddle and slowly lost touch with us. I watched them steadily fade through the rear window then let out a huge gasp when they finally disappeared.

Heaven's above! Somehow we had survived the frenzied attack. And at the hands of hardened Illuminati agents. I could not believe our good fortune and instinctively began to pray, "Thank you, Lord for protecting me as I walked through the valley of the shadow of death..." but came to a stop when I noticed Danzer sitting opposite also solemnly jabbering to himself with his hands up to his face. I pulled myself together, made sure the book was safe and sound and stuck my head out of the broken window to check if our driver was all right, or even still there. He was as relieved to see me as I him and shouted out, "We'll carry on this way, sir! It's a little longer but I wager we'll meet less trouble!"

I waved to him that I understood and, obliged by his earnest efforts, called, "Thank you... Heinz!" before pulling my head inside. I took one last look at the book and was about to stuff it in the deepest pocket of my fur coat when I noticed Danzer's beady eyes coveting it. He stuck his hand out and huffed with dubious self-importance, "I think *I* should take that now, Christian."

Though I neither liked him or the fact that he was nominally in charge of our mission, he was still a Canon priest and, not wanting to overstep my mark, or upset Van Halestrom, I begrudgingly gave him the book. He took it without taking his eyes from mine then leaned back amongst the shattered glass and wood splinters, jealously clutching its worn cover to his chest and blessing me with his other hand, "You have reserved yourself a special place in Heaven tonight, Christian. Well done, well done. Yes, yes. Well done."

I collapsed in the opposite seat, pulled my coat around me, stuffed my fur hat back on, retrieved the leather keg from under the piles of wreckage and helped myself to a long, stiff drink. Though he was still a fellow agent too so, after almost being killed at least half a dozen times in his service, I felt more than obligued to add, with more than a touch of vexacious sarcasm,

"As we can no longer close the windows, sir, may I suggest that you don't leave it on the seat again because the next time it falls out I will make you go and fetch the damnedable thing yourself."

32

Chapter 5

The Book of Servants

The journey back to the castle was short but very, very cold. With both windows gone, and a good deal of the doors to boot, I almost froze to death and I am sure that it was only a combination of my fur coat and copious amounts of brandy which saved me. With the book in his hands Danzer was transformed. Indeed, such were his high spirits that he seemed impervious to the elements and spent the entire journey joyously singing hymns at the top of his baritone voice and quaffing the remaining brandy and even, at times, though less often, thanking me. You could not say that he did not take the fight to the Illuminati with a passion. In fact, he seemed to be one of their most ardent enemies.

We rattled into the castle's courtyard two minutes before I died from frostbite to find our loyal comrades waiting by the front door with the Professor holding out a lantern like a beacon in the night. The exhausted horses had not even staggered to a halt before I had jumped down from the carriage, run up the stairway and crashed into Francesca's waiting arms to share a very long and meaningful embrace. It was clear to all, by the state of the battered carriage, and me, that we had run into serious problems on our supposedly 'simple errand' and my friends gathered round welcoming me home with sincere oaths and many kind words. Though there was much to tell and the moment I had finally pulled my lips from Francesca's, I blazed away, "Why didn' t you give me a gun, Professor? The biggest one you have?"

"Why did you not ask for one, Sebastian? I have several."

"There were Illuminati agents everywhere. Four, five. perhaps more... maybe six. Experienced riders, powerful weaponry, mighty blunderbusses and led by an evil moustachioed devil with the look of death in his eyes. We only escaped by the skin of our teeth. It is only by the grace of... of... of... good fortune that we are alive."

"Count Massenhausen," concluded Van Halestrom darkly, "It must have been. Illuminati treasurer, original member and despicable fiend with the blood of countless souls on his hands."

"I should have known," I quivered, recalling his cruelty. *[3]

"Sacré bleu! I knew there would be trouble," stamped Francesca. "But you're not injured? No?" she begged, checking my limbs to see that none were missing. "I would not trust that Danzer with his own mother. Priest or not. Ooh. Putain!" she spat as Danzer wobbled up the stairway humming another hymn to himself.

She faced him as he came up the steps with her fists clenched behind her back and seethed, "How could you take my Sebastian to that... that whorehouse when you knew there would be trouble?"

"Good evening, my dear. Yes, thank you, I *do* have the book," he gloated imperiously and clasped the little black book to his chest as he walked past her through the open door.

The Professor attempted to keep the peace and suggested to us all, "The library will be the best place to check the book's authenticity."

---

3. **Illuminati Chief Treasurer Count Anton Massenhausen 'Ajax.'** A former student of Ingolstadt University, by 1787 Count Anton Massenhausen appears on all published Illuminati membership lists and was chief treasurer from the inception of the organisation and also one of the five original members along with Weishaupt whom he met at the university. Massenhausen had operated a lottery, amongst other things, in his time and had a reputation for drinking, gambling and womanising. Though this, by all accounts, is thought to have been spread by Weishaupt, but he was also rumoured to be a 'poltroon' (coward) and if S. Drechsler recollections are reliable this would seem to be untrue.

He herded us in from the cold with his cane and lantern and we followed Danzer along the hallway as Francesca harangued him for all she was worth. "All you men think about is your own part in these escapades. One of these days one of us will be killed. Damn you, Danzer."

"I assure you there will be no need to check the book's authenticity, Professor. And I would like to remind you, young lady, that I am an honourable Canon."

Francesca boiled like a kettle, "I am fully aware of *what* you are your mighty... eminence..." but stopped herself after receiving a stern frown from Bacon.

The five of us scaled the stairs and entered the cavernous, circular library where we all crowded round the central desk. Danzer finally passed the book to Van Halestrom who laid it down where we all could see. He opened the cover then read out the inscription on the first page which was written in particularly elegant handwriting, "*Eternal Survum Suum*: His Master's Eternal Servant." He paused for thought and said, "I believe, in this case, that the master is Lucifer, and as you can see, the servant has signed himself '*H*'."

"Who could it be, sir?" I asked with a gulp.

"The Order's codenames usually reflect a high regard for the enemies of ancient Rome, as Rome represents the West, or the current order which, of course, they intend to destroy."

"Hector? Hercules?" guessed Danzer, "He is obviously of the highest rank."

"Then Hannibal seems the most likely conclusion, sir," cleverly interjected Bacon. The inscrutable old scholar did not even take his eyes from the book but nodded at it, urging Van Halestrom to continue. I almost gasped when I saw at the top of a long list of names on the next page and penned in the same exquisite handwriting, *Adam Weishaupt - Spartacus*.

"Incredible," breathed Van Halestrom. "Here is the proof in black and white." He ran his finger down the page. "Ah ha. Kolmer, Frank, Baron Knigge - Philo. Yes, they are all here." He flicked over the page reading out; "Baader, Bode, Massenhausen, Dacshel, Meggenhoff, Professor Kundi... Ha. I always suspected that idiot was an Illuminati reptile. Well, well, well. Who do we have here? Remember Lange, Sebastian? Codename Tamerlane? Your friend who was killed by lightning? Here he is." He scanned the next page silently before suddenly declaring, "Look, Bacon. The Marquis de Constanza has chosen the name Diomedes for himself. All the planets. Only the most respected commander in the Trojan War would do for that fat, lazy, aristocratic fool."

Bacon leant closer and even the imperturbable old man seemed to rear up in alarm as Van Halestrom turned the next page.

"Good Lord, sir. I am greatly saddened to see Herr Johann Wolfgang Goethe's name here. I suppose one cannot always tell the strength of a man's virtue by the character of his work, however worthy."

"I fear not, old friend. It seems no rank, or position, or high office, or even acclaim, is impervious to the Order's lure." *4

"Oh yes. They are all there my friends," assured Danzer. "It was sworn to me when I first brokered the deal to get the book.

---

4. **Bavarian Illuminati Membership 1787.** The Illuminati's ranks had swelled to over three thousand by this time. Although there had been many arrests and defections the list still included; aristocrats, judges, councillors, Barons, Counts and men from every possible walk of life and position. Johann Wolfgang Goethe, the author of *Faust*, in which the tragic character sells his soul to Mephistopheles (the Devil), was famously a member and recruited in 1784. Jacob Lange's (Tamerlane) death by a lightning strike in 1785 led to Adam Weishaupt's banishment from Bavaria after authorities found incriminating documents with his body.

Every single one of them; professors, scholars, judges, priests, councillors, magistrates, librarians, historians, financiers, diplomats writers even dukes and barons, all in one little black book. Now we have the godless plotters in one place we can oust them once and for all. Either by showing the book to Duke Theodore along with the other evidence seized from Weishaupt, Lange, Zwack and the others or, as we have done before, assume the role of judge, jury and executioner and smite the evil heathens ourselves." Seemingly satisfied with his night's work he smacked his lips, scratched his protruding belly, spied the Professor's brandy decanter on its usual table and went to help himself.

The Professor continued leafing through the book until he paused then moved it closer to the candlelight and murmured, "What's this? A page seems to have been torn out."

Danzer almost dropped his glass and thundered, "It must have been that bit..." he glanced at Francesca and continued more courteously "...woman back at Madame Zukkerburg's. That harlot would have done anything to betray me."

Francesca scowled at him all the same and I bit my tongue remembering the poor woman's expression as she was so unnecessarily slaughtered in the priest's brokered deal gone so tragically wrong.

"But what of it?" he shrugged offhand, "We have all the other names of those of serve the Order throughout Bavaria - and beyond. What should we care if one or two of the vermin are missing?"

"Plus Hannibal's identity?" reminded Bacon.

Danzer ignored him and took a hefty swig before carrying on, "Do you not see? This is our chance to lance this festering boil forever: for us, for the great Mother Church, for Christians and Christendom everywhere. To rid the world of this insidious cancer before it infects the very heart and soul of humanity. For that is what they plan." He faced Francesca and continued in the same ominous tone, "You may not fear God's wrath, my dear, but if you fear for the fate of your unborn child, you should, for soon and very soon, all of us will suffer the evil they plan."

She remarked, "The finest political minds in Europe agree the Order plan to cause three great wars then trap everyone in perpetual slavery to their fraudulent debt. I have read much on the subject."

"Yes, my dear, but there is more."

"More?" She wrinkled her pretty nose.

"Yes, my dear," he said, for once his eyes filling with stern conviction and he ended, "To take over our very minds."

There was a foreboding pause which I felt obliged to break, "And how do they plan to do that, sir?"

The Professor took up the going. "Ah that is the strangely simple part of the plan, Sebastian. With these." To my surprise he patted a pile of books on the table.

"Books?" I could not help but scoff.

"Yes, Sebastian: books. Well, the ideas in them anyway. And, in turn, education, newspapers, political discourse, the printing press, theatre, the arts even music. For these are the true weapons of their revolution. There is a limit to what can be achieved even with war and debt. So, to accomplish their new world order they must mount a war on culture.

I failed to believe that music of all things could be used by the Illuminati as a weapon to 'take over our very minds' and Francesca scorned, "Pah! They will never take over my mind or my child's."

"On the contrary, Francesca. The social movements hoped to usher in your long-awaited equality with men will be infiltrated by their agents and exploited to exacerbate the existing differences between men and women to generate a war between the sexes. This is their plan: to ferment conflict throughout civilisation but always in the name of freedom and liberty."

Francesca seemed unusually crestfallen and before she could mount a counter argument Danzer leapt into the saddle. "The Professor is right. They plan to create revolutionaries of all kinds: atheists, apostates, nihilists and demagogues to destroy the six existing orthodoxies; papacy, aristocracy, family, property and sovereignty. And with these foundations demolished they scheme, even now, by infiltration, to set the Holy Catholic Church and the Muslim caliphate on a collision course to start a cataclysmic struggle after which the splintered remnants of these ideologies will be brought into one dissolute, conflicted world consciousness: The International Mind. Then, with their new technologies, weapons will be created to exploit the New Citizens' particular weaknesses. That's right!" he exclaimed, impassioned by his own sermon, "I have heard it. A vice for everyone."

His eyes darted between us checking to see if we were listening. He need not have bothered. We were hanging on his every word and he preached on, "Vanity for the exhibitionists, greed for the materialists, oblivion for the aimless, gluttony for the undisciplined, depravity for the lustful and wrath for the fearful, the blind and the hateful. For the children of the new age these sicknesses will not be seen as weaknesses but as strengths or dismissed as mere growing pains as they adjust to their new intoxicating freedoms and succumb to utopian political ideologies which disguise the Luciferian dogma of the self and the unholy. Why, I even know of evil machines that are dreamt of to bring a portrait into every man's hand so the famous can lead the dissolute masses into this dystopian future which only they would have the arrogance to blasphemously call 'The Great Work.' Where humanity will finally tear itself apart in a rage of self destruction like... like..."

His eyes searched the room until suddenly focusing as though he could see exactly what he spoke of standing right before him and he proclaimed, "Samson, Aye! That's it. Like Samson. Driven to madness by the desire for immoral abominations, they will eventually bring about their own downfall and just as when the blinded Hebrew judge brought down the temple at Gaza, all will tumble down on their heads."

He gasped and had to steady himself on the table before chucking his remaining brandy down his throat then compulsively refilling his glass from the decanter. He might have been a lascivious, contradictory, untrustworthy, old drunk but he could certainly rattle the rafters. You could not deny it. *5

5. **Illuminati & The Great Work (Hermeticism).** The Great Work is a term used in Hermeticism from which the occult traditions descend. On a personal level Magnum Opus (Latin interpretation) means the spiritual path towards self-transcendence and attaining this most revered metaphysical state represents the culmination of the spiritual path, the attainment of self enlightenment and the rescue of the human soul from the unconscious forces that bind it. Globally applied, it could be fairly described as a utopian internationalist single state which, merely by its very nature, could only be bought into existence by revolutionary practices to accomplish a 'One World One Collective Conscience.' Or in a corporate, cultural, geopolitical sense: Globalism.

Chapter 6

Secret in the Stars

Danzer's Nostradamus-like prophecy seemed to exhaust the conflicted, old fellow and, after downing the rest of his brandy, he collapsed into a chair and stared disconsolately into space.

"That was very articulate, Joseph," observed the Professor, "No one could doubt the strength of your resolve after such a speech." He addressed us all, "But let us not underestimate tonight's achievements my friends. We have won a major victory over our enemies and we should be thankful for that."

"Wise words indeed, sir," concluded Bacon. "Now, it is getting late and I still have chores to complete. So, if you will excuse me."

The old butler quietly slipped away but not before courteously stopping at Danzer's side to assure the tired cleric that everything possible would be done in order to bring the book to the authorities' attention.

Francesca squeezed my hand and muttered under her breath, "I knew it would be a woman's fault in the end."

"Eh?" I whispered, still dazed by Danzer's ominous sermon.

"Delilah, you idiot," she teased, moving her fingers like a pair of scissors. "Come to bed soon, darling. Don't worry. I won't chop off your hair. You might need your strength." She giggled then kissed my cheek and ran off after Bacon.

I was just about to follow her when the Professor hobbled over and discreetly suggested, "I think we should leave Danzer with his thoughts," and gestured at the door leading onto the terrace.

I sighed with rueful frustration but obediently followed him as he limped outside into the blustery night. The North wind had blown away the remaining clouds and now a sea of stars radiated across the night sky. I took a deep breath of the chilly air and we crossed the terrace to admire the spectacle from the balustrade.

He stared up into the heavens and began, "You have done well tonight, Sebastian. I cannot thank you enough."

I seized this opportunity to air my thoughts about changing my terrifying style of life. "Sir, I fear with Francesca pregnant..."

He knew exactly what I was going to say and interrupted me, "Sebastian, I promise you that for the foreseeable future your life will be as calm as a summer meadow. Of course, you will be paid for your recent labours and, please forgive me as I did not have time earlier, but I wanted to say... well, I hope this will be a good year for us."

He shook my hand and quickly changed the subject, "Now then, I also brought you out here to show you something." He scanned the stars muttering to himself, "Now then, where is it? Where is it? Somewhere over here. Ah ha, there!" He pointed out into the constellations and asked, "Can you see the Winter Triangle pointing down with Sirius at the tip?"

"As clear as day," I nodded.

"And to the east: the three kings of Orion?"

"Why, of course, sir. The Winter Triangle and Orion's Belt are the best known asterisms in the northern sky."

"Very good, Sebastian. Always best to have a keen knowledge of astronomy. Now, what you might not know is that around the winter solstice, the alignment of Sirius and Orion's belt points down to indicate the position of the sunrise on the horizon."

As he suggested, I was surprised that I did not know this but he was not done yet.

"Now tell me, lad, what does 'solstice' mean in Latin?"

"That's easy, sir," I offered, "Sun-stands-still."

"Correct. But did you know this is because the sun's downward passage stops at the winter solstice on the 21st and appears to stand still for three days before rising again, one degree, on December the 25th? Interesting eh? But this is where it gets really interesting. The ancient Egyptians believed the sun embodied the life-giving principle so this upwards movement represented the reincarnation of Osiris's son Horus. Thousands of years after this the Christians believe that three kings followed a bright star in the east to witness the birth of the son of God, or The *Sun* God, who later dies but is then reborn three days after."

He took a timely pause while the wind whistled around us and the stars shone above before he finished, "The parallels speak for themselves. Many, many other religions are enshrined in similar myth and superstition but all are based on this same occult celestial knowledge and, I assure you, it is definitely *not* a coincidence."

I had neither expected a lesson in astronomy nor theology but this particular revelation, at this particular moment, instantly resonated with me. It was obvious what he was insinuating and its magnitude. Only that the entire Christian creed was based on something else; a much older, and higher, level of understanding.
*6

6. **Illuminati Hermetic Mystery School Religion.** The Ancient Egyptians, including several other arcane religions, Greek, Roman, Assyrian, Babylonian, anthropomorphised (personified) the stars and interpreted our own sun's passage at the solstices typically as God's or God's son or, as S. Drechsler states, 'The Son of God's' reincarnation. The iconography and personages of many contemporary faiths derive from ancient celestial observations. For example: twelve signs of the zodiac, twelve apostles. Orion's three stars, the three wise men. Occult astronomical knowledge creates another level on which religions can be considered and, in this case, establishes the backbone of the occult Hermetic Mystery School Religion practised by the Illuminati. The Winter Triangle, made from the family trinity of Illuminati favourites: Horus the son, Isis the mother and Osiris the father, can be viewed here on the StarChart app.

He was a shrewd old bird. Looking back now I am sure he well suspected the experiences that I had gained while in his service had, as much as I had fought it, forced me to seriousl question my religious beliefs. No small matter for a man of my strict orthodox upbringing: Age of Reason or not. This new exciting revelation not only further undermined years spent in front of the pulpit but destroyed what remained of my disintegrating Christian credo and a moment of profound contemplation passed before I eventually reasoned, "Is this what I need to understand to reach the next level, Professor?"

"Yes, my boy. But remember it's merely another step up the ladder and there's always another," he pondered, "As above, so below."

No one could make me think like the Professor when he was on form and he was not finished. While he had my attention and we continued to gaze into the eternal heavens he mentioned, "There is one last thing I wanted to share with you, Sebastian." He took a moment to collect his thoughts before asking "Tell me, who do you think you are?"

I did not know what he was driving at and chuckled, "I beg your pardon, sir?"

"Yes, perhaps I should rephrase that. Let me see... Do you think you know yourself? How's that?"

"As well as any other twenty one-year old, sir. Why?"

"I was afraid you would say that," he chuckled and carried on, "There is an engraving, thought to predate the pyramids, over the entrance of the ancient Greek temple in Delphi that simply says 'Gnothi seauton' or 'Know thyself.' If I ever teach you anything this is the most important. Without it; self knowledge, everything, and I mean everything, is meaningless." At this moment he faced me and, with the oddest look in his eyes, asked carefully, "You do understand don't you, Sebastian?"

"I think so," I slowly nodded and echoed, "Know thyself."

"Good lad," he said and smiled wisely to himself. We stood appreciating the mighty cosmos for a meditative moment before he prompted "Now, before you go to bed, I think Bacon has something to show us."

Once more, I did not question but dutifully followed him back through the library where Danzer was now sound asleep and snoring loudly in his chair. We made our way up the hallway and came to a stop by an old door which I had noticed many times but through which I had never been.

'More secrets?' I wondered as the Professor steadied himself on his cane and, using a key chained to his waistcoat, opened the door and led me down a steep, spiralling staircase into the very bowels of the castle. As we descended I could hear a repetitive clanking noise gradually becoming louder and could smell a most pungent odour. Indeed, it was so strong that I had put my hand over my face long before we finally reached a studded door with an eerie, silver light flickering from underneath.

"Here we are," coughed the Professor and gripped the door handle then loudly added over the din coming from the room, "You might want to cover your mouth and try not to breathe in the fumes! They're extremely poisonous!" and he hobbled inside.

"Is nothing ever simple with these eccentrics?" I wittered and took a deep breath then followed him through the door.

Well, more secrets was right. Inside the cramped, deafening chamber I was amazed to find Bacon, adorned in a strange, goggled, leather hood with matching gauntlets going all the way up his arms, pouring a glowing silvery molten metal into a row of small moulds on the floor. I quickly realised that he was making the arrowheads for our destructive multiple shot quadre bows and that the molten metal was silver.

"So this is where they come from," I murmured to myself behind my cupped hand and watched in fascination as Bacon moved down the line, meticulously pouring the shimmering, spitting metal without wasting a drop. In the flickering light at the back of the chamber within a barred vault I began to make out piles upon piles of silver ingots. In fact, there was so much I had to look again whereupon I was certain that I could also see gold bullion and bags upon bags full of coins. Incredible. It must have been the loot the Professor had 'confiscated' from his numerous Illuminati enemies. He had clearly been very successful in his labours and, no doubt, become extremely unpopular in the process as there was enough cash there to settle Bavaria's entire national debt and, I wagered, several other countries into the bargain. And, for once, I am not exaggerating.

I had to rub my eyes but perhaps more because of the pungent fumes spewing in my face. The Professor nudged my shoulder and shouted out over the din, "Bacon has a steady hand does he not?" admiring his friend's craftsmanship.

"... Yes!" I gagged as the vapours almost overwhelmed me.

"We thought you should see this!" he ironically shouted, swiping at the clouds of thick smoke with his cane. "Sorry about the racket! That's the steam pump working the bellows!" He flapped his hand dismissively at the rattling contraption next to the furnace and shouted, "I have to redesign it!"

Bacon put down his ladle, lifted his hood and raised his voice amid the cacophonous row, "What did you say, sir?"

The Professor shouted in his ear, "I told him that we wanted him to see all this!" He gestured around the smoky room then pointed at the vibrating engine and yelled, "But that I had to redesign the bellow pump because it was too noisy!"

"Yes, sir, about ten minutes to cool but tell him to put his hand over his mouth because the fumes are extremely poisonous!"

There was a confused pause while they both stared rather nonplussed at each other.

"Right. We shall go now!" relented Van Halestrom but his old friend shook his head and pointed to his ears then pulled his strange hood back on and waved goodbye.

We left him to his work and steadily climbed back up the spiral staircase and finally out through the door onto the landing. Van Halestrom relocked the door, brushed down his cravat and stated matter-of-factly, "Well, goodnight, Sebastian," and with this remarkably understated farewell, bowed and limped off. I stared into the place where he been standing utterly unable to fully comprehend everything that I had seen when he softly called, "Oh, and Happy New Year."

Remember, this was only one night at the Castle Landfried. Though I did not spend every night there, and, perhaps understandably, not all nights were quite like this, it is a perfect example of my astonishing time there. I wandered back to my room along the empty corridors in a profound daze, worrying that if I tried to squeeze anything more inside my bulging head it would burst over the fine portraits and rugs. Also, I wondered, what more incredible secrets and adventures the next day, and indeed the next year, held in store. Little did I know that I would not have to wait that long to find out. *7

---

7. **Hermetic Philosophy 'Know Thyself.'** The ancient Hermetic aphorism 'Know Thyself' is recorded by the Greek Writer Pausanias circa 100 B.C. to have been inscribed in the forecourt of the Temple of Apollo at Delphi in ancient Greece. The timeless maxim is considered to be the crucial philosophical prelude before transcendence which cannot occur, without this ancient challenge being accomplished first. Adepts of the occult tradition are expected to fully come to terms with this idea before achieving illumination.

Chapter 7

New Year's Resolutions

The next day was far less eventful. How could it have been
otherwise? After all, it *was* New Year's Day. Though there were
still all the usual pitfalls to leap, delicate intricacies to navigate
and nasty surprises to crash straight into. After completing
my usual morning regime; braving the toilet, putting on some
tasteful clothes, drinking a pot of coffee, braving the toilet again
and eating a hearty breakfast, I kissed Francesca farewell at the
top of the stairway before boarding the Professor's coach to
head back to Ingolstadt.

Danzer rode up front with us leaving his driver to bring up
the rear in his beleaguered carriage. Though the turbulent priest
was still muttering to himself and grinding his teeth, he was a
sea of calm compared with his vexatious mood of the previous
day. Van Halestrom took pains to reassure him that he would do
all he could to get the book to the authorities, and also to find out
through our networks if anyone had any news of Massenhausen.
On the whole Danzer seemed content with this state of affairs but
as we reached the city gates he grumbled with an air of disquiet,
"I'm still worried, Professor. The authorities move too slowly
rounding up the Order's agents. Even those they have already
identified. I fear the delay is allowing someone friendly to their
cause to give them refuge and safe passage from Bavaria."

"I wholeheartedly agree, Jacob," nodded the Professor, "And,
as such, I have an ingenious plan to find out exactly who and
where. I think it would be fair to assume that the 'who' and the
individual who signs themselves 'H' are one in the same. But
the 'where,' now that is another question altogether."

Danzer's eyes lit up at this and he suggested, "Perhaps get
Christian here to investigate, eh? He's a resourceful fellow."

I was as much surprised to hear this glowing compliment as I was unhappy to be volunteered to go chasing after the Illuminati.

"No, no. I have other plans for Sebastian. He needs to get on with his studies. I have already taken far too much of his time."

This was the biggest surprise of all. For a moment I thought that he was talking about a different Sebastian as he had never said anything as remotely understanding about my studies before.

We pulled up in the street outside the university and transferred Danzer into his carriage. Though it was a holiday there were still a few students around but we did little to hide our activities. I was a senior undergraduate now which made it more acceptable to be seen fraternizing with a master. Also our friendship was as common knowledge as our opposition to the Illuminati and our connection with the Elector's ongoing case against the secret society. It was all big news back then and filled the pages of all the newsheets, especially in Ingolstadt; home of the Bavarian Illuminati.

Personally, I enjoyed the notoriety and being seen as a local hero of sorts. Though the previous night's escapades had scared the living daylights out of me, as had all my escapades to be truthful, I relished pretending they had not with manly indifference but secretly brimmed with pride as a couple of first year students nudged each other upon seeing the fabled Illuminati Hunters in the street, no doubt back from another exciting mission. It was even true. Though a bit more fame and admiration and a little less adventure would have suited me better but there you go.

Danzer was soon ready to depart and as his driver whipped the horses he leant out of his broken carriage window and huffed, "So where do you think they are escaping, Professor? Stuttgart to the west, or perhaps Bremen to the east?"

"Possibly," called Van Halestrom as the carriage rattled away.

The Canon was confused and called out, "Maybe Hamburg to the North? That's where Baader is. Perhaps there are others too?"

"Perhaps to the North, the East and the West! Yes. Farewell! Farewell!" Van Halestrom called out almost laughing, "Peace be to you brother in this New Year!".

Danzer gave up in a fluster and withdrew his head as his battered carriage wobbled off up the road. The Professor sighed, "There's a good man in there somewhere trying desperately to get out. Let's hope that one day he succeeds."

He looked me up and down and announced, "Right, Sebastian. We have work to do."

"Work?" I winced. "But it's a holiday."

"Ha. Young men don't need holidays, Sebastian. They need work. Come on."

He waved Willy away to stable the carriage and tottered off on his walking stick through the gates. *[8]

To be fair, work for us third year students before graduation was pretty easy. We prepared our dissertations and sought experience of work in our chosen subjects in the outside world.

---

8. **Illuminati Court Cases, Banishments, Confessions & Runaways.** Several arrests and court cases involving the Illuminati had taken place by 1787. Notably, three professors, Cossendy, Renner and Grünburgen, (see *Illuminati Hunter II*) who defected from the organisation when they did not receive the 'special powers' that they had been promised, were interrogated and gave extensive and damaging confessions. Weishaupt himself fled when threatened with arrest. Once, reportedly, even hiding in a chimney to escape the authorities. After first fleeing to nearby Regensburg he later ended up being given refuge by sympathetic Duke Ernst II of the Sax-Gotha-Altenburg family which in 1825 became the Sax-Gotha-Coburg line, intriguingly direct ancestors of the United Kingdom's Royal family.

This usually amounted to much sitting around in beirkellers talking a lot but completing very little and, if we did find real employment, more often than not, it was for family or friends. To be truthful, I had not yet organised this part of my curriculum having no family or friends in Ingolstadt and it was something that I had promised myself I would do the moment I returned to university in January. Remember, throughout all my adventures I was a busy undergraduate and, while some of my contemporaries found it hard simply completing their studies, I had many other extracurricular activities to accomplish.

After making our way through the unusually empty corridors we reached the Professor's study. "Right, Sebastian, there is much to do," he said, hanging up his coat, disposing of his cane and plonking himself down on the corner of his desk.

"Much to do?" I asked, thinking where I might go for another breakfast after completing whatever he had planned for me.

"Yes. You're going south to Switzerland."

"I'm sorry, sir, I thought you said I was going to Switzerland?"

He looked blank faced at me and repeated, "That's right. You're going to Switzerland."

"Switzerland?" He was serious. I gawped so deeply I subsequently found it impossible to close my mouth. Well, this was too much. I had to sit down.

He lit up his pipe with his ingenious miniature flint box and started, "Yes. As I said, I want you well out of the way for the foreseeable future, for Francesca's sake and your own. With murderous Massenhausen on the prowl I'm sure it's for the best."

I glanced apprehensively out of the window. I was not sure which I found harder to believe, that I was being taken out of action or that I was going to Switzerland? He had promised my life would become like a summer meadow. Perhaps, at last, he was keeping his word.

"As you know you also require some work experience as a final year student with regard to completing your graduating dissertation." I nodded, suspicious that, once again, he had been reading my thoughts as he continued, "With these factors in mind, I have chosen to send you to the sleepy town of Poschiavo in Switzerland where you will assist a friend of mine, Count Thomas von Bassus, to catalogue his extensive library on behalf of the university here in Ingolstadt, of which he is a former student. This task will take you from January to April whereupon you will return here to complete your dissertation in May and to be with Francesca in time for the birth. In the meantime, while I make the final arrangements for your journey, you will visit your mother and father back in Tuffengarten as you have never missed a Christmas with them before."

"Tuffengarten?" I blurted, but he raised a finger and carried on unabated.

"You will leave on today's only stagecoach north for which Willy is currently booking you a seat. After this you will return here, shall we say in four days, to collect your things and the letters of introduction which I am about to write. Then you will leave immediately for Poschiavo. There is one proviso."

"One... proviso," I stammered, trying as usual to keep up but failing dismally.

"It would be better if you did not tell the Count of our friendship but instead tell him that we are... mere acquaintances."

"But why? Why this complexity? Why cannot one thing be simple?"

"For the simple reason, Sebastian, that we were once good friends, very close actually, but as can sometimes happen with good friends, we fell out and never made up our differences. Sad really, a bit like you and Jan eh?"

The mere mention of my not-so-dear and departed friend, Jan whom the Professor had killed to stop him from killing me, caused me to flinch with morbid regret.

"Trust me, Sebastian, it will simply make your stay more congenial without an air of animosity hanging over it, however long ago its origin."

He smiled reassuringly and, at last, I begrudgingly parroted, "Mere acquaintances."

"Excellent, my boy," he slapped his good thigh and enveloped me in a lingering cloud of smoke then had the audacity to ask, "Any questions?"

Given the circumstances this was the most absurd question of the entire eighteenth century and I gave up before I started. I tried to clear the air as he snapped his fingers. "Ah, I almost forgot." He lifted himself up and hopped over to his bookshelf where he tilted back his threadbare copy of Sun Tzu's '*The Art of War*,' causing the ingenious bookshelf to gently swing open and reveal his secret cabinet of weapons. It was only eight o'clock in the morning and we were already going through his private arsenal.

A tiny burst of excitement stirred in my belly and I leant back in my chair to peep inside. But to my surprise it seemed quite empty. In fact, I could not see anything at all. I wondered if he had finally seen sense and cleared it out. He disappeared inside for a moment then came back out holding what appeared to be a simple brass-tipped black walking cane with a black ivory handle. He hopped back to his desk and I japed, "I had not planned to break my own leg, sir."

"Ha, very good, Sebastian. Now, I'm sure you won't be needing this where you're going but I have been meaning to give it to you for a while now." He winked, "You know? Just in case."

He held the stick with both hands around the shaft then rotated the handle and said, "Observe." He let it fall through his fingers, tapping the brass tip on the floor and with a 'Snap!'

a six inch metal spike jutted out of the top of the handle with devastating force.

"Good Lord!" I gasped, jerking back my head. "That's awesome, Professor."

"Oh yes, but the real trick is that if you turn the handle anticlockwise then tap it twice you have two seconds before a pistol's charge of gunpowder blasts out the spike fast enough to take a man's head off," he rocked his hand from side to side, "At maybe twenty yards. Here. Feel it. She has a wonderful balance."

He plonked the terrifying thing in my hands like a rifle and I pretended to test its equilibrium.

"I have already told Francesca of your travel plans. You will leave your horse here so she can be rested and shod for your upcoming journey. Bacon has already stowed a bag of your things in the carriage and Willy will be back outside the university gates in five minutes. I will inform your tutors to make the necessary amendments to your curriculum and, I believe, all other eventualities have been considered."

Once again in the Professor's service I was utterly silenced upon discovering what he actually had planned for me. No second breakfast then. He lifted himself from his desk and stuck out his hand whereupon I jerked up like a puppet pulled by invisible strings, shook his hand, bowed, said farewell - as sincerely as I could given my discombobulation - and closed the door behind me as he encouragingly called out, "Good luck!"

I met Willy at the front gate as planned and less than an hour later I was regarding my startled refection in a stagecoach window as I pounded up the northern road with a bag of my belongings under my arm, my exploding walking stick on my lap and a ticket to Tuffengarten stuffed in my top pocket.

The subsequent gruelling sixteen hour journey might have been boring for a normal student going home to visit his folks, stuck in the back of a juddering, draughty stagecoach with a random collection of, for the most part, glum strangers. But in a fashion to which I had become accustomed, I was far too busy turning over the tumultuous aspects of my life to be bored and, as such, spent most of the journey dramatically casting myself as mighty Atlas burdened with the entire weight of the world upon his shoulders.

Nonetheless, as I walked the final mile from the coaching inn to my parent's house and past the familiar landmarks of my youth I was reminded that, in the bigger scheme of things, I had not done badly over the past two years and that, despite these adolescent foibles, all was still well.

Chapter 8

The Prodigal Son Returns

It is always difficult to know what to expect when returning to the place that you grew up. Though I had hardly imagined the muddy streets to be lined with childhood friends celebrating my long-awaited return, it would have been pleasant if just one person had said hello or even recognised me as I trudged along Tuffengarten's main street in the fading evening light and knocked on my parent's front door. My mother soon answered and, as my unannounced arrival came as some surprise, her eyes did moisten and, at last, I was recognised and given the loving hug that every good son expects upon seeing their mother after a prolonged absence.

I spent the evening at the kitchen table warming myself by the stove as she fed me up and we caught up with news, in her life and in mine. Obviously, when it came to mine, though what I told her about the academic side of my life was mostly true, pretty much everything else was a lie. I could not tell her about my love life and, despite promising myself a hundred times on the way there to summon up the courage to explain about Francesca and my ensuing fatherhood, I claimed that I had no time for love but, laughably, only books.

This may seem unworthy, and even unlikely, but I dared not cause a commotion, an easy thing to do with my strictly catholic mother. Francesca and I had been so preoccupied by our fight against the seething powers of darkness that we, understandably, had still not found the time to propose, let alone arrange, marriage. With the foolhardiness typical to a man of my years I convinced myself that somehow there would still be time during the next six months to either tie the knot or explain why I had not.

As for my mother, nothing much had changed. Her hands hurt more each day and she worried that father was finding it harder to get out of bed due to his gout. This had led to an unsupervised apprentice in the gunsmithys making a mistake which had lost him a valued customer. On the subject of my father, and an indication of the crippling formality in our household, I was told he would see me tomorrow as he was particularly busy working on his accounts.

As we talked she mused that, one day, she hoped to see me step down from an expensive carriage. I reminded her that I already possessed Petrova my wonderful horse - an extravagant gift from her and my father - which was far cheaper. In her wonderfully illogical French manner she said she estimated 'a carriage less expensive for it did not need to be fed.' I had to point out that one still required, at least, one horse as a carriage was useless on its own and we both laughed deeply at her absentmindedness.

The next day promptly after breakfast, I was finally granted an audience with my father. After knocking smartly on his door I was invited inside and found him sitting upright in his neatly made bed surrounded by his accounting books. I clicked my heels, bowed then stood, as I had been taught, with my hands behind my back, my chest out, my chin up and where he could see me. Though that now appeared to be at the foot of his bed.

He examined me for a whole minute before noting in his usual disparaging tone, "You look tired and in need of a week of your mother's cooking. But I hear you're not staying that long." He adjusted his spectacles, "I am told your studies go well."

This seemed almost like a question so I ventured, "Yes, sir. Broadly speaking all is well and I hope to graduate with honours." Broadly speaking this was true with, of course, a little help from my new fund friends and particularly the genius, Bacon.

He solemnly raised a hand to halt this unwarranted sign of confidence. "We'll wait to see if you graduate before jumping to any conclusions about your brilliance. Then you'll have to decide what you intend to do. Eh? You can't be a free and easy student all your life: going here and there; doing this and that." He peered over his spectacles and sniffed, "I hope you haven't forgotten that you must repay your student's loan to Count Friedrich?"

"Financially speaking, sir, I am pleased to say that I am solvent and can now support myself and intend to honour all my debts..."

"Uh! You do, do you?" he grumped at my presumption. "What does a man of your age know of solvency? Or honour? I want you to know this family has never owed money and God willing we never will. I suppose you found a simple job in the city? Doubtless it did you good to see what it is to have a proper job and see how the rest of us manage. Never forget Romans verse 2:1 'perseverance comes from piety.' Remember, it's useless being a flash in the pan. Right, you'd better go back to your mother. I'm sure she'll want to feed you up. I've my bookkeeping to finish."

Having just missed sharing our first Christmas together since I was a boy, I had hoped to talk for longer and was somewhat downhearted to be dismissed so offhandedly. I was about to leave when I remembered the present that I had brought him and laid out the pair of fine clocked stockings at the foot of his bed but he was already buried in his books. Maybe he said goodbye. Maybe he did not. I walked from his room and realised that, though I knew I would never be able to share with him all the incredible things that I had seen and done, I would always want to - like the little boy I would always be on his knee.

Of course, if I had taken him for a beer at the village tavern and told him straight, 'Look here, old man, this is what I've really been up to,' and explained a fraction of the truth he would have had a seizure on the spot.

The next morning, after barely going out or even seeing my father again, my mother escorted me back up the main street which was now a river of mud to the coaching house to begin my journey home. While we waited in the rain she told me all the things that she had forgotten to mention over the past day and a half. After a while her thoughts inevitably turned to those of my future and 'in her eyes' my pre-ordained first steps toward eventual priesthood.

"You know, Sebastian, your father and I have always prayed for you to become a priest. Such a noble thing to do with a life," she began piously, "You're always guaranteed respect from those you meet whatever you do, and you'll always know that you can expect forgiveness whenever your time finally comes. ... Not that you'd ever do anything wrong." She looked at me sideways, sniffed and, with brimming eyes, implored, "So we wanted to know, my sweet, if you had decided yet to dedicate your life to God?"

Her confounded emotional bribery made it impossible for me to tell the truth. I tried to rid my mind of the image of 'Priest' Danzer slapping the ill-fated whore round the face and replied, as politely as I could through gritted teeth, "I will give it my sincerest considerations, mother dear."

My journey back to Ingolstadt was mainly uneventful. I say mainly, because on the second day I fell asleep aboard a stagecoach and, perhaps because I was in a strange place (and there can be no stranger place than a strange stagecoach, full of strangers, passing through a strange town) or maybe because of everything else going on in my life but, for whatever the reason, I had the most hideous nightmare. Such was the vision's potency that it moved me greatly and I have seldom had one as prophetic before or after.

I dreamt that I was walking along the pavillion of a superb palace. Beneath my fine shoes the floor was decorated with black and white chequered tiles and I was dressed in the most elegant clothes. Rows of graceful columns flanked my sides and beyond them perfectly tended green gardens dotted with trees spread out to the horizon. A graceful woman wearing a bright pink dress and matching parasol crossed the lawn and disappeared momentarily behind the columns. Strangely, I knew that it was not Francesca but before I could see who it was behind the parasol she giggled and ran through a door which somehow replaced the pastoral scene. Upon finding it locked I barged it open with my shoulder only to tumble helplessly into a black void towards the face of a hideous laughing goat. I tried to stop myself but saw that my hands and feet were tied to a crucifix and, struggle as I may, I could not stop myself falling, falling ever downwards into the demonic eyes of the beast.

I awoke screaming for mercy and grabbing at my hat, causing great consternation amongst the other passengers on the morning coach from Wurzburg. Despite apologising to everyone and calming down the squawking chicken in its basket and paying for the broken egg and persuading my fellow travellers that I was not an escapee from the asylum, not even the chicken was convinced and I swore to myself that I would never ever fall asleep on transport that is public again.

The bells of Ingolstadt's St Maria's church chimed twelve o'clock as I strode back through the gates of the university. I was eager to organise everything as quickly as possible so I could get back to the castle to see Francesca one last time before my forthcoming journey. I hastily went about my business collecting the cataloguing books from the doddering old head Librarian, my letters of introduction and map from the Professor's clerk, a few clothes and my quadre bow from my quarters in town and my beautiful five year-old white mare Petrova from the stables;

watered, fed, shod, brushed, saddled up, happy to see me, her favourite human, and raring to go. The evening dusk was already gathering as I galloped her out through the city gates and up the road to the castle.

Night had not long fallen by the time I arrived in the castle courtyard and, having noticed a lonely figure waiting in the light of the open door, I flung Petrova's reins at the stable boy and bounded gleefully up the stairway only to be met by wrinkly old Bacon.

"Ah ha. Fashionably late, sir. How novel," he remarked in his usual sarcastic tone. I went to ask where Francesca was but he was miles ahead of me and offered, "My lady is awaiting your presence in the banqueting hall, sir."

"Awaiting my presence?" I panted, taking off my gloves.

"Yes, sir. She has been there for some time. So I would hurry if I were you, sir."

He gestured towards the banqueting hall with an unbecoming sideways jerk of his head. After crooking an eyebrow to show that this had been noted, I strode off up the corridor. "Francesca!" I called and swung open the door to find her seated at the far end of the grand table. Much to my delight she was dressed in a fabulous, blue satin frock with her new earrings twinkling in the candlelight and her hair stacked above her head, exactly the way I liked it and, spread across the table between us, a feast fit for a king and, appropriately, a queen. I quickly surveyed the table settings to see where best to ravish her that very moment but she forestalled my intentions and raised a spoon.

"If the first course gets any colder I will be extremely upset." Next to the bowl of soup at my end of the table I saw my pocket watch. "Ah yes," she added, "I found that for you so you're never this late again. Now sit down or else I will be very cross indeed."

Though it was hard, very hard, I controlled myself and did what I had been told. I pulled a chair up to the table and tasted the soup. Though it was very good I knew it would not fully satisfy my ravenous appetite so I asked, "What's the second course?"

"Beef," she replied with a simmering grin.

"And the third?" I asked, coming to the boil.

"You will have to work that out for yourself," she said and, putting an extra long frankfurter in her mouth, looked me straight in the eye, and bit off the end. Well, rather obviously, that night we both feasted as never before. All I can say is that I am glad that the carpenter who made the bed in our room was such a fine craftsman for had he not been we would have reduced his handiwork to a pile of kindling.

Come the first light of day I gathered my scattered clothes from the foot of the bed and quietly got dressed. I took one last longing look at Francesca fast asleep on our sun-kissed pillow and gently pecked her cheek. I was halfway to the door with my boots under my arm when she said, "Weren't you going to say goodbye?"

"I didn't want to wake you, my sweet. You looked so peaceful."

She frowned. "You must always say goodbye, Sebastian. Even Russians say goodbye." She lifted her head. "When will I see you again?"

"As I told you, my love, as soon as I finish this one simple task."

She squinted in the bright morning light and asked with uncharacteristic doubt, "I will... see you again won't I? Only, some men say things they don't mean."

I had no idea where this had come from especially after our antics the previous night but I did my best to allay her fears.

"Thunder and lightning, woman," I guffawed, "Of course I'll be back." Realising this perhaps a tad ungracious, I plunged back to her side and implored, "Darling, would I be here in the first place had I not proved my undying love for you a thousand times? Over and over and over again?" I took her hand and kissed her fingers as I had the night before which brightened her expression and transformed her frown to a smile. "Well, believe me, my love, I'm more than prepared to do that all again. And again, and again... and again... and again..."

This time I kissed her properly on the lips and for a goodly moment. After which, I stood up, blew her another kiss for good luck and strode manfully from the bedchamber then hopped down the stairs trying to put on my boots and thinking very highly of myself.

Bacon and Willy had been busy since dawn attending to matters in the stables and I found Petrova saddled up with my quadre bow in its large leather holster on one side of her withers and my cataloguing books over the other. She knew we were off somewhere on our travels and eagerly scraped her hooves on the cobbles while they strapped a large wooden cage containing five cooing messenger pigeons over a blanket across her rump.

I checked once more that I had everything and that was that. There was nothing else for it. Having found that for prosperity's sake it is always best to start your next adventure with as picturesque a vignette as possible, I mounted my awaiting steed with a youthful leap, reared her up as she liked, wished my friends a hearty farewell and galloped off out through the open castle gates with one hand on the reins and the other waving romantically goodbye behind me.

Chapter 9

On the Road Again

With fair weather, Petrova in excellent form and mostly dry roads we were in our element. Man and horse in perfect unison. My senses always revelled in the freedom of the open road; the enlightenment of travel, the purpose of mission, Mother Nature's beauty unfolding at a pace, my soul at liberty. I tapped my spurs into Petrova's flanks and, inspired by heroically pounding her through the Bavarian countryside, involuntarily yodelled with delight. I was back on the road again.

The Professor had written me two introductory letters; one to Count Bassus and the other to a Giuseppe Ambrosini, the owner of a bookshop in Poschiavo where I was going to stay. He had also penned me a short personal letter and I went through it in my head as I thundered on my way.

Dear Sebastian,

I'm sure you will find the Count most hospitable. Be careful to work hard, stay out of trouble and keep your nose clean. Let me know when you have arrived, then send one pigeon on the first day of every month after that. We will take great care of Francesca while you are awayt and look forward to your safe return in May. Good luck my friend.

Professor Van Halestrom.

According to Van Halestrom's map Poschiavo was a daunting three hundred miles away. As the crow flies. I planned to take ten days to get there, maybe less if the going was good. Who knew how long if the going was bad and the weather turned? I had never been further down the southern road than Augsburg before but that was only fifty miles away and I planned to be there later that night, all being well.

The rest of the journey would have been far quicker, and a lot less daunting, had it been over the rolling countryside usual to Ingolstadt. However, and this was the predicament, I was going over the Alps - in winter - like good old Hannibal no less, and along a route on which many had fallen by the wayside. Nevertheless, I was a tenacious student back then, further emboldened by my master's faith in my abilities and, no longer sitting on a stagecoach worrying about something I could not effect, I was relishing the challenge. Anyway, the mountains were a long way off. Now I wanted to ride.

Having no wish to test my luck once more and inadvertently run into a gang of Illuminati killers outside the university, I skirted Ingolstadt to the west and crossed the Danube at Neuberg. Though this was a new route for me the decision proved providential. Everything went according to plan and, as I had estimated, we reached Augsburg just after nightfall and found suitable lodgings.

The next day was as easy as the first and we got another fifty miles under our belts before we stopped off at a place called Memmingen. At this early stage of the journey the further I got from Ingolstadt the better I felt. In those far off days most folks never left the village in which they were born, whereas my adventures had taken me as far as Vienna and even the distant shores of the Baltic. Oh yes, I had travelled quite a bit for a man of my age and felt more than comfortable doing so. If I completed this next monumental journey I could claim to have traversed the whole of continental Europe from the north to the south, or as close as damn it. Some accomplishment. That was if I succeeded.

With the weather still holding we set off early the next morning to start our ascent into the foothills and by sundown reached the town of Lindau by Lake Konstanz which nestled at the very foot of the great Alpine range. I had to drag a blacksmith from a tavern to change Petrova's rear shoes but noticed the tired man was a trifle slapdash. So the following morning I hardly let her run at all and we took it very easily. However, at lunchtime when we stopped to ask where we were, I discovered that we had fallen well short of our expected target so I reluctantly increased our pace.

Petrova was in fine fettle but it was unseasonably warm and she soon needed a drink, so I pulled her up at a convenient brook crossing the road. She took a tentative lick and stamped her foot. I knew what that meant; she did not fancy this muddy stuff and could smell some better upstream. I let her lead me into a small clearing twenty yards from the road where a babbling brook flowed into another pool and she drank to her heart's content.

"Good girl," I said and slapped her shoulder, "Have as much as you like. I'm not sure where we'll find some more. Unless it rains."

That very moment, as if God himself was listening, there was a distant rumble of thunder amongst the gusting wind. But strangely when I gazed above the treetops, what clouds there were looked unlikely to create a storm. Still, amongst the breeze, I distinctly heard it again. Petrova tossed her head and pricked up her ears.

"There, there, my beauty. Only some thunder," I soothed, knowing that all animals were spooked by thunderstorms. But as I dismounted my ears pricked up too as I recognised the unmistakable sound of clattering bridles amongst the thunder. It was not thunder. It was horses. Several horses. Up until that point I had only seen a few travellers on the road and all but two of them had been farmers. All farmers have one thing in common: they always go everywhere as slowly as possible. Whoever this was, they were in an awful hurry. I watched the road through the gap in the trees as the pounding steadily grew louder until it sounded like an almighty cavalry charge. Good God! I got the shock of my life when Count Massenhausen flashed by at full pelt with his moustache and cloak blowing in the wind and four mean looking riders on powerful steeds galloping behind him.

Though the son of a bitch tore by like a cannon ball he still somehow registered me out of the corner of his eye and I uselessly squatted down in the undergrowth as they thundered past. I stayed there anxiously biting my nails as they pounded on up the road and when I was sure that they had gone, I rubbed my brow and promised myself to be more vigilant in the future. Buoyed by my apparent lucky escape, I was about to give the evil bastard the finger but my heart skipped a beat when I was sure that I heard a faint shout hanging on the breeze. Had the hoof beats also come to a stop? I strained my ear again but Mother Nature had other ideas and stirred a gusting wind. I cursed her inconsistency when, all at once, the wind suddenly dropped and I heard them straight away. They were coming back.

I jumped up and dragged Petrova into the trees then threw myself into a hollow covered with pine needles. I motioned her to do the same; one of our most practised stable tricks and, much to my relief, she obediently toppled over. But much to my despair this threw the pigeons into a wild panic. I tried to hush them as the motley crew reappeared at the edge of the clearing and began watering their horses from exactly the same spot where we had been only seconds before. While they dismounted and indulged in a little horseplay Massenhausen pushed his way through them and stood with his hands across his brow unnervingly scanning the undergrowth in our direction.

"Damn his hawkish eyes! Go away. Go away," I hissed and lay as flat as a leaf while the damnable pigeons flapped and cooed away like there was a fox in the cage. He stayed there staring directly over our heads for an intolerable two minutes while his men idled around and played the fool. Finally, as he could not find whatever he was looking for, he summoned them to saddle up and, after a rallying call, they set off as sharply as they had come. I held my breath as they rode away until, this time, I was positive they were gone for good, I gasped, "Damn you all the way to hell and back," and wondered if that was where he was going?

I stayed in the hollow for perhaps an hour. This might sound over cautious but - here's the trick - one of his men might have left his tobacco pouch or his gloves and, believe me, in this line of work, it is exactly the kind of thing that can get you killed. In the end, Petrova pulled herself up to get another drink and feeling a tad uncomfortable myself I followed her back to the clearing.

Now I was in a fix. There was only one road south and Massenhausen was on it. If I continued I risked running into the bastard who might stop anywhere for any reason; a lost horseshoe, to rest, to eat or drink, or even beat up an old lady. Who knew? After another hour or so I decided that I must get going again. I could not sleep outside and we both needed to eat so, ignoring my reservations, I gambled on travelling to the next village but upon my arrival, after discovering there was nowhere to eat or sleep and still a little sunlight left, I cast the dice once more, pulled my scarf over my face and went the extra ten miles up the road to the bigger town of Feldkirch. I arrived in a fluster, in total darkness and, looking like a desperate highwayman, had to wake the owner of the only inn and beg him to let me have a room.

Taking this small chance proved to be the right decision in the end and when I woke in the bed of my new pleasant lodgings the next morning, I excitedly yanked myself up to the window to gaze in awe at the inspiring mountains which now seemed in touching distance. Over breakfast I spent a thoughtful moment staring at the rugged peaks contemplating the next potentially perilous part of my journey; traversing them.

This was fast becoming of more concern than even Massenhausen, whom I hoped by now had taken one of Feldkirch's many junctions and was half way to hell. Though, of course, I could not be absolutely certain and dreaded to think what would happen if I ran into him. Adding to my woes I discovered that one of my pigeons had died in the night and discreetly buried the animal behind the stables at my lodgings. I checked the other birds but being no ornithologist had no idea if they were at the peak of health or also about to drop down dead.

After purchasing vital supplies from the village shop I loaded my gear onto Petrova and got ready to travel to the next stop; Vaduz in Lichtenstein. All the locals were in agreement that, though it was biting cold, it was as clement as it ever was at this time of year. So, keeping one eye on the clouds, I made my way over the top.

This was the thing; the weather in the mountains could turn in an instant and when it did, no matter how experienced a traveller you were, you could get caught out and both you and your horse could be dead in a matter of hours. Despite the worst horror stories of the locals the fair weather continued and I was not slain by a 'deadly ice storm.'

The magnificent views afforded me as I climbed the twisting mountain road were some of the most dramatic that I had ever seen and made all the hard effort worthwhile. Every now and then there were places of convenience to rest and recuperate and share food and stories with other travellers. But I never stopped for too long to ensure that I made solid progress throughout the day and, though there was a little snow in the afternoon, the miles slowly plodded on and the hours steadily mounted up. After another punishing twelve hours in the saddle, I was extremely glad to see the welcoming travellers' lodge in Vaduz and later that evening rested in my bed, preparing myself for the final push.

Remarkably, the next morning the skies fully cleared and for that whole day it was perfectly warm and still. This was indeed fortunate at this most critical part of my journey, crossing the highest ground. For I was now truly amongst the mountains in the heart of Lichtenstein and, mesmerised by their awe-inspiring spectacle and beauty, I felt like a tiny speck of dust faced by the magnitude of heaven's work.

In the afternoon we wound our way along the famed and astonishing canyon known as The Bernina Pass and I understood why when my breath was taken away as I first came across Lake Bianco. We skirted the superb lake and, at the bottom of the valley, turned back to see one particularly majestic peak set against the pure azure sky perfectly reflected in the mirror-calm waters. As I marvelled at the pure symmetry of the illusion, the Professor's words resonated within me as if they were in the very mountains themselves: 'As above, so below.' *[9]

I sat upon Petrova for a contemplative moment admiring the view and eventually wished that I was an artist on The Grand Tour with my easel and brushes for I would have loved to have painted that extraordinary spectacle and hung it on my wall. Though I can still picture it today as clearly as if it were before me now.

---

9. **Illuminated Philosophy 'As Above, So Below.'** Perhaps the best known of all philosophical aphorisms 'As above, so below' is associated with Hermeticism, sacred geometry and Tarot. The philosophy generally attributes a reflective quality to nature from the tiny to the universal. In the secular context, the phrase can refer to the idea that microcosm reflects macrocosm. For example; that the ills of the individual can be reflected in the ills of society at large. In Hermeticism, the phrase can be taken to mean that earthly matters reflect the operations of the astral plane and, perhaps its most commonly known usage in western religious text would be within The Lord's Prayer: 'On Earth as it is in Heaven.' A good example of the concept in a contemporary form, can be seen in fractals and the Mandelbrot Set, wherein the same patterns exists on all scales fom the largest to the infinitely small.

At dusk we reached the alpine village of Chur and later that night I stared into the fire of the local tavern considering the tantalizing prospect that the very next evening I would reach my destination. And so it was, I woke on the last morning of my journey to find myself once again blessed with another crisp winter's day. I must have been the luckiest man alive to ever cross the Alps in January as, up to this point, I had only seen two showers of rain and one light dusting of snow. Knowing Mother Nature's volatility, I hastily readied myself before she could change her mind. We soon began our descent and before long the countryside softened into sloped pasture dappled with clusters of pines which was in pleasing contrast to the bleak, barren otherworldliness of the higher ground.

Late that afternoon we came to a narrow bridge spanning a fearful gorge. Even though the structure appeared sound in every detail, I still brought Petrova up to consider my next steps carefully. This was due to my overwhelming fear of heights. An irrational fear from which I still suffer to this day, and which I overcome with mixed results. The precipitous nature of this particular gorge gave me the trots so badly that I wanted to gallop all the way back to Ingolstadt. Indeed, when I squinted over the side I could hardly see the tumultuous river crashing on the rocks below. Eventually, I crossed by successfully fighting the urge to look down again and, upon safely reaching the other side, was rewarded for my bravery when I came upon a milestone which read, under the sign of two crossed keys, '*Poschiavo 15 miles.*'

"Nearly there my beauty." I encouraged and we trotted down an inviting road that weaved off though a beautiful forested valley. An hour or so later, as the sun set over the mountainous western horizon, we turned a corner and found ourselves on a broad plateau in the middle of which lay, like a jewel in the twilight, the picturesque town of Poschiavo; its multi-couloured spires and rooftops an inspiring sight to the weary traveller.

With the last embers of daylight fading fast from a dramatic sky we finally rode into the town and stopped in a large square to get our bearings.

I told Petrova, "We're looking for Ambrosini's Bookshop." She neighed to say that she had got me here and finding where we were staying was my job.

I looked around the square from one house to another until I slowly realised that the one we were standing right outside had a grand sign over the door advertising, '*Ambrosini's Bookshop.*'

"Ah. Well, that was easy," I told her and she scraped her foot on the cobbles to say that I was stupid. There was lamplight falling onto the street from the cellar window so I dismounted and led her over. When I crouched down to get a better view and wiped the dirt from the glass I could not quite believe my eyes. In the shadows, I was sure of it, was a Guttenberg printing press. I quickly rubbed away some more dirt and muttered to myself, "What in Heaven's name is the crucible of the enlightenment and spreader of its news doing here?"

Ingolstadt had a printing press but it was a city. These machines were as rare as cathedrals so it was very odd indeed to find one in this 'sleepy town.' I saw someone moving about so I tapped the window and instantly heard steps running up the cellar stairs. Before you could say 'Gesundheit!' a slightly agitated, bald man answered the door and stood on the threshold wiping his hands on his apron.

"Good evening, kind sir." I breezily began, "I'm looking for Giuseppe Ambrosini?"

"Aye," he replied in a stern tone.

"Excellent," I said, holding my most charming smile, "My name is Sebastian Drechsler. I am here on behalf of Ingolstadt University to catalogue Count Bassus' library. I believe that I am staying here... tonight?"

I felt myself frame this last part as a question because he looked as though he had no idea what I was talking about and was most unhappy to find a presumptuous, grubby student banging on his door at this late hour. I fumbled around inside my coat and produced the Professor's letter of introduction which he took off me. I was about to curse Van Halestrom for sending me on this fool's errand when Ambrosini tapped the letter with his inky finger.

"Ah. I remember," he granted, "Only got told a week ago. That's right; room ready for you upstairs. I'll get my boy to look after your horse and bring your bags."

He stuck out a hand so I gingerly gave him Petrova's reins and, after giving her a thankful kiss on her nose, unhitching my quadre bow holster then unloading my largest and most dangerous bag, I went inside. Upstairs, as promised, I found a tiny bedchamber but which contained nothing other than a small truckle bed, a jug of water and a pot to piss in. His boy soon came up with my other bags and, as the realisation that I had arrived struck home, my excitement waned and my fatigue took over, compelling me to rest. I did not even have time to piss in my pot or take my boots off before I fell fast asleep. *[10]

---

10. **Poschiavo. Giuseppe Ambrosini & The Printing Press.** As S. Drechsler recalls Giuseppe Ambrosini owned a popular bookshop in Poschiavo in which a Guttenberg printing press, an anomaly for a town of Poschiavo's size in the late 1700's, operated and printed many important works of the day including several criticizing the church and the pope and, interestingly, the Italian version of Goethe's seminal work *The Sorrows of Young Werther* (1774 revised 1778) in Italian.

Chapter 10

Poschiavo

I awoke instantly possessed by a desire to explore my new surroundings which was to be home for the next three months. Doubtless this was because my bedchamber was as Spartan as a nun's underwear, lit only by one tiny arrow slit window and with a bed as comfortable as a kitchen table. I pulled my sore body up from the plank, filled my pot, splashed some water on my face and went downstairs. I could hear Ambrosini banging away in the cellar but there was no one else around so I stepped out of the front door into the sunshine and went for a walk.

I crossed the picturesque square with a whistle and meandered through the winding streets, going this way and that with no real plan or direction. It soon dawned on me that Poschiavo was quite unlike anywhere else I had been and rather like walking through a fairy tale. Brightly coloured eccentric half-timbered houses lined a maze of narrow intertwining lanes and charming squares. It was quite magical and not what I had expected at all. The townspeople of this intriguing place were also oddly welcoming and nearly all wished me 'Good morning' as I strolled by. The town was a true gem and by the time I found myself back at the bookshop I was thoroughly uplifted.

In my absence a number of people had gathered in the square and stood chatting and warming themselves in the pleasant morning sunshine. Judging by the number of expensive carriages parked at the kerb I guessed that it was a meeting point for the local gentry. I decided that this would be a perfect opportunity to discover more about my host so I approached a group of four gentlemen involved in lively conversation outside the bookshop. I stood politely a few feet away where I could hear them but not cause offence and my eyes naturally fell on the biggest.

He was a handsome fellow. He had the air of a fifty year-old but the looks of a much younger man and, though only an inch taller than me, with his perfect gentleman's posture; one gloved hand poised rakishly on a gold handled cane while the other casually rested in his waistcoat pocket, he somehow seemed larger than life. He wore a stylish, blue morning jacket cut from the finest cloth, fashionably short breeches over bright white stockings, silver buckled leather shoes, an impeccable powered wig and, to top it all, a dashing blue tricorn hat with a grandiose black feather. I watched him for a while as he confidently laughed and joked with his friends and, in my young impressionable eyes, I could not help but think that he was exactly the kind of man that, one day, I wanted to be. He must have felt my gaze because he winked at me, causing me to baulk, 'Who is this bright spark?'

I overheard his friend berating him and paid closer attention.

"But you never take my advice you old buzzard. I say again, for the third time. If the Germanic speaking peoples are to be unified in nationhood then surely the Swiss must also take the plunge and become one with us at the heart of Europe."

"One day your obsessive nationalism will get us all into terrible trouble, Herr Bahrdt. Where next?" quipped the charmer, "Poland?"

The men all laughed at this apart from the excitable fellow who saw me watching and asked, "What is it my friend? Have you come to ridicule my ideas of the greater Germany too? I would not try it. I have had two large coffees already."

The men chuckled again and, seizing my chance, I stepped forward and began, "Sorry to interrupt, Gentlemen, but I could not help notice that you were... of a certain standing and therefore might know a local chap of some import?"

"Some import eh?" said one and sniffed, "Who is the fellow?"

"Come on, man. Speak up," urged another.

The men seemed helpful so I asked hopefully, "... Count Bassus?"

To my surprise they all roared with laughter except for the tall handsome one who seemed to take great offence and, while the rest of them fell about laughing, beheld me as though I had insulted his mother.

"The man is a monster!" he seethed and grabbed my arm, "A selfish, depraved animal that should never be trusted near decent folk and especially children. Why, if he were here now, my friend, then we would have a fight on our hands." He pushed his head over my shoulder and shouted, "Quick! Quick! Sergeant at Arms! There's a killer on the loose!"

His friends laughed uproariously as he pulled his head back to reveal a boyish grin. I realised that I had been fooled and felt my toes curling painfully inside my boots as he introduced himself. "How do you do, sir: Thomas Franz Maria Count von Bassus at your service." He removed his feathered hat and bowed with flamboyant distinction.

"Sebastian Pierre Drechsler," I muttered quietly.

He took my hand without rising as though I were a cardinal and gushed with much faux humility, "It is indeed an honour, *Sir.*"

With my humiliation complete he came up smiling when a sudden look of recognition crossed his face and he exclaimed, "Wait a moment! You're the student from Ingolstadt University here to catalogue my library. Oh dear. Please, please forgive me. You have come all this way and I have done this." He winked and grinned, "I promise I'll never do it again. Let me introduce everyone; this is Herr Goshen; bookseller, atheist, writer and critic. Next to him we have Herr Johann Mayr, here to compose his next opera and, I believe Herr Bahrdt has already introduced himself."

Bahrdt shook my hand and smirked, "I don't suppose we could have expected anything more refined from a *Woodturner*."

He was referring to the meaning of Drechsler and I had heard the taunt many, many times before.

"Leave our guest alone, Bahrdt," scolded the Count, "Not everyone has had as much coffee as you." He flashed a winning smile. "Welcome to humble Poschiavo, Herr Drechsler, our own little piece of heaven hidden up here in the mountains; refuge for hermits, poets, artists, politicos and theorists alike and, of course, those who *can* think properly." He looked me over curiously, "Speaking of refugees, sir, prey where are you staying?"

"That's easy, sir" I said with a smirk of my own and nodded at my front door not five yards away, "There, in the bookshop."

This drew a pleasing laugh from the men and now it was Bassus' turn to look surprised. Indeed, he looked a little shocked for a second but laughed it off, "Oh no, no, no. That won't do at all." He beckoned to a uniformed, young servant waiting by a fancy, open-topped carriage and insisted, "You will stay at my house. We have a reputation for hospitality to maintain. I'll have your things taken there now." He gestured at the bookshop door and, as the attentive servant ran inside, pulled on his other glove and inspected me. "Anyway, you look as though you could do with a hot bath, some clean clothes and a square meal. So, what do you say fair traveller? Are you game?"

I may have been a little grubby and certainly hungry but I was not stupid. "Yes, sir," I heartily replied and clicked my heels.

Ambrosini came outside and stood watching us and wiping his hands. He nodded to Bassus as the servant boy laboured out with my heavy things and carried them to the carriage.

"Right then," said my new host, "Forgive me, Gentlemen, but I promised my old faculty back in Ingolstadt that I would look after young Herr Drechsler here so, I'm afraid I must bid you farewell."

"Before you go, Bassus," piped up Bahrdt, "Please explain to us, properly this time, just why you think Switzerland should not join the great unification experiment?"

The Count raised a gloved finger and decisively proclaimed, "Because, my Teutonic friend, the European body politic, like any other body, needs a head, a clear head, from whence only truly neutral emanations can originate."

The men all gravely nodded in agreement at this insightful yet poetic remark and even testy Bahrdt conceded somewhat. Before the Count could leave I interrupted, "I have a horse, sir."

He laughed, "Well, I didn't think you walked here, Herr Drechsler. I'm sure we will cope, good sir." He summoned the servant once more who seemed to instinctively know to run to the stables behind the shop.

"That's right, Herr Drechsler," nodded Goshen confidently, "Used to be Mayor you know? If Bassus can't do it no one can."

"Oh yes. You're in safe hands with Bassus," agreed Mayr.

"Indubitably," said Bahrdt, going with the tide.

Bassus humbly resigned to the praise, "How can the multitudes be wrong eh?" He tapped his cane twice on the cobbles with a flourish and finished, "Abracadabra. I create what I speak," then struck his gentlemen's pose and leant rakishly on his cane.

I worried that had he done that with my exploding walking stick his hand would have ended up in Lake Geneva. He gestured for me to join him and, feeling like a cat that had fallen from moderate height onto its feet but next to a huge bowl of cream, I accompanied him to his waiting carriage.

"Forgive my ostentatious transport, my friend," he apologised, opening the door to an upholstered velvet seat, "But I feel it is important that the good townspeople see me, and I see them."

I hopped aboard and he followed me in while his servant panted back across the square leading Petrova by her bridle. The exhausted young man tied her to the back of the carriage, pulled himself up onto the running board and wiped his brow.

"Right then!" hailed Bassus, "I trust everyone is sitting comfortably?"

I had not been this comfortable for quite some time, so I kept my mouth shut and he cheered, "Then let us be off."

With this the driver flicked his whip and the carriage trundled out of the square. *[11]

11. **Poschiavo & Count Bassus.** Thomas Maria Baron von Bassus was born in Poschiavo in 1742 and attended Ingolstadt University and, upon his return, was promptly made mayor of the ancient town at the tender age of twenty six, He had inherited huge tracts of local land and many properties from his wealthy parents much of it in Switzerland but also Sandersdorf in Bavaria. Bassus was a politician and philanthropist and organised many cultural activities in the town and even procured a printing press for the place which was unheard of in those days and this was operated by Giuseppe Ambrosini from his bookshop which had a reputation for selling and printing controversial works. Bassus was regarded as having the fine manners 'befitting his experience of German court.' The influential Count was also a close friend of Charles Friedrich Bahrdt a 'German Unionist and Professor of Sacred Philology at Leipzig University' and Johann Simon Mayr the famous composer who penned over seventy operas.

Chapter 11

The Library

We trotted through the pleasant town, weaving past beautiful fountains and a pantheon of wonderful statues. In the end I gave up noting the wondrous delights hidden throughout the lanes but one thing I could not fail to notice: everywhere we went the townsfolk waved to Bassus. In fact, such was his fame, that it was like being in the presence of a Saint, or a Pope, one of the popular ones, and I resigned to leave my hand on the carriage's side where it could be seen perpetually waving back.

We turned down a road leading us past an entire street of new houses under construction and he wafted a finger at the vast forest of scaffoldings. "Forgive me but we have to go the long way to my house because of the building works. Gentrification, I prefer to call it. An expensive pastime it may be, too expensive my closest friends keep telling me, but I feel it is important to ensure the man in the street remains happy with his lot. Ah, but such are the burdens of the modern philanthropist eh?"

So it seemed that he was paying for all this work himself. I calculated that he must be extremely wealthy and could see why he was so adored by the townsfolk. We bumped down the road past yet more building works and a line of dirty workmen who briefly stopped what they were doing to watch us go by.

"Who are they?" I asked, looking at the dusty faces.

"They're the Latin itinerants. From the next valley. Catholics mostly. Well, all really. They come here to do the work."

We wound our way to the edge of town and up along a sweeping avenue bordered with grand houses set in fine gardens. At the end we came to a palatial villa resembling a Greek temple and, much to my delight, gently rattled into the driveway.

"Ah ha, my humble idyll," sighed the Count with a nonchalant yawn as we came to a rest outside a stunning white neoclassical mansion flanked by an elegant colonnade. Rising up at the back above the shallow, leaning roof, I could even see an impressive dome gleaming in the sunshine.

And I was staying here? Yahoo! I coughed to discreetly conceal an enormous whoop of joy as I recalled my gloomy bedchamber back at the bookshop. Two footmen ran down the broad flight of steps to help us from the carriage and, while one of them led Petrova away, the other leapt back up to the porch to open the doors then stood to attention as we entered the house.

The Count escorted me down a meticulously clean hallway lined with all kinds of fascinating artefacts, from exquisite chairs and paintings to suits of armour and old weapons. He noticed me take an interest in one particularly haunting portrait; a mysterious, red haired woman staring poignantly into the distance.

"Ah. You have a keen eye, sir. A gift from a friend, one favour for another, if you will. The Roman Tiburtine, Sibyl: famous for her apocalyptic prophesies in which the last emperor of the world slays the Antichrist. If one believes in such things. Personally, I do not. But I feel it lends the place a certain je ne sais quoi. Don't you think?" He covered his mouth and whispered like a naughty schoolboy, "And the friend would have be furious had they not seen it hanging here upon their next visit." *12

We strolled on and he asked with genuine interest, "So, sir, where do you hope your studies will lead?"

I saw no reason to lie to my charming host so I told the truth, "My parents wish me to become a priest, sir."

12. **The Roman Tiburtine; Sibyl.** Amazingly this mysterious painting by an unknown artist still exists today in Poschiavo in the Hotel Albrici which was also owned by Count Bassus and can be viewed here by E Book readers.

"I see," he kinked an eyebrow, "Many of my friends joined the church after university to serve country and countrymen. But I myself chose a different path and entered the world of politics, for I felt there lay my true calling."

We had come to some impressive black double doors at the end of the hallway and he gripped both handles, beaming, "But it never stopped my desire to learn."

With this he dramatically heaved open the doors to reveal a room of such outstanding beauty that I thought I was in heaven.

"Welcome to your office for the next three months!" he announced and led me into a spectacular library comprising two levels of packed bookshelves covering the walls, the top level being a balcony that one reached via a superb spiral staircase and, set in the ceiling at the far end, the magnificent dome that I had seen from the front of the house suspended on six pillars, between which glorious stained glass windows allowed sunlight to fall onto a welcoming fireplace, sofa and reading plinth below. It was the library of my dreams, made a reality. He eased along the shelves brushing the book spines with his fingertips.

"The library crowns my family's heritage and was gathered together from the four corners of the world over seven centuries. Oh yes, my friend, you'll find everything here. What's your fancy then eh? Alchemy? Politics? Morals and dogma?" He glanced at me and surmised, "Architecture?" then tapped his finger on one particular spine.

He was either very insightful or very lucky because he was spot on, I was indeed very interested in this topic. "I thought so," he said with a grin and pulled out the old book then flicked through the opening pages. "Then this will interest you. Do you recognise this building?" He turned the open book towards me.

"It is Herod's Temple in Jerusalem," I answered and joined him.

"Correct, my learned friend. Distinctive is it not? A copy of Solomon's Temple destroyed in 637 BC by the Babylonians. The structure also symbolises much in the hermetic traditions; a society, the world or even the mind itself. But how about this?" He turned to an illustration of the Temple's floor plan showing the surrounding outer portico penetrated by the inner chamber: The Holy of Holies.

"Tell me what you see here?" he asked and watched my eyes. Unsure of what he meant I let him continue and, after a pause, he mused, "Is it not the sexual act? The male entering the female? And see the columns; Jachin and Boaz, leading to the Holy of Holies, when seen from above, are they not the testicles?" He gave a shrewd smile and flicked his eyebrows.

I supposed he was right, to an extent, but his frank manner caused me to recoil with embarrassment. I had not even had breakfast yet.

"No need to be coy, boy. You will never learn anything of real truth if you let polite sensibilities prevent you. The truth is that these ancients were all sex mad. What else was there to do back then, eh?" he reasoned with a playful shrug. "After all, is it not the oldest pastime?" I relaxed slightly and he suggested, "Here, let me show you something else." *13

13. **Solomon's Temple** & **The Pillars Jachin & Boaz.** Both these icons feature heavily in occult symbolism. The original name for the Masons, often associated with organisations such as the Illuminati, was the Templars after Knights of The Temple reffering to Solomon's Temple. These warrior aristocrats became wealthy during the crusades defending pilgrims to the Holy Land and were thought to have found occult secrets in the ruins of Herod's Temple in Jerusalem which gave them great powers. The Templars were finally rounded up and burned at the stake by Pope Clement III in 1413 for heresy and Devil worship in the form of the Baphomet when Jacques De Molay was their leader. The legendary brass columns outside the Temple's entrance known as Jachin and Boaz were thought to be indestructible on Solomon's original building and are familiar in Tarot and represent opposing aspects.

He slid the book back in its slot then took a couple of steps down the shelf where he pulled out another, urging, "Here. Come and see." He fingered through the pages until he came to an illustration of a hexagram. "Of course you are familiar with this geometric shape: the hermetic symbol for Saturn, The Star of Remphan. But look again. Tell me what do you see?"

Unsure again of what I was meant 'to see' I declined to answer though I was certain that, this time, it had nothing to do with sex. But apparently I was wrong again as he traced the top triangle with his finger he mused, "Is this not the male?" and, tracing the bottom triangle, said, "And this the female? And brought together in union?" He traced the whole hexagram, "As above, so below."

I stared at the shape and had a tiny inkling that I was beginning to grasp what he was getting at.

"Sex mad the lot of them," he chuckled and, prodding the picture again for extra emphasis, he elaborated, "Now here, inside the hexagram is the hexagon, which stretched out of the paper becomes the cube. Thus, the culmination of these two dimensional opposites, is three dimensional life itself, or creation: The Kabbalah." Seeing my face light up upon hearing this he asked, "You have experience of Kabbalah? *[14]

---

14. **Sacred Geometry: The Hexagram.** The most commonly known occult symbol is the union of opposing triangles 'of the upward fire or male and the downward watery female (male/female).' The hexagram represents the maxim 'As above so below,' and produces a three dimensional cube in the centre. Hermetically known as the Star of Remphan or the Seal of Solomon (sometimes referred to as The Star of David, though, surprisingly, this has no biblical reference) it occurs in several cultures from the orient to the Middle East and also in western mysticism. The Hexagram, with its six points, six triangles and six-sided central hexagon (666) is the arcane occult symbol for Saturn and, geometrically, shows a hexagon in its centre identical to the gas cloud situated on the planet's North Pole which, mysteriously, was only first observed by man with the Voyager Probe in 1977.

I was finally certain of something. I did, indeed, have *profound* experience of Kabbalah. Though, aside from briefly mentioning it to Bacon, I had told no one and it had been plaguing my thoughts for the past two months. Bassus seemed open-minded, in fact, perhaps a little too open minded and, though I had only known him a short time, I felt there was little I could say that would shock him. So I plucked up the courage and ventured, "I have seen the eternal Adam Kadmon at the very end of the universe, sir, and the being who forms our very souls on the anvil of destiny."

Unsurprisingly, his eyes lit up like candelabras as I thought they might. While I had his attention I hurriedly described my transcendent experience during my pursuit of Kolmer in which, after freezing in a snowdrift, I had felt myself die and go to heaven, only to be brought back to life by Francesca's warm touch and quick thinking, to return a changed man with my Kabbalist insight. He took great interest in my story, as I had hoped someone would ever since it happened. So, it was with great relief that when I came to the end, he touched my shoulder and sincerely said, "You're a very privileged man, my friend. Many would trade their very souls to see what you have seen, if only to prove that what they'd studied and worshipped all their lives was true." He carefully put his fingers together and added, "Then the truth has been bestowed to you, the young journeyman? How poetic."

He replaced the book and took a stroll around the room. "Well then, it seems you have come to exactly the right place, my friend. For everything is here that a gentleman of your... how shall I put it?" He tapped his cane on the floor, "Spiritual aspirations could wish." He gave the smouldering logs in the fireplace a prod and coughed, "I'll get Gretchen to show you to your room and make you something to eat.

He pulled a bell rope hanging from the ceiling and offered his hand as he finished, "If there is anything else I can get to make your stay more congenial then please don't hesitate to ask."

"I... don't know what to say Count..." I bumbled, eagerly shaking his hand.

"Then don't say anything," he interrupted, "It is merely what one member of a fraternity does for another." He gave me one more winning smile and offered, "Until the next time then, Herr Drechsler." With this he turned on an expensive heel and strode out of the double doors.

"Thank you, thank you so much, sir," I gushed and followed him over the threshold, rubbing my hands in glee when, from nowhere, a huge, stone-faced frau with blonde plated hair stepped into the doorway and stopped me dead in my tracks. She crossed her arms and pulled a face much like an obstinate cow blocking the road. Being a guest I did not tell her to get out of my way but called past her, "Thank you again, sir."

He waved a glove over his shoulder and the solemn frau nodded to an archway at the bottom of the corridor. After one more peek at the tantalising room, I closed the doors and followed after her.

I was overjoyed to discover that my quarters were as sumptuous as the rest of the house and decorated in the same immodest baroque finery. I had three vast rooms, the extraordinary luxury of my own toilet and bath, a huge wardrobe, several beautiful rugs, a long elegant mirror and even my own glorious, gold painted furniture. While I tested the mattress on my grand four-poster, curtained-bed with my tender backside and ogled the idyllic view of the mountains from my window, I could not help but murmur, "How could this excellent set of circumstances be better in any single way?

You lucky dog!" Apart from the frightening frau this place was perfect. I even felt a little guilty that the next few months of hard graft was starting to look more like an extended vacation. Hoorah!

In my rapturous state I had overlooked one thing and I quickly ran downstairs to locate the stables. I need not have worried as my bags were safely piled up and Petrova was also living in the lap of luxury with her own clean stall lined with fresh straw. I helped the young uniformed servants, none of whom was older than fourteen, unload the pigeon cage and, after grabbing the healthiest looking animal, took it off to send Van Halestrom a message and let him know that I had finally arrived.

Over the next few days I was made most comfortable; fed beyond the dreams of gluttony, rested beyond those of sloth and bathed and pampered way past my vainest fantasy. The gracious Count took me on the several tours necessary to view the entire sprawling house and extensive grounds. During one such tour of the cellars I was most pleased to discover an entire brewery dedicated to the production of a golden beer more delicious than any other I had ever tasted. Though unfortunately, as I realised after a few glasses one afternoon, it gave me terrible wind. *[15]

There was also an observatory with a telescope that the Professor would have envied, a music room complete with harpsichord and, in the endless gardens, even a modest chapel.

On another tour of the grounds the Count and I came across Gretchen practising falcony with a young golden eagle. Though the beast was only an adolescent it was already almost too big for the huge woman. Bassus explained that she had named the bird Barabbas, after the murderer spared by Pilot instead of Jesus,

---

15. **De Bassus Beer.** The De Bassus name has enjoyed a long success in the brewing industry and De Bassus beer is still brewed today in Sandersdorf Bavaria.

because when she found him there had been another chick in the nest which she had killed. I only ever saw her smile twice and when she overheard Bassus mentioning this was one of them.

Despite the gruesome servant lurking about, after a few days I settled in and so, after arranging my things about me one morning; several quills, some ink pots and one huge, empty catalogue, I set about recording the contents of the library. My task was made easier when Bassus allocated me two of his brighter young servants who proved most helpful. Surprisingly, both of them were literate and helped no end to transport the piles of heavy books back and forth to my table.

The Count paid me frequent visits to see if I needed anything when he was not busy travelling somewhere or meeting someone or hunting something and we soon became good friends. It was impossible not to. He was more like a fellow student than a supposedly dignified aristocrat such was his amenable manner and riotous sense of humour. Not that he was without his serious side too and took to his studies, which centred around mystery, symbolism, history, allegory, poetry and art, with the most rigorous scrutiny.

He took pains to explain his fascination with the pyramids at Giza, a fascination which, I have to admit, he subsequently inspired in me. He achieved this with countless diagrams, plans, and lists of dimensions and statistics, and speculated on the intentions of the architects and even their ability to have built the extraordinary edifices in the first place. A riddle to which he could find no logical explanation. As a mark of our growing friendship he gave me my own library key, and, as expected, soon asked me if I knew Professor Van Halestrom but seemed completely unsurprised when I told him, as instructed, that we were 'mere acquaintances.'

My work went well and I soon got to know my way around.

My frequent and long conversations with the intriguing Count did not hinder me but, if anything, aided my task and, such was my speed, I calculated that I would finish much earlier than expected. This pleasing state of affairs meant that I was able to spend a great deal of time reading and absorbing the extraordinary texts that lay around in abundance.

One evening during one of our after dinner conversations, Bassus drew my attention to his three volumes of the Karma Sutra in which, as any man would, I took an avid interest having never seen such erotica before. He also showed me a limited edition of John Cleland's The 'Adventures of a Woman of Pleasure' or 'Fanny Hill,' illustrated by a very talented and *highly* imaginative English engraver whose name escapes me but which I considered of far superior quality and found almost impossible to put down such was its power to arouse.

Late one evening, about a month or so after my arrival, I was putting away some books that the boys had overlooked when I noticed the copy of Fanny Hill lying all alone on the table. After a quick look around to check Gretchen was not loitering in the shadows, I popped it inside my jacket and tip-toed out of the library, locked the doors and hurried upstairs to my chambers.

After all, my work was going well, as was everything else, I had sent my messenger pigeon, behaved myself, kept my nose clean, even told Van Halestrom about Poschiavo's printing press and, to top it all, no one had tried to kill me since Christmas. So in my eyes I had earned myself a little celebration.

Suffice to say, I do not need to tell you what happened next as it should be obvious. I was a young man, on his own, hundreds of miles from his lover and with the keys to a library full of exotic erotica in his pocket.

Chapter 12

The Nightingale

The morning after I woke a little less rested than usual and sidled downstairs with the book tucked tightly under my arm. I wanted to return it before someone noticed that it was missing and peeked up the hallway towards the library before turning the corner. The coast seemed clear so I stepped out but to my horror walked straight into the Count coming the other way.

"Ah. Good morning, Herr Drechsler." he halooed. "Where have you been hiding?"

He was in his usual fine spirits that morning and dressed in an impeccable silver grey suit with a voluminous white cravat. I squeezed the book under my armpit and replied through a feigned yawn, "My apologies, Count. I have been up all night reading."

He spotted the book straight away and said with a knowing wink, "Your *insatiable* desire to learn has been noted young man."

Humiliated beyond my wits, I attempted to change the subject and remarked, "I thought you not due back for two days yet, sir?"

He frowned, "Don't be ashamed, my friend. While under my roof feel free to do whatever you wish, and *educate* yourself in whatever way you see fit." He gave a childish smirk, "As long as you do not break anything and upset Gretchen. Now come with me. I have a most excellent surprise for you."

I glimpsed the library only yards behind him but he urged me with a hand on my elbow and, after heaving myself away with gut-wrenching embarrassment, we finally strolled up the hallway.

I thanked God that no one could see me promenading through this fine house with this charming aristocrat with my one-off, limited edition, illustrated, pornographic book stuffed under my arm and I vowed to never tell a soul about this horrid experience as long as I lived. Bassus remained perfectly oblivious of my intense shame and chatted away as ever, "As artistic custodian of this cultural outpost I am entrusted to arrange a series of events; music, performances, plays, readings and so forth, throughout the year and, as such..."

His voice faded away to be replaced by the most sublime sound drifting down the corridor. At first, such was its pure ethereal beauty, that I thought it was a bird. Perhaps a skylark or a nightingale I mused, even an angel such was the heavenly trill. Then as we turned a corner the sweet song resolved into the strumming of a harpsichord accompanied by the soaring tones of an exquisite female soprano.

"... And that's why she's here," continued the Count as we stopped outside the door of the music room. Uncertain of what he had said I let him finish, "So, would you like to meet her?"

I cannot remember if I nodded or not but I will never forget what happened when he opened the door. For standing next to the harpsichord, with an old duffer at the keys, was the most incredibly captivating young woman that I had ever seen.

The stunning creature was wearing a towering blonde wig and a scintillatingly low cut, pink gown, was about my age, maybe a year older, had piercing sapphire blue eyes, one of those well bred noses that turns up at the end and a pair of lips sweeter than the sweetest valley rose. Her dainty features and snow white skin were reminiscent of a porcelain figurine on a music box, but with a bosom protruding like two alpine peaks and a cleavage ample enough to park the Professor's birota, she was beyond compare. Oh yes, a prettier picture I had never seen and I knew, right from that very first moment, that I was smitten with the biggest smite that anybody had ever been smote.

"Sebastian please allow me to introduce Tatyana von Schumann, gifted operatic soloist and her teacher Herr Donizetti. My sweet this is Sebastian Drechsler; student of Ingolstadt University here to catalogue the library."

She noticed me staring at her as would have a blind man facing the other way and asked with a coy smile, "Are you all right, sir?"

I wiped my mouth in case I was drooling and she continued with an air of haughtiness, "A *librarian* eh? How exciting." Then achieving a level of humiliation I had never imagined possible, she twisted her refined nose at the book under my arm and observed, "You obviously take your work very seriously, Sir. I wonder to what category you would attribute *that* particular novel?"

She stirred an immaculately drawn eyebrow but before the ground could swallow me whole Bassus offered, "Tatyana is playing the lead in Handel's Alcina at our opera house here in Poschiavo next month. Perhaps you would like to attend?"

I was about to tell him I would kill myself if I did not when the fossil at the harpsichord griped, "If she wants to perform at all without losing her voice after the first act then she'd better start practising right now. So if you will excuse us please, Gentlemen."

"You have been told, *Gentlemen*," she purred.

"Yes, my sweet. Well, we wouldn't like you to lose your voice would we now and let down your adoring audience?" judged Bassus wisely.

She offered him her hand which he kissed then never once taking her eyes from mine, she very deliberately smiled and curtseyed low enough for me to gaze lustfully between her mountainous summits.

I might still have been there today staring had the Count not put his hand back to my elbow and firmly led me from the room. Once outside he explained that there was much he had to arrange for the darling's upcoming performance at the festival (though he did not put it quite like that) and that he would see me when these duties allowed then left me in a state of wild romantic delirium. I ran back to the library to finally return the book but noticed that I could still hear her angelic singing. So, overlooking work, or even pulling the bell rope to summon Gretchen with my breakfast, I crept upstairs from where I could listen to the nightingale properly.

She was a prodigious talent that was for sure and, even though, frustratingly, I could not see her, I was bedazzled by her performance. When the rehearsal finished and I heard the sounds of her departure I ran to a window overlooking the front steps. Seeing her as she stood talking for a moment with Donizetti before mounting her carriage caused my heart to flutter like the wings of a bluebird in May. When she glanced up at my window I pulled back into the shadows then stepped forward again as her carriage rattled away. I knew I had to see her again and, though I only had to wait a few weeks, even that was far, far too long.

I tried my best not to think about her or the upcoming festival too much over the following weeks but kept my mind on my work. The cataloguing continued to go well and, with my keen young assistants now doing almost everything themselves, and having to spend only two or three hours a day supervising them to confirm all was in order, by the end of February I started to spend my afternoons playing billiards on the Count's new table or exploring the town.

I had heard nothing back from the Professor and felt no pressure to return to Ingolstadt. Though Francesca was, of course, always on my mind, I knew she was being well looked after and, realising that it was useless to worry about something

I could ill affect, I tried not to think about her or the birth. In short, I sought out distractions during these days to take my mind of such quandaries; riding, reading, chess, billiards and drinking mostly but also, of growing importance, shopping. For with my pockets relatively bulging, I was determined to buy some new clothes. As my bags had allowed nothing more I had come to Poschiavo with the most meagre of wardrobes.

When I had mentioned this to the Count after I thought he had noticed, with some sadness, that I only wore one jacket, I had been most surprised when he had simply instructed me to visit his tailors in town to be 'fitted out' and to put these purchases on his account. Though I could easily afford my own new clothes from any old haberdashery, in my mind the Count's tailor was worthy of a medal, perhaps several. While pride had made me reluctant to take him up on his generous offer until now, the thought of making a grand arrival at the opera in a dashing new outfit guaranteed to outclass all the other brutes proved a prospect that I could no longer resist. So, one day, I visited the shop.

The perfectly groomed tailor was so gay that it was impossible not to let his high-spirits affect me. While being measured for an entire new wardrobe with intimate, and probably unnecessary precision he gave me all the local gossip; who was marrying who, who was having an affair, who drank too much, who drank too little and how much everyone was looking forward to the spring festival and I left his shop in a dizzying state of excitement. As I had come to notice more and more, everyone in Poschiavo was the same. From the butcher to the baker, the cobbler and even the undertaker, everyone seemed to share the same cheerful optimistic manner. During those heady weeks before the festival, as I mingled in the squares and the coffee shops with the happy townspeople, I have to admit, I felt the same gay, care-free attitude infecting me.

I often found myself in the company of open-minded strangers with whom I quickly felt at ease and spent my time laughing and joking with these care-free, bohemians who, in the most part, seemed to spend the entirety of their nights drinking and dancing along to the many musicians who frequented the bierkellers. I marvelled at how sophisticated and cultured and socially relaxed it was. Even compared to Ingolstadt which I had found a revelation coming from stuffy, old, humdrum Tuffengarten. Perhaps, more importantly, I eased into a pleasant, if a little lazy, routine because I knew that no one in this gentle cosmopolitan place was really a secret Illuminati agent who, at every moment, was conspiring to do away with me.

Chapter 13

A Night at the Opera

As always when waiting with high expectations time seems to stand still. The week before the opera was no different and passed extremely slowly. During these days I almost entirely neglected my librarian's work, preferring instead to spend my time socialising in town and especially at the cafe next to Ambrosini's bookshop, which seemed a beacon for the characters peculiar to Poschiavo. I frequently met there with Bahrdt and Mayr who introduced me to all manner of intriguing oddballs including runaways, military deserters and political refugees from all corners of our troubled continent.

One morning, after a particularly late night out with Bahrdt, I answered the door of my chambers to a well-mannered young man who delivered my new clothes which I was delighted to discover were even more glamorous than I had hoped. This put me in an excellent frame of mind and I dressed up and paraded about my rooms pretending to be one of Bassus' privileged young acolytes who I had seen about town, busy doing nothing. Yes. That was the life for me.

So heartened was I by the clothes, my general mood and Tatyana's imminent performance, I realised that I had become slightly dissolute in my ways and decided on the spot to make a new start and to give up my drinking nights with Herr Bahrdt and my bedtime reading with Fräulein Hill. With these resolutions firmly in place I concluded that all was definitely well.

At last it was the Sunday of the Opera. I lazed around the house all day until it was time to get dressed then spent hours deciding what to wear and arranging my hat, jacket, pocket watch and chain and cravat until they were all just so.

Once these vital tasks were complete I proceeded to pace around the room constantly checking my pocket watch until I drove myself mad. An added frustration was that I had forgotten to purchase a walking cane which all gentlemen in Poschiavo seemed to have. I could not find the Count to borrow one and it was too late to buy one as all the shops were shut. I dared not take mine for obvious reasons. I could not remember whether to the turn the handle clockwise or anti-clockwise and had no idea whether it was set to explode or not.

I inspected my reflection for the hundredth time in my mirror and sighed deeply. My clothes, which seemed most excellent two hours ago, now seemed a little baggy and ill-fitting. I shook my head and sighed, "What shall we do with you eh, Seb?" Five minutes later I was sitting on a barrel in the cellar having a few tankards of beer to calm my nerves and trying desperately not to spill any on my new billowing cravat.

The opera house, though comparatively modest, was huge for a town of Poschiavo's size. Another gift from the philanthropic Bassus, the graceful building was fittingly built in the same classical style as his own house: fluted Corinthian columns and all. Not that I could see the damn things as I had to alight from the carriage halfway up the street upon finding a milling throng waiting outside which block the road. I was a little alarmed to find an even bigger crowd in the foyer, making it almost impossible to enter the auditorium. Thankfully, the Count had reserved me a seat in the centre of the second row, as only dignitaries such as Barons, Dukes, Generals and the like, filled the first. I felt most privileged and extremely fortunate, as the stalls, the place from where I usually watched any performance, resembled a cattle pen on market day.

I was handed a programme by an usher; a single piece of paper, no doubt from Ambrosini's printing press, which read:

'Alcina: An Opera Seria by George Fredric Handel 1729. Adapted from Ludovic Ariosto's epic poem Orlando Furioso. Roles: Alcina, A sorceress soprano - Tatyana von Schumann.'

That was all I needed to know and I squeezed my way down the row to find my seat, being careful not to crease my jacket. I could not see Bassus amongst the hats and feathers ahead of me but I could not see the faces in the boxes either so I presumed that my benefactor was up there. The conductor soon walked out before the orchestra and the crowd gradually hushed as some of the lights were snuffed out and the smaller chandeliers lowered. After a settling pause the curtains swept back and, with one mighty blast, the opera finally began.

The story of Alcina centres around two young lovers who become stranded on a mysterious island ruled by a powerful sorceress who seduces everyone that journeys there but quickly tires of them and turns them into statues, or animals, or plants or anything else that takes her fancy. After the usual melodramatic rigmarole all is resolved; Alcina finds true love thenceforth all characters, including the original young lovers, are turned back into humans and everyone lives happily ever after. Or, at least, that is what I took to happen because it was in Italian which I cannot understand even when spoken very softly and slowly. So please forgive me if I cannot be sure. *[16]

Though I was certain of one thing: from the moment Tatyana von Schumann strode out onto the stage in her dramatic makeup

---

16. **The Illuminati in Music & The Opera Alcina by George F. Handel.** The opera, also known as The Sorceress is, generally, as S. Drechsler describes and available to E Book readers who wish to share the author's night out. The Illuminati has always been associated with music, never more so than today but rumours abound from Mozart to the Beatles and Beyonce. Whilst many maybe difficult to substantiate, and even harder to believe, there can be no question that a sinister group wishing to control the world from behind the scenes would seek to control popular musicians for their own devices.

and costume; a female Pan with antlers and even a fetching tail, along with the entire audience, I was utterly bewitched. Even without the music, which, to be fair, is not the best opera ever penned, she was mesmerizing and used her athletic supple body, revealed by means of a skimpy costume, to great effect. She was the perfect operatic actress. But with the music, she was phenomenal and I was almost moved to tears by her gorgeous soprano. Good Lord, she could sing. Also, like all the best performers, she knew how to hold an audience. Throughout the entire performance I was convinced that she was looking straight at me but when I glanced around I saw several other men, young and old, who were under the same illusion, and her spell. I even saw one ancient general seated in front of me get thumped by his wife for licking his lips though, I am sure, such was her tantalizing performance that I may well have licked my own.

All too quickly it came to an end and I leapt to my feet along with two hundred other men, who were joined moments later by their slightly reluctant wives. For Tatyana had stolen the show and soon came out from between the curtains to enjoy the applause and, to my surprise, a shower of spring flowers. This seemed quite the fashion in Poschiavo, though unheard of in more reserved Bavaria so I had not thought to bring any. I looked enviously at those who had because I wanted to show my admiration too, and so much so it riled me. She led the rest of the cast for a final bow and although I shouted louder than everyone around me, now she did not seem to see me at all. I was still shouting fanatically when Bassus joined her on stage and triumphantly held up her hand, a gesture which was greeted with a tremendous cheer and even some more bouquets.

A line of men started to form at the side of the hall next to the orchestra pit. I noticed some of them preening their hair and others waiting with flowers that they had stolen off the stage.

Excusing myself as I did so, I barged my way through the departing guests and pushed my way into the queue before it stretched out of the auditorium and into the foyer. Our patience was duly rewarded when Tatyana appeared from the side of the stage along with Bassus who began introducing her to the young bucks and some ancient codgers who obviously still fancied themselves. Some of the men looked far too dashing for my liking as they posed about in their military uniforms. I did not enjoy the way she giggled and swooned as they boasted of their latest campaign or cavalry charge. Finally it was my turn and Bassus jested, "Ah ha. I think you two have met already."

At last her dazzling blue eyes met with mine and she offered her bejewelled hand, smiling, "Did you enjoy the show?"

"Of course I did. I didn't want it to stop?" I kissed her hand being careful not to suck off any of her rings.

"Did you hear that, Tatyana?" chuckled Bassus, "He didn't want it to stop."

"Yes I heard him," she beamed sympathetically.

I went to say something wittier but Bassus whisked her away to greet the next man in line and, though I tried hard, I could not catch her eye again. After a while the line broke up and everyone followed her into the cramped foyer where it was impossible to get near as the other remaining guests flocked to her like moths to a candle. I pushed my way to the bar and had a drink and a secret fart and generally loitered about waiting with some of the others to see what would happen next.

There was a rumour of a celebration in the big house over the street and about half an hour later we watched through the windows of the foyer as Bassus and Tatyana's entourage crossed the street from the stage door and entered the house outside which I now noticed two burly footmen. I quickly drank up, left my glass tottering on the table and trooped into the street with the rest to join a crowd, perhaps fifty strong, which formed another line that slowly shuffled towards the house.

From somewhere behind I heard a voice call, "Woodturner! Where's your ring?"

It was Bahrdt waving his hat. I gestured him to come and join me and after a bit of fuss from the men behind us he squeezed in.

He gave an oily smile but warned me, "They won't let you in without a ring you know?"

He showed me a ring on his middle finger. I leant closer and saw that it was engraved with a hand holding a hammer.

"You're not a member?"

"A member of what?" I asked, peering back toward the open door.

"A member of the society."

"What society?" I said, vaguely remembering him mentioning a club of which a 'certain select crowd' of the locals were members but it had been during one of our longer nights out spent propping up the bar and I had not paid too much attention.

"You must be a member to get in," he stated categorically.

As he said this the men in front went inside and finally it was my turn. I came up to the door and the large servant pointed to my finger. Damn it. Bahrdt was right but I complained, "I'm staying with the Count; Count Bassus... at his house... the big one."

The man looked blankly at me and shook his head.

I protested, "Surely that's enough man?"

"You must be a member to come in, sir," he insisted.

I looked past him through the crowd and glimpsed Tatyana laughing and welcoming the guests as he said, "Sorry, sir, but you'll have to step out of the way for the next man."

"Curses!" I fumed but gave in, "Yes, yes, yes. I will go. Let the next man in, why not?" I huffed and stormed away.

"I told you," called Bahrdt. Then the blaggard showed his ring and stepped inside.

I trudged off in a terrible mood, shouting up at windows and kicking at the ground. By now I had imagined myself fully ensconced in Tatyana's dressing room toasting her in champagne, admiring her bouquets and gossiping about the production; whether she thought that the violins had played with too much vibrato and if the old conductor needed to be replaced by a younger, more virile man, while, of course, constantly complimenting her breathtaking performance. Bugger the Saints! I had an especially loud fart and, finding myself in the square overlooking Ambrosini's bookshop, stopped behind a tree for a well-needed piss. As I relieved myself I spied a wagon drawn by a single horse waiting outside the shop and noted that the cellar light was still on, as usual. "That old Giuseppe works too hard," I grumbled to myself, "That's why *he's* always miserable."

As I shook my manhood dry a shadowy rider trotted up from the stables round the back. When he drew up next to the wagon his face briefly caught the light from the cellar window and I instantly recognised him. It was Massenhausen! I almost pissed my new breeches putting my manhood away then made myself as thin as possible behind the tree. What in God's name was the murderous son of a bitch doing here? Of all places. I deeply suspected that he had not come for the cultural festival and peeped out to see what he was up to. Ambrosini had appeared and was directing his boy to help the driver of the wagon load several bound stacks of paper aboard. 'What's this?' I thought. I doubted that they were spare copies of the opera programmes. So what were they?

With the mysterious cargo loaded Massenhausen grunted his goodbyes and led the wagon away while Ambrosini ushered his boy back into the shop. After a moment I came out from behind the tree and crept across the square. Unfortunately, they had not dropped any of the pamphlets so I could not find out what it was all about. I crouched down to peep through the dusty cellar window but had no luck there either because, as I did, the light was snuffed out. There was nothing else that I could do, so I quietly slipped away.

I traipsed back to the Count's house anxiously glancing over my shoulder every time a coach clattered past carrying the last of the late night revellers in case it was Massenhausen. Shit. What an awful night, when I had had such high expectations. Not only had I been completely overlooked by that gorgeous woman but I had discovered that I was still haunted by the Illuminati and the next in a long line of evil bastards. I looked up into the night sky and cursed my luck. I had come all this way, hundreds of miles, to this beautiful place, to an entirely different country, where finally everything was all right, well, partially all right, and now even this beautiful idyll had been ruined. Bugger the Illuminati! It seemed that nowhere, not even this island of peace and tranquillity was safe from their scourge. How could I relax here now knowing that, at any moment, the fiend and his friends could jump out from round a corner and slit my throat?

I had a spark of inspiration. I would tell Bassus what I had seen. Yes! Of course. That was it. If anyone could sort out Massenhausen it was the influential Count and his minions. Though I was initially encouraged by this plan, I worried that a man of his jovial disposition might be sceptical of my wild conspiracy theories and by the time I had got back to the house I had returned to my previous low ebb. I went directly to the library, found what I was looking for then slipped upstairs to take out my anguish and frustration.

Chapter 14

Siege Mentality

The next morning I awoke in a foetid, sweaty mess and so nauseated by my foul smelling flatulence that I thought I would be sick. I lay there scratching myself for a moment before the previous night's memories came clattering back through my consciousness like a stagecoach full of bad dreams and I fairly threw myself back against my headboard in a fit of feverish vexation.

I sprang from my bed, splashed some cold water on my face, pulled on a pair of clean breeches and ran downstairs. After discreetly replacing the book, I went to find the Count to tell him what had happened. Though I searched high and low I could not find him anywhere and guessed that he had still not come home from the celebrations. I hurried back to my room and unpacked my quadre bow from its holster. Simply seeing the menacing weapon made my heart start to race and I carefully checked it over with my trembling fingers. Everything seemed fine so I loaded it with four silver-tipped bolts and sat on the bed staring at the distant mountains with the fearsome thing resting on my lap.

This was ridiculous. I could not just sit here armed to the teeth waiting for Massenhausen to reappear. Anyway, the evil son of a bitch was probably over those hills and faraway by now. He certainly was not taking coffee and strudels in town. My stomach rumbled as the smells from the kitchens wafted upstairs and, realising that I could not take the weapon to breakfast, I looked for somewhere safe to hide it so as not to alarm the chambermaid who might tell Gretchen. In the end, when the smell became too much to bear, I gave up and left it conspicuously on top of my wardrobe and ran downstairs.

After eating I went to the stables to get a pigeon but upon finding that the idiot young servants had let another one die, I lost my temper and gave them a hearty tongue lashing. I returned to my bedchamber in a foul mood with one of the more fortunate animals under my arm and immediately penned a message to the Professor which read: *Work going well but seen Massenhausen leaving P in cart full of pamphlets. Printed Here! Flight or fight? Please advise!!!*

This seemed to eloquently describe my position so, after checking that no one was looking, I released the bird out of my window and wished it Godspeed.

The next few days were dire. Count Bassus did not return and, in my solitude, I went over my dilemma a million times until I started to develop a siege mentality. I finally resolved that, while I could not guarantee Massenhausen would visit Ambrosini's again, I could certainly guarantee that I did not. If I had to go out, I would go somewhere else and, wherever that was, I would take my hunting knife with me. The only thing that truly worried me was if, unbeknownst to me, Bassus and Massenhausen were friends and the brute turned up one day for a tour of the blasted library. As Bassus was not there I could not ask him, so I resolved to keep my knife with me at all times in my discreet underarm sheath. During this time I became a virtual prisoner in the house, preferring now to work alone as Bassus had inexplicably changed my young servants before leaving and it was not worthwhile training their slightly duller replacements. When I peevishly asked the youths what had become of their predecessors they told me that they had been required at another one of the Count's estates.

As my work continued my reading took me to a darker place. I read Milton's Paradise Lost, Dante's Inferno and amongst others a treatise of Isaac Luria's Kabbalah which seemed to suggest that, because both good and bad acts hastened the coming of God, Moses' Ten Commandments could be inverted wherein thou shalt *not* kill, becomes thou *shalt* kill, etcetera, etcetera. *[17] Though it was all serious stuff, I did not baulk and tried to remain 'open minded' as the Count had recommended. But in the end, perhaps because of my reading matter, my enforced solitude or perhaps because of my low esteem after being ignored by Tatyana or perhaps, moreover, because I felt it morbidly fascinating, I began to take the copy of Fanny Hill to my bedchamber every night. Though this constant self-pleasuring was something I had never done before, and I was concerned that it was becoming a habit, I consoled myself that my urges would dwindle the moment I saw her again.

Then two weeks to the day after my night at the opera, I knew this because it was Sunday, I was busily working away in the library when I heard a carriage pull up in the driveway and Bassus hailing his staff. I threw my quill in its pot and ran off to investigate and found him outside chatting with someone through the window of a pretty pink, two-wheeled barouche carriage drawn by a pair of frisky white ponies. Certain that the buggy was far too gay to be Massenhausen's, I came up close where I could be seen and brimming with eagerness to tell him about Poschiavo's new and most unwelcome guest.

"Ah. Sebastian! We were just talking about you," he welcomed and turned around to reveal Tatyana sitting in the carriage swaddled in an alluring white fur cape and hat.

"Hello, Librarian," she smirked.

---

17. **Lurian Kabbalah.** Isaac Luria (1534 -1572) developed his version of Kabbalah in the sixteenth century. Luria's idea suggested that man was moving through time to eventually become God himself, lends itself to the philosophy of spiritual autonomy popular in the renaissance. Though it is not difficult to imagine how, in the wrong hands, such spiritual 'freedom' could be problematic.

Thank God I had worn one of my new frock coats, a clean shirt and my new extremely tight breeches that morning and looked presentable. "Good day, Fräulein Schumann," I replied with a bow, trying to hide my delight upon seeing her though my heart was galloping like a highwayman's horse.

"I have a problem," sighed the Count, "I have booked luncheon for myself and Tatyana in town but I have remembered that I have another appointment here so, I ..." He gave her a complicitous smile, "... *We* were wondering if you would like to go instead?"

All I had wanted to do for the last two weeks was talk to him about Massenhausen but felt my resolve crumble like a castle made of sand as I glimpsed Tatyana's glistening lips. I started, "There was something I wanted to talk to you about, Count..."

"Something about the library? I'm sure it can wait, my friend." He patted his waistcoat and fretted, "I'm late already and I fear you might be too. Damnation. Where's my watch?"

Without thinking, I took out my own and noted, "Half past the hour of twelve, sir."

He stopped what he was doing and stared at the silver timepiece then laughed at Tatyana with an air of vindication, "I told you he was an interesting one, this student of Ingolstadt."

"Most interesting," she agreed, arching an eyebrow.

Conscious that I had mistakenly revealed too much I conceded, "...Of course I will go, sir. How could I refuse?"

I tucked the watch back in my waistcoat, felt to see that my knife was secure and pulled myself into the seat next to her.

"Good idea, my learned friend," jollied Bassus, "One cannot work all day. Abracadabra," he tapped his walking cane, "I create what I speak. Enjoy yourselves," and closed the door behind us.

The driver flicked his whip and the pink contrivance pulled off up the driveway with a spritely jolt. Yes! This was the life!

Not hiding in a library like a fearful hermit but the life of a proper gentleman, riding in a luxurious carriage with a beautiful woman by my side. A little overwhelmed by my sudden change of circumstances, and now with the beautiful woman *right* by my side, I could not remember any of the wonderful witticisms that I had dreamt up and rehearsed every day since meeting her. She noticed me struggling for conversation and broke the ice, "I'm glad you decided to join me, Librarian. There is much I wish to talk to you about."

At last I had the excuse to look right into her beautiful eyes and, determined not to mess things up, replied as cool as a cucumber, "My name is Sebastian, my lady and there is much I wish to talk to you about too."

"Good," she grinned, "Then we will not have to listen to each other chewing all the way through dinner."

She appeared to bite her lip and turned to look out of the window, showing off her stunning profile. It might sound arrogant but, as much as I fought it, I could not help feel that she was attracted to me, though presumably took it for granted that all men were attracted to her. Such was the flirtatious atmosphere between us that any further conversation seemed unnecessary, until we pulled into one of the town's many squares (this one appropriately boasting a statue of Cupid complete with archer's bow) where we stopped outside a delightful little restaurant and she chuckled with delight, "Ah ha. The Garden of Paradise. You'll love it here."

A footman promptly opened her door and I followed her inside. She confidently informed the maitre'd that we were the Count's guests and required the best service and soon we were sitting in a corner at our own table, romantically regarding each other over a bottle of wine and tucking into a lavish meal. We conversed politely at first and she told me about her career and her upcoming performances in Vienna, about which she was very excited and that she enjoyed Tarot and the artist Durer. I was pleased to tell her that I shared this last pleasure and we chinked our glasses in happy irony that Melencolia was our favourite piece. Wonderful. By the time we had finished the meal, washed down with two carafes of claret, we were both relaxed and well at ease with each other. After looking me over for the umpteenth time, still attempting to size me up, she said sardonically, "I feel there is more to you than a normal librarian, sir."

"I wouldn't have thought you had too much experience of librarians, normal or not, my lady. And please, call me Sebastian."

"Why did you not come to our little party after the opera - Sebastian?" she asked jokingly and added with a charming smile, "And please call me Tatyana."

Merely hearing her say my name made it hard to concentrate but I explained, "Because I am not a member of the society."

"Why not?" she scoffed, as though it was as common as wearing socks.

"I didn't know that I needed to be," I replied with a sigh, remembering my disappointment that night.

"I see," she took a sip of wine, "Members can attain many things, you know? Many advantageous things. Favour, privilege, money, knowledge."

"Ah. I'm sure there is much I should know," I wagered. "After all: salvation through knowledge eh?" I toasted my witty observation and she raised her own glass in appreciative accord. I probed, "So what *should I know* to become a member?"

She gave me a questioning glance and asked, "Well, that depend doesn't it? Do you wnat to be man or master?"

Seeing my puzzlement she took an apple from the bowl on the table and held it out before me. "Cut it in half," she said with a smile.

Intrigued, I took the apple and, as the table had been cleared of cutlery, I absentmindedly took out my hunting knife. She looked at it as though it was a crocodile and sarcastically flustered, "Goodness me. What else do you have in there?"

I passed it off with a manly shrug and went to slice the apple along the stem but she placed her hand on mine in a fashion that I am sure she knew arousing and said softly, "No. The other way."

I tried to keep my composure, turned the apple around and chopped it in half. She picked up one of the pieces and explained, "See the seeds make a five pointed pentagram? This pentagram symbolises man, the microcosm, and the six pointed hexagram the universe or the macrocosm. Embracing this elemental relationship between five and six man becomes master and achieves the mystic eleventh point within The Tree of Life: Da'ath - one more than ten, Kabbalah's number for God - or The Magician in Tarot: he who possesses the spiritual insight, higher intuition and alchemic abilities to control both worlds: As above, so below. But to do so he must first taste the forbidden fruit of knowledge." She looked deep into my eyes and took a bite from the apple so seductively that I felt my breeches tighten. She chewed it up and swallowed it then asked with a wanton pout, "Are you ready to become master, Sebastian?" Now it was my turn to swallow. I nodded with transfixed anticipation and, like Holy Eve herself tempting Adam, she slipped the slice in my dribbling mouth then whispered softly, "Because the day ye shall eat thereof your eyes will be opened and ye too shall see as Elohim."

This mixture of biblical and hermetic texts was spellbinding and, along with her alluring lasciviousness, I was pawing like a rampant bull in a dirty field. She knew it and, seemingly satisfied with her work, abruptly sat back in her chair and said rather curtly, "I think you should take me home now."

She stood to go and in my haste to follow her I almost knocked over the table. She glanced at my bulging breeches and, mistakenly thinking that I had done so with my increased manly proportions, giggled with glee all the way out of the restaurant leaving me shamefully bringing up the rear, hastily buttoning my coat over my pantaloons.

This embarrassing state of affairs continued all the way back to the Count's mansion where she finally chuckled with her hand over her mouth, "Well, I hope I will see you again soon, Sebastian, the librarian *full* of surprises."

She gave me her pretty hand to kiss. I obliged and, though I wanted to beg her to stay so I could show her a few more, I stepped out and watched her carriage pull away. *¹⁸

18. **The Eye of Elohim - Da'ath.** Da'ath (Daat) is the mystic or invisible eleventh sefirot, or point, in Kabbalah's Tree of Life and has similar qualities in western new ageism to the The Third Eye. The other ten sefirot represent God; 1 being the masculine principle and 0 the feminine, thus the eleventh, which is created when connections are made between the second, third, fourth and fifth sefirot, becomes transcendent to God. It is said that when Da'ath is achieved so much light is radiated that the other sefirot become indistinguishable and become 'as one.' The Eye of Elohim (or The Eye of God) is mentioned by the serpent in The Garden of Eden from the book of Genesis as it tempts Eve to eat the apple and refers to the transcending of the soul as self-realisation. The Master or Magician card in Tarot is traditionally depicted with one hand pointing up and the other down in classic 'As above, so below' pose.

Chapter 15

Defend the Fort

I brushed myself off, made damn sure my coat was buttoned all the way down and, bristling with a fresh determination to protect not only myself but delicate Tatyana too, purposefully strode inside the house to find the Count. I knocked on the door of his study whereupon he bade me enter and I marched inside to find him standing at his desk inspecting some documents.

"Have fun?" he asked and I rudely muttered my thanks. He took his attention away from his work and, noticing my pensive expression he asked, "Is something troubling you, Sebastian?"

This time I was not going to be distracted and came straight out with it, "Do you know Baron Massenhausen, sir?"

"Maybe I have shaken his hand somewhere. The name certainly sounds familiar. But then I am a politician, I shake a lot of hands." He came round the table and offered me a chair. "Tell me? Who is this man to you?"

"I don't know him well, sir, but well enough to know he cannot be trusted near decent folk. I saw him at Ambrosini's after the opera collecting some stacks of printed papers."

"Giuseppe's an extremely busy man, my friend. He has lots of customers. After all, he has the only printing press for miles."

Seeing that I was not fully satisfied he added, "I will ask Ambrosini what he was doing there if it reassures you."

"That would be very kind, Count," I said more humbly, "It would put my mind at rest." My thoughts returned to my fabulous afternoon for which I had not properly thanked him and I said, more timidly, "There was something else, sir?"

"Anything, my friend."

"Why did you not tell me about the society when you have told me about so many other things?"

"Ah yes. Forgive me yet again. I noted your absence at the gathering after the opera. It was my fault. With everything else I simply forgot that you would not be granted entry. Please allow me to explain. I did not feel it necessary for you to know about our little society as you were only here for a short time and, as such, would not truly benefit from membership. It is merely a group of like-minded libertarians such as myself, some with hermetic leanings, some not, who come together once a month on the full moon to share ideas and mutual understandings. That's all really. Oh, and members generally help one another in business and, shall we say, other areas where possible."

As I contemplated this he offered, "If you wish I could organise your enrolment? That would be a formality with me as your sponsor." He watched my eyes.

Though I had not expected him to say this it was exactly what I had wished, and my troubled expression broke into a smile.

"Ah. Of course," he acknowledged, "I will make the necessary arrangements. Now, let me see," he inspected a diary on his desk, "The next meeting is in three weeks on..." he looked genuinely surprised, "Oh. The 22nd of March. Well, well, well. If you're not a student of Gematria then I should tell you this date is particularly auspicious. Indeed, perhaps the most auspicious of all. There is also a little introductory handbook for initiates to read and I will make sure you get one. So shall we say then? Yes?" He picked up a quill and scratched a note in his diary in his effortless but beautiful handwriting.

And apparently that was that. Voila! Surprised at the ease with which my problems had been solved, I slowly lifted myself from my chair and, taking my leave, gazed at the profusion of framed pictures, certificates and paintings covering the walls of his office. Amongst etchings of lions, tigers, and many elephants, I spotted a print of Durer's Melencolia. The incredible coincidence brought me to a sudden halt.

Bassus noted, "Ah yes. Tatyana likes that one too. Durer was a genius. Apparently, the winged maiden Melencolia is the least desirable muse. However, the initiated understand that only the melancholic possess true intelligence and creativity." He gave me a learned nod. "Beauty often hides where least expected, eh?" He seemed to allude to something positive that I would, no doubt, soon discover and mentioned, "May I recommend a wonderful alternative critique on the subject by Johann Winckelmann. There's one in the library." *[19]

With this he showed me to the door and I left his study considering my life was much like the view from my window: one moment in the deepest darkest valley, the next atop the highest sunniest peak.

I kept myself to myself over the next weeks, stayed away from the beer, the pornography, and Gretchen and her damnable bird and carried on with my work in the library. I considered my own dissertation while delving into many texts during my long nights by the fire: Hermetic, Alchemic, Gnostic, Kabbalistic, Geometric. I explored the fascinating critique Bassus had recommended which, in turn, led me to Solomon's pillars Jachin and Boaz and, eventually, after seemingly scores of other tomes, I found myself, once again, exploring Gematria, the method of ascribing numbers to letters and, in turn, meanings to numbers.

---

19. **Melancholia Hermetic Insights.** The hidden meanings, allegories and plethora of symbols in Durer's masterpiece of the androgynous angel Melencolia have baffled and intrigued art historians for centuries. There were thought to be four humours controlling our state of mind according to German thinker Cornelius Agrippa, Melencolia was level one and pertained to artists.

I discovered the reason why Bassus had been so excited about the date of the society's next meeting - and my initiation - In Gematria twenty two is a Master Number, as there are twenty two letters in the Hebraic language of the Old Testament, the number represents the word of God, also the Tree of Life has twenty two paths connecting its points, or sefirots.

This intriguing topic fast became a particular favourite of mine which I took upon myself to study avidly. Late one night with the candles burning low, I came across a rare text explaining how tantric repetition of these Master Numbers could produce spells. For example; three elevens make thirty three, a most powerful numerical spell with ominous aspects because 3x3=9, and God is symbolized by ten: 1 the masculine and 0 the feminine in balance, nine symbolises fallen and as all numbers multiplied by nine add up to nine: once fallen, *always* fallen. *[20] I found the subject most fascinating and developed a deep empathy with the heretical ideas, as one new breakthrough quickly led to another they built up and up like a wall - the wall of a temple. During those long nights I reflected how far I had come from the little boy holding his mother's hand in church. For I now considered my previous beliefs to be those of a child and, since I had grown up, I now sought out the ideas of a man.

One day, as promised, I found my initiate's handbook left

20. **Gematria & The Occult.** Gematria originated in Assyrian Greek Babylonian culture and is the method of ascribing alpha numerical code to letters, though the technique is often adapted to ascribe meanings to pure numbers. Tarot uses a form of numerology similar to Gematria. Six, six, six is meant to signify man in his lowest beast form, hence the number of the beast, whereas seven, seven, seven signifies man exalted. John Dee the first controller of MI5 and renowned hermetic Kabbalist referred to himself as the first agent or 007. It perhaps then can be no coincidence that MI5 is the national intelligence service five representing microcosm and MI6 international intelligence when six represents the macrocosm and, of course, together, as S. Drechsler explains, they would be eleven, or the Magician in Tarot.

on the plinth in the library. Upon opening it I saw that it was printed by Ambrosini. Who else? On the first page, underneath the emblem of the hand holding the hammer, in a grand font it introduced, *Guidance for Initiates of The Craft*. 'The Craft' I presumed referring generally to all labour undertaken by members. Interestingly, I noted that there were eleven rules: Cause the society no harm, a bible must be open at all times in all meetings, no lie must knowingly be told to another member, the meeting area was sacrosanct and therefore the consumption of intoxicants was prohibited and, though I cannot remember them all, intriguingly I recall the eleventh stated that all initiates must believe in a celestial master, or grand architect as the handbook put it, though, as an indication of the growing free-thinking spirit in those enlightened times, it did not specify the Christian God.

I closed the booklet reflecting that it was all good clean fun between gentleman with their quirky rules and traditions and that, if it included running round the countryside with my breeches round my ankles while they all drunkenly mocked me, I was prepared to do it to get closer to that darling woman. For I was convinced that my membership of the society would grant me some sort of new level of intimacy with Tatyana. How, I could not think but I guessed that it must be some subtle understated secret that was never discussed but always known; a nod, a wink, a tap of the nose - like the Professor and me. I stopped to think about him for a moment, and Francesca, whom I had been intentionally keeping from my mind. I considered sending my last pigeon but what should I say? That everything was 'probably' going to be all right? I had still not received a reply which convinced me that I cared more than they anyway. Also, I felt no need to mention my membership of this organisation. Anyway, that was rule number six of the society: Never mention the society.

So, at sundown on the 22nd of March Bassus knocked on the door of my chambers to take me to the chapel in his grounds where my initiation was to be held. He smiled approvingly upon finding me smartly dressed with my new cane, of the unexploding variety and, without further ado, escorted me downstairs.

We strolled leisurely through the house and out into the garden where the rich aromas played my senses like a violin concerto. He sniffed the air and, nodding reverently to Sirius twinkling in the twilight over the horizon, observed, "Ah ha. Our celestial mother blesses us with her perennial fertility." He inhaled the seductive scents once more and asked, "Are you ready, Sebastian?"

"Of course, sir," I replied as we came to a timely halt at the chapel door. He checked me over one last time and, as he brushed my lapel, advised with strangely uncharacteristic caution, "One thing my friend, whatever you do, don't let them get your goat. All right?" He checked to see that I was paying attention so I nodded. His boyish grin returned and he smiled, "Right, here we go."

He opened the door and we entered the vestibule where I was surprised to find - of all people - Bahrdt and the butcher waiting in the shadows. Bahrdt gave me a discreet nod and I stood alongside Bassus in front of the door leading to the nave with them slightly behind. The Count gave the door three distinct knocks and there was a notable pause before a slow and steady voice called out, "State your name and your business."

"I am Brother Bassus and I bring an initiate wishing to gain admittance."

We lingered in the shadows for a moment until the voice chanted once more, "Does he possess the three virtues: God's will, a sound mind and a good personage?"

Bassus gave me a cheeky nudge then called out, "He does!"

and, prudently remembering the society's prohibition of weapons, snatched my cane off me as the bolt slid back and the door swung open.

I stepped inside and approached maybe a dozen men at the end of the candlelit aisle, three of whom were seated: one in the centre, signifying the North; one to the left, the West; and one to the right; the East. I did not recognise the first two but was a little perturbed to see Giuseppe Ambrosini the designator of the East. The rest gathered behind them and included Mayr and Bassus' tailor and some others whom I recognised from around town, and before them all, lying upon a lectern as prescribed, an open bible.

I came to a halt before them and Brother North pointed a judge's hammer at me and declared, "Prepare the initiate to show he is of sound body and feeling but suffers the darkness of ignorance."

The Count pulled a black silk scarf from his pocket and tied it over my eyes while Bahrdt rolled up a leg of my breeches and the butcher pulled open my shirt exposing my chest. I clenched my fists as I heard a sword being drawn from a scabbard and a hand pressed down on my shoulder to push me to my knees. The cold tip of a blade pressed into my chest and I was asked, "Do you feel Brother initiate?"

"Yes," I replied with a rather flimsy gulp.

"Do you suffer from the darkness of ignorance?"

"Yes...I suffer..." I stumbled over my much-rehearsed words and felt the bible being pushed under my hand and someone pressing my palm down upon the pages.

"Do you swear to uphold the rules of the society and preserve its secrets or suffer our most severe and capital of punishments?"

There had been no mention of anything 'capital' in the introductory booklet but being blindfolded and held at swordpoint did not seem the time to argue, so once again I gulped, "...Yes..." in the same self-conscious tone and a ring was rather ungraciously pushed onto my middle finger.

I heard three resounding raps of what I took to be the judge's gavel and was told, "Stand on your feet, Brother."

I gratefully got off my knees whereupon my blindfold was removed and Brother North acknowledged me with a stern nod, "Welcome to the Society of The Craft, Brother Drechsler."

I bowed and composed myself while furtively rolling my breeches back down and buttoning up my shirt. A seat was provided for me and some of the others acted out the story of Hiram Abiff with Bahrdt playing the lead role of the chief architect of King Solomon's Temple who was killed by three ruffian builders because he would not divulge the Master Builder's secret password. The story ends when King Solomon finds Hiram's body and catches the ruffians whom he tortures to death after which he replaces the rest of the workforce, secure in the knowledge that the passwords are safe. Though some of the acting was questionable, the importance of the allegory was not lost on me: fidelity and serious punishments for those who divulged secrets.

With the play over, the atmosphere lightened. More candles were lit and my fellow Brothers split up into small groups with some coming over and informally introducing themselves. After Bahrdt and Bassus and a few of the others had shaken my hand, I noticed Ambrosini standing on his own obviously feeling less obliged to say hello. Not wanting to pass up the opportunity of questioning him about Massenhausen, and testing rule number three: do not lie to another Brother, I was about to take the initiative but another man stepped up and began talking to him.

I decided that it was probably best not to cause any trouble on my first night and better to let Bassus get to the bottom of the murky business. After a quick chat with the others, in which I attempted to share my new-found hermetic insights but instead learnt more about the price of mutton, I waited till no one was looking then discreetly slipped outside into the garden and plonked myself down on a bench to take stock.

On the face of it, it seemed nothing more than a group of haberdashers and green grocers chatting in a tavern with a few odd arcane rules and traditions thrown in for good measure but there was still something tangibly idiosyncratic about the group's ethos which I could not quite put my finger on.

I pondered what Bassus might have said had I told him that today, the 22nd, was my birthday and, perhaps, of even more note, that I was twenty two as well. 'Maybe on another day,' I considered. 'Even good friends have secrets,' and quietly wished myself, "Happy birthday Seb. What a time to be alive, eh?"

I gazed up into the heavens noting that The Winter Triangle had shifted lower in the sky and, as I contemplated its distant eternal light, just for a moment, I felt something faintly stir in my deepest, darkest recesses. As though a single, cradled candle of inkling had been lit. Such was this feeling that I stopped to check myself, but still there it was, somewhere deep inside me. Not visceral, or physical but nevertheless something: something important. As much as I attempted to define what it was, it remained a secret to me and I guessed hopefully, as the Count had hinted, that it would soon reveal itself.

*21

---

21. **Secret Societies &_Initiations.** The 18th century was perhaps the zenith of the secret society with most gentlemen of means, if not all, affiliated to one group or another. The benefits of membership were not exclusive but could vary from business, political, cultural to simply social. The practice was widespread in the middle European capital states in those days and especially prevalent within student communities. Though S. Drechsler's initiation most resembles that of the Masonic tradition many societies would have observed similar rituals with similar themes. While the play of the myth of Hiram Abiff is particular to Masonic initiations the three strikes of the judge's gavel is not but is said to, in some ceremonial traditions, symbolize the three nails used for the crucifixion.

Chapter 16

The Tarot Tells All

One thing about my time in Poschiavo is that, as I recall, it was always sunny. Despite knowing that it must have rained at some point during my stay, I cannot remember seeing one drop but only that every day seemed oddly bathed in bright sunshine. The Count once told me that the plateau around the town possessed a 'microcosmic climate' and that a professor of the atmospheric sciences had come there the previous summer with something called a balloon to which he attached a thermometer and flew around the hills and completed many measurements proving that the region was two degrees warmer than the neighbouring valley.

Fittingly, as April bloomed we were treated to almost constantly beautiful weather and, with my work all but completed, I was in excellent spirits. Along with the magnificent splendour of spring bursting into new life all around me, I was overjoyed to be invited to a soirée at the end of the month at Bassus' house. And the best part of all, it was to be hosted by Tatyana. The Count had arranged this prestigious cultural gathering for thirty or so dignitaries from the courts of Europe who were coming to enjoy some hunting and feasting plus some music recitals and, on the last day, Tarot reading. No surprises as to who would be involved with this and with my membership of the society granted I began to chomp at the bit with fresh excitement at the thought of seeing her again.

By this stage I was using Fanny Hill habitually and taking it to my bedchamber every night, sometimes even the occasional afternoon too and then not even returning it the next day but lazily hiding it under my pillow. I had begun to imagine Tatyana as a character in the stories as I ogled my favourite passages and found that this only heightened my pleasure. The Count had recommended that I consider it 'the liberation of my sexual desires' but somehow afterwards I still found myself lying under the covers racked by guilt and memories of Sunday school warnings about 'wasting my seed.' I told myself that I was being prudish and that my urges would fade the moment I saw her again.

At last it was the weekend of the soirée and I waited with bated breath by the upstairs window constantly checking the driveway. Eventually, her pink barouche rattled into view and a couple of young servants readied themselves at the bottom of the steps. I raced downstairs checking my ring was on my finger and that my coat was buttoned down over my tight breeches and, as I was both extraordinarily keen and fit, I was at the door with the Count and some of the others in time to welcome her as her foot stepped onto the gravel.

She took an age saying hello to everyone including Bassus and some old Baroness whose carriage was also being unloaded who stole her attention for an inordinately long time, explaining the myriad ailments of her tiny annoying dog. Finally, she came over to me and flashed her beautiful eyes, jesting, "Hello, Sebastian. I hope you're not hiding anything from me this time."

"Only my overriding joy to see you again," I beamed and kissed her hand, appreciating the opportunity to be entirely truthful.

"I must say, I'm looking forward to spending some more time with you this weekend, in between all my other exertions."

I could think of a few exertions of my own and, as another carriage arrived, I took my chance and led her by the arm into the house. "Ooh, Sebastian," she cooed, "I love it when you're so masterful," and saucily put a finger on her lip, though my eyes were drawn like magnets to her bosom nestling in a low cut scarlet costume.

We were passing the music room and she said, "Ah, maybe I should check inside..." she grinned, "To see that all is ready?"

I looked back up the hallway at Bassus welcoming more guests and the servants bringing in their things but before I knew it she pulled me inside. She closed the door behind me and led me over to the harpsichord by my arm so I took the opportunity to draw her attention to my ring, almost holding it in front of her face. Although I knew that she could see it, she disregarded it with a wrinkle of her nose then wistfully touched a black key leaving a minor tone hanging in the air. "Do you play?" She asked with a note of dreamy nonchalance.

"I have never tried..." I began but she took my hand and placed it on her right breast causing me to shut up and my pulse to thump like the guns of a Spanish Man of War. She sighed in the same absentminded manner, "I think you have the hands for it," and offered up her rosy lips. My loins exploded with excitement but when I leant forward to taste her kiss she pulled her head away as another carriage noisily rattled up outside and a familiar baritone boomed, "Blessings Christians! I trust God has kept you well!"

I froze as stiff as a conductor's baton and murmured, "Danzer?"

Compounding my surprise Tatyana wriggled out from underneath me and gasped, "Uncle Danzer is here. Oh, how he makes me laugh. Come, I'll introduce you. You will love him. Everyone loves Uncle Danzy."

I must have stayed there for a whole two minutes staring in shock at the black and white keys in disbelief as Tatyana's squeals of delight and Danzer's deep voice reverberated down the hallway. At last I heard then coming down the corridor so I managed to pull myself together and over to the doorway where, at least, I had the vengeful pleasure of seeing Danzer's face when he saw mine. His eyes fairly fell out of their sockets as the Count introduced us, "Ah. Yes, this is Sebastian Drechsler: Student of Ingolstadt University here to catalogue the library."

"We... have met," croaked Danzer and I stiffened in horror as I thought the idiot was going to give us both away but he recovered and improvised, "At some... lecture I gave on Catholic morality in Ingolstadt. Yes... I think that must be it. Is it not, young man?"

He implored me with his crazed eyes to help him.

"That's right, Canon Danzer: Catholic morality," I dryly retorted and shook his sweaty hand, noting, "How could I forget?"

"Guess what, Sebastian?" trilled Tatyana like an excited schoolgirl as she escorted him off down the hallway, "Danzy is going to sing for us. Won't that be wonderful? He has such a rich baritone. Don't you, Uncle Danzy?"

Such was my surprise at Danzer's appearance from out of the blue that I spent the next hours in a trance, only capable of slowly repeating what was said to me and staring opened-mouthed into the near distance. This first stage of disbelief was soon replaced by seething jealousy, as I came to understand that 'Danzy' and Tatyana were like uncle and niece and, as such, inseparable. She was either sitting next to him laughing at his stories, by his side singing at the harpsichord, at his feet listening to his wisdom or even sometimes, infuriatingly snuggling on his lap, soothing him with motherly advice and daughterly affection. He was a drunken, lectherours buffoon thirty years her senior, at least, yet she seemed drawn to him like a butterfly to a sweet flower.

It was infuriating and I nearly lost my temper on several occasions. After the way she had acted seconds before his arrival I was dumbfounded at my apparent demotion in her affections and to become a mere spectator of their close, and rather overly-affectionate, companionship. Especially when, if his crazed driver had taken one wrong turn and got lost on the way, I would have had the opportunity to prove my undying love for her right there and then in the blasted music room on top of the damnable harpsichord.

It was a severely frustrating afternoon which turned into an intensely annoying evening. Along with the other more dignified guests I was forced to listen to the two of them sing a hundred boring duets and other dour recitals then hold court until the early hours as they reminisced of their seemingly endless adventures; drinking and revelry mostly, after which the party was broken up without anyone else getting to say a word. The finishing blow came when she bade me goodnight with a single dismissive waggle of her finger and without even looking at me, something she had not done since Danzer's untimely arrival some eight hours previous and I went to bed in the foulest of moods.

To make things worse the temptress was put in the room next to mine and I could hear her singing an old folk song as she prepared for bed. Listening to her seductive voice wafting in through my window was maddening. I felt like Odysseus being lured onto the ruinous rocks by a siren but with no mast about which to tie myself, I covered my head with a pillow.

In the end I could bear it no more and strode masterfully from my bedchamber to go and have it out with her once and for all. But as I turned the corner leading to her room, I froze like one of Alcina's statues when Danzer traipsed up the stairs onto the landing as though he were walking in his sleep. I searched his listless face but there was no sign of compos mentis whatsoever and he walked right by me without a flicker of recognition. Adding to my confusion he stopped outside Tatyana's chambers and knocked on her door in the same listless fashion.

I could not see the door from round the corner but I heard her singing stop and, after a moment, she opened it and whispered, "Ah, there you are. What took you so long? Come in."

I watched with furious envy as Danzer wandered inside and the door closed with a gentle click. I punched the wall next to me causing me great pain and a little plaster to fall away then crept over to the door and listened but all I could hear were muffled voices. After a short silence she started singing the same hypnotic song so, keeping one eye on the corridor, I crouched down and put my ear to the keyhole. Behind her singing I could hear Danzer ranting as he had at the castle but this time more softly and amongst the bars of the rhyme; quoting the bible, wailing for pity, sobbing like a child and even, at times, climatically moaning obscenities. In the end, it was all too much and I returned to my room, slammed the door and the window shut then threw myself on my bed like a heartbroken adolescent and covered my head with a pillow. But it was still no good and overcome with seething envy and twisted pride, I spied Fanny Hill amongst the bedsheets and, once more, succumbed to her addictive lure.

Quite understandably, I did not sleep well that night what with my own nocturnal endeavours and the noisy frolicking next door which continued until sunrise. My emotional turmoil only deepened when, after a particularly late breakfast, I went to the library to replace the book and found Tatyana there - in my inner sanctum - giving Danzer a damnable Tarot reading. Although she sulked in protest of my presence and I fibbed that I had much important work to do, I surreptitiously replaced the book then watched from behind Danzer's chair. He did not care. He did not care about anything. He was still lost in his bewildered, dreamlike state and already drinking heavily though it was not even lunchtime.

I chuckled openly at his cards which I knew, even in my ignorance, were terrible: The Ten of Swords, which featured a man lying face down with ten swords stabbed in his back - hardly a good start I thought and obviously indicating some nasty future surprise. The Five of Pentacles, the loss of money, faith, or a lover, as Tatyana explained. The Hanged Man, signifying entrapment, sacrifice and compromise. Next; The Devil, who needed no introduction then; The Tower, which, for me, with its depictions of destruction and chaos and figures tumbling to oblivion, is the most frightening card in the deck and finally his last card; Death, which again I felt required no explanation.

By the end, even I started to feel sorry for the mad old drunk and I noticed even the imperturbable Tatyana tense a few times when she turned them over because, from what I could make out, it was the worst hand anyone had ever been dealt in the long history of Tarot. Although she tried to interpret it differently, and Danzer spent the entire reading staring into the fireplace mumbling nonsensically to himself, I could tell that she was lying. *22

---

22. **Illuminati & Tarot.** The belief in Tarot's divinatory meanings was developed widely in the 18th century by protestant preachers and the Masons. The themes and imagery are essentially linked with Illuminati symbolism and elements of the Ancient Mystery School Religion; the tower, the pillars Jachim and Boaz and The Magician. As contemporary philosopher and Tarot historian Michael Dummet notes 'it was only in the 1780's when the practice of fortune telling with regular playing cards had been well established for at least two decades, that anyone began to use the tarot pack for cartomancy' (fortune telling).

Chapter 17

The Hunt

After lunch we prepared ourselves for the hunt. For many this was the main event of the weekend and accordingly Bassus had assembled a party of his more sporty friends who seemed a serious bunch, none of whom I recognised but who gave me some strange looks when I indicated that I was coming along. I guessed this was because none of them thought that a *librarian* could ride. I would put that right. After changing into my new riding gear I met up with everyone and we went to the stables to collect our horses. Petrova neighed a laugh when she saw me coming in my jaunty new hunting costume but I told her to be quiet and that she would have to expect such things now that I was a gentleman. I bellowed at one of the stable boys for being sluggish helping me into my saddle and to remind everyone that I was not to be belittled.

Danzer ungainly mounted up next to me along with a handful of the ladies, including Tatyana who had bravely decided to come out with us. I was a little surprised when Bassus asked me to escort them and Danzer in a procession slightly to the rear of the action but pretended that my pride was hurt and that I had yearned to show everyone what a fine horseman I was by bounding off through the trees chasing some terrified animal. Secretly, of course, I had wanted to stay as close to Tatyana as possible, if only to ensure that she did not sneak off into the bushes with Danzer for another *duet*.

The word went round that we were hunting wild boar and the gamekeepers and the young servants were going to beat the animal through the woods before us. We gathered on our horses in front of the house along with a pack of baying hounds then made our way out into the forest. As I had known full well, there were plenty of ways to show off my horsemanship to Tatyana without gallivanting off with the rest. So, whilst remembering to keep it subtle, I performed a few of my favourite stable tricks on Petrova: walking her sideways, having her open gates with her nose and, when given a treat, asking her to neigh 'Thank you.'

Drunken Danzer, on the other hand, was not getting along at all well with his feisty mare. He got his coat caught in the bushes and a stirrup on a gatepost and looked as though he would fall off with every clumsy bounce in the saddle. Though Tatyana was fully aware of my superior skills she pretended that she was not and encouraged and complimented Danzer as though he were her only son out on his first hunt. When the pack of dogs got the scent the serious riders, including the Count who was quite a horseman himself, flew off into the dense woods and, though we could hear them shouting and the dogs barking and their bugles echoing through the trees, we did not see them again for two hours.

For once, Tatyana and Danzer stopped talking to each other as his stupor deepened and she fell in with the rest of the ladies who were generally trying to keep out of the way and not fall off. Finally the bugles reached a frenzied climax before being replaced by the furious baying of the hounds and we came out of a thick copse to find the dogs and a group of five or six hunters at the prey with the rest of the men standing back. Bassus rode over to us as the dogs ripped the quarry apart and recommended that I should keep the ladies back at a safe distance. I did not fancy the idea of seeing this animal torn to shreds anyway and the ladies seemed to share my distaste so I led them back to the house. Tatyana had said nothing to me during the entire outing but I must have caught her peeping at me a dozen times. Though I fought it, I still could not help but think that she was fond of me in some way and promised myself that I would try one last time to get back into her affections.

So, later that evening, I arrived at the feast dressed fittingly for a formal dinner and to win a young lady's heart. Unfortunately, the young lady in question was seated at the head table at the far end of the room and almost impossible to even see, let alone talk to. So, after dinner, I sought her out amongst the crowd but as I reached her table the band struck up and she went off twirling about with clumsy Danzer. Though many other chaps had asked her for a dance - I knew this because there was a queue of them impatiently waiting for her - she faithfully stayed by Danzer's side for the next hour making sure that he did not fall down or knock someone over. In the end, feeling both deeply disappointed and highly strung, I spotted Bassus sitting on his own watching the dancing from a window bay. I slumped into a chair next to him and upon seeing my forlorn expression he beseeched, "Heaven's above, man. What's wrong with you now? Surely you can't be unhappy here. In the midst of all this frivolity?" He was right. The music was merry, several couples were vigorously romping round the room and everyone else, including many other very attractive women, were happily clapping along and enjoying the festivities.

Not wishing to offend my honourable host I humbly began, "I do not wish to seem rude, sir, as you have already given me so much, almost all of of which, I have not even asked, but I thought..." I came to a halt unable to decide how to broach the subject.

"Yes, Sebastian?"

"I thought that as I had joined the society then I'd be granted... certain... certain privileges."

"Yes?"

"Favours..."

At this point Tatyana and Danzer waltzed by causing me to heave a sigh and saving me the trouble of having to explain.

"Ah, I see," he grasped what I was about. He tapped his finger on his knee then began, "There are many degrees within our society, Sebastian. And I know what you're thinking, but it is unnecessary for initiates to know how many. Know only this: each brings more entitlement, money and access to that which members desire. You scratch backs, your back gets scratched. In Brother Danzer's case he has been a member for some years and has achieved much distinction from his labours and, as such, has attained our highest degree. Now, without being impertinent, I believe it's my turn to excuse myself for seeming rude but do you not think, at this point, Tatyana a little, how should I put it, out of your league?

"I see," I gulped, feeling my guts turn to lead and knowing all too well that I was showing it.

Bassus put a consoling hand on my shoulder. "Sebastian, you're an excellent fellow, a very excellent fellow indeed. More importantly, you're my friend, and, as a friend, I can tell you that you possess all the necessary qualities to proceed very quickly through our ranks. Then who knows what you might achieve, eh? The world, I'm sure, would become your proverbial oyster. But at this moment, you're still only an initiate and as an initiate you have limitations. Don't you see? As I told you: the initiates are merely the portico of the temple protecting the inner chamber."

Considering his ideas regarding the symbology of the temple this left me feeling like a proper...

"Uncle Danzy! Ow!" yelped Tatyana as the comatose Danzer stepped on her feet for the hundredth time.

I gestured at them and asked, "Is the ballerina a member of our society too?"

"Strictly speaking, women are not allowed to join. Hence the symbolic bearing of your breast to check that you're a man. Although there are a few women like Tatyana who hold a, how should I put it, *honorary* role. Do you see?" He flicked his eyebrows and gave a-not-so inscrutable smile.

If he meant what I thought he meant my manners prevented me from saying; namely that Tatyana was some sort of prostitute who was passed around between the higher members of the society. I was flabbergasted and choked when I understood how naïve I had been. Too overwhelmed to pry any further I shrank back in my chair and, seeing Gretchen approach us, Bassus observed, "Ah. I am needed elsewhere. I must go now to organise the night hunt: A more private affair for some of the more hardened riders." He rose and patted me on the back, musing, "There's never enough time eh?" before walking off with Gretchen who gave me an icy stare as she followed him.

I grabbed a bottle of wine from a passing servant and nearly slapped the little turd when he complained that it was for someone else. I sat sulking on my own guzzling the wine and watching Tatyana dragging Danzer through another polka. Such was my unbridled angst that I emptied the bottle in a matter of minutes and, unable to control myself any longer, as the next dance came to an end I barged my way over through the other couples and rudely stood in front of her. She looked straight through me as though I was not there and in desperation I glared at Danzer who, perhaps, less surprisingly, did exactly the same as her. I went to confront her but regained my composure seconds before I made an even bigger scene and angrily strode off through the shocked guests.

I went straight to the library, got what I was looking for and carried it in clear view back to my bedchamber along with another bottle of wine. I was going to pleasure myself and I did not care who knew. I flung open the door, flopped through the curtains of my bed and, after taking a hearty slurp, went straight to my favourite passages.

Perhaps because of all the noise in the house, or perhaps because I was a little drunk, I could not become aroused. I got frustrated and, in my haste to get more comfortable, I knocked over the bottle soaking the pages in red wine. Thunder and lightning! I frantically tried to clean up the mess but it was no good. The priceless, limited edition, one off, irreplaceable book was ruined and, feeling suddenly extremely sober, I paced round my bedchamber in a cold sweat wondering how I was going to explain myself.

Along with this excruciating problem keeping me up half the night, the mysterious hunt with their noisy activity around the house kept me up the other. Though fortunately this time there were no trumpeting bugles or howling dogs, the riders made one hell of a racket coming and going and shouting strange oaths at each other. I wondered, when hunting in the daytime was dangerous enough, what strange passion possessed them to partake in such a risky nocturnal pastime? Wallowing in my grief-stricken mood as I was, I wondered whether I should seek out a less risky nocturnal pastime myself and tried desperately to get some sleep.

Chapter 18

The Grande Tour

Somehow I must have slipped off but with my mind beset with hellish dilemmas, I hardly slept a wink and the next morning I felt even worse than the day before. On my way to breakfast I came across Danzer in the hallway adjusting his belt under his robes. When he saw me coming I noticed his eyes shifting around like a pair of flags in the wind and I gleaned some small comfort to see him back to his twitching, mumbling self.

He checked that we were alone before demanding under his breath, "What in Hell's name are you doing here, Christian?"

"I may well ask you the same thing, Canon," I countered, "I take it not to deliver a lecture on *catholic morality*."

"You have not told anyone... about our little secret?" His bloodshot eyes scanned mine.

"If I told everyone all my secrets, sir, it would never end."

"Good, good. Well done, Christian."

He produced a hip flask from under his robes and took a slug.

"Are you... drunk, sir?" I asked. He reeked of brandy and it was now before breakfast.

"Of course I am, you idiot!" he spluttered, "How else do you think I make it through the day?" He twisted his bulbous, reddened nose as if I had claimed the bible was full of nursery rhymes and rumbled on, "I don't know whether I'm more surprised to discover that *you* are not, or that you had to ask?" He had another swig and gasped, "You'll have to excuse me, Christian. I have to go and talk with Count Bassus."

He glimpsed my ring and stared at me with a startled expression which slowly changed to an uneasy grin as he tentatively offered his hand. Innocently thinking that he was being conciliatory, I took it but for some reason he bent his ring finger double. I found this most strange but he seemed even more surprised than me and, after another uneasy grin, he departed. It was all extremely odd and I could not make hide nor hair of it. *[23]

I mulled it over during breakfast then decided, right there and then, to get out of the house altogether. Everyone was so preoccupied with their own little worlds that they would not miss me and the thought of spending another day with this particularly peculiar crowd was more than I could bear. Tatyana was not even up yet. I decided that I would go hunting myself. Yes. A little target practice in the woods would do me good. So, I went upstairs, collected my quadre bow in its holster and, managing to avoid everyone on my way, collected Petrova from the stables and slipped her out into the countryside. Hooray. I was free.

We left the town behind us and travelled north up the pleasant winding road in the direction of the bridge. The freshly blossoming valley was even more beautiful than I had remembered and, as Petrova wanted to stretch her legs, I let her. It was good to be out and feel the wind in our hair. She galloped for a good three miles then trotted for another ten after that and, before I knew it we were nearing the bridge. Not wanting to go near the frightening chasm if I did not have to, I rode her into the trees and, upon finding a secluded clearing, I dismounted and took out my bow. The awesome weapon was less overwhelming outside and I loaded up four silver-tipped bolts from the quiver then swung the ungainly thing about.

23. **Secret Society Handshakes.** Secret societies have always used clandestine messaging systems for a variety of reasons: not least signalling for help and obviously to check so see whether strangers are possible initiates. There are no end of complex hand movements within this article for EBook readers. Perhaps the most well known secret hand signal is 'the hidden hand' present in photographs and portraits from Napoleon to Stalin and Marx to Churchill.

"To Hell with it," I muttered. I was angry. I squeezed the trigger - 'Zut! Zut!' - and blasted a couple of bolts up into the trees. I got the fright of my life when an enormous, old, dead branch came crashing down to the forest floor not six feet away, causing me to put an arm over my head and all the birds to jump and squawk and flap about for miles around. Petrova neighed at me to stop being an idiot and wandered off in a huff. Maybe she had a point. I did not mind her going for walk. I could give her my special whistle and she would come back from a mile away.

I slung the quiver over my shoulder and stalked off through the trees using the bow's telescopic monocular to aim at birds and branches and anything else I could target. I had neglected my training since coming to Poschiavo. My legs were not as fresh as they were a few months ago when Bacon and the Professor had me running about the castle courtyard and exercising every day. I was only young like Petrova, I wanted to stretch my legs too. As the mood took me, I set off at a pace, sprinting through the bushes, dodging this way and that and hiding between the trees. I even took an athletic forward roll over a bush and sprang out of it to land flat on my stomach with the bow out before me and my eye squeezed tight on the monocular. It was all quite exhilarating and much like being on a mission.

As I lay there panting in the undergrowth, I saw something dark past the lens protruding through the grass only a few yards ahead. So I got up and went over to investigate and was shocked to find a rusty, old bear trap: a big one at that, primed and ready to go off. Shit! I had nearly jumped straight into the thing. I crouched down to examine the menacing contraption and saw that it was connected to a chain running over to a nearby tree around which it had been tied. I followed the chain then slapped my hand over my mouth when I found a tiny bloodstained shoe at the base of the trunk. I was nearly sick in my mouth and, as I imagined this appalling accident, I stumbled backwards and fell over, landing awkwardly on my side with the bow dangerously trapped underneath me. I went to pull myself up but froze when I heard a voice shout, "Nothing here either!" I tried to control my breathing so I could hear better. Who the hell was that? And what were they doing here?

"Where are the others?" Shouted the voice and, over the sound of my panting, I was sure that I heard another more distant voice yell, "Over there! By that tree!"

I stopped breathing altogether and slowly pushed myself up to see who was making all the noise, but, as I did, I felt a chain under my side and something jagged brush my wrist. Now I stopped moving too.

"Not that tree. That one!" wafted the second voice on the wind as a bead of sweat fell from my nose and a chill ran up my spine. I slowly inched my head around to see my hand lying precariously between the jaws of a second bear trap with my wrist pressing on the rusty spikes. I started to shake from holding my position and heard the first voice ask from a lot closer, "This one?"

"Yes, that one!" Came the faint reply.

I gently lifted my wrist from the spikes but caught my elbow in the bow's shoulder strrap. One of the chain links slipped under my side as I nudged the edge of the squeaking trap.

"Come on!" shouted the faraway voice as I strained against the strap and, at last, wriggled my hand free. I dragged myself away as fast as I could but stopped dead when a boot almost trod on me as the telltale tinkle of spurs strode past.

Good God! Whoever it was must have been looking the other way. I tried to control my fear but almost wet myself and had to grip the bow hard to stop my hands from shaking. I groped around in the quiver on my back to count exactly how many bolts I had: Four, five, six and there were two on the bow. I prayed that I would not need them all and cursed myself for wasting the others.

"Nothing here either!" Shouted the owner of the boots from barely six feet away. "That's all of them!"

He crunched back through the twigs and I rolled over to see one of Massenhausen's henchmen looming up to me. His eyes widened when he saw me lying there and he threw his hand under his tunic for his weapon but he did not stand a chance. 'Zut' The arrow whipped into his chest and his face twisted with despair as he lurched backwards out of view. 'Crunch!' I heard the bear trap snap shut and a spine-chilling whimper. The horror of it compelled me to sit up and I gasped to see him stricken in horrendous agony against the tree with his leg pincered in the trap as he choked his last breath and died right there in front of me.

"Reinhardt!" rang out a piercing cry and I turned to see two more brutes with muskets sprinting in my direction from a nearby road. I suddenly realised that I was right next to the bridge and, as I found my bearings, I saw Massenhausen on the other side looking over from his horse next to a small covered wagon.

There was no time to think. I put the bow to my shoulder and found the nearest henchman in the monoscope but he saw me aiming at him and dived into the undergrowth.

"Get him!" distantly raged Massenhausen as the next brute fell into my sights already pointing his musket at me. 'Zut!' I fired and watched the bolt fly into his face. He flailed backwards as the powder puffed from his flintlock and I heard the bang a second later as red hot shot tore through the shoulder of my jacket. It grazed me badly but I gritted my teeth and pulled out a bolt from the quiver

Feeling my training come to the fore, I speedily reloaded the bow with its clever system of levers and pulleys and threw it back to my shoulder with my eye fixed on the monoscope. "Where are you? Where are you? Come on! Come on!" I fumed and scanned the bow only to see his raging face appear not six feet away. No! 'Zut!' I fired and dropped the bow as he crashed into me and had to grab his wrist to keep the tip of his knife from plunging into my face. He glared at me with blood erupting from his mouth and we wrestled briefly until he gave a stunted gasp as his strength wavered and collapsed onto my shoulder.

I pushed him off and jumped up, roaring towards the bridge, "Yah! Take that Massenhausen! Pig dog! I've killed these fools and I'll kill you too! You piece of shit!" I loaded up two more bolts and aimed at him as he obviously did not fancy coming and fighting me one to one. Though I did see him taking note of exactly who I was before he gestured to the unseen driver of the little wagon and they both set off up the road. He must have been a hundred and fifty yards away when I fired but I still only missed the son of a bitch by ten feet. I roared with defiance when I saw him flinch and ran down to the road preparing to fire again but he cantered out of range with the wagon.

"You won't even fight me!" I roared, "Then who are you? Who are you? Come back and fight pig dog! Come back! Come back you son of a bitch! Come back!" Violence always makes me angry and I stood there ranting and bellowing obscenities in the road at the base of the bridge for some time. After a while my throat hurt too much and I bent over to get my breath back when an almighty whack round the back of my head sent me crashing to the ground.

Chapter 19

Out of the Frying Pan

I must have passed out briefly because when I regained consciousness my head felt like a blacksmith's anvil after a hard day under the hammer and all I could hear was a man screaming from far away, "He's killed Reinhardt too! All three of them dead! Dead I tell you! I don't believe it! Kill the bastard! Kill him now!"

I tentatively touched my bleeding head and peeped out from under an eyelid to see a filthy dog of a man staring me right in the face. He called out, "He's not dead. He's alive. I can see his eyes moving."

My faculties suddenly returned in a rush of delirium and I realised that more of Massenhausen's men must have sneaked up behind me and knocked me out while I was having my tantrum. No! I was in deep, deep, deep shit and, when I heard the other voice yell from much closer, "Good! Then I can kill him myself!" I nearly soiled my new hunting pantaloons with a great deal more. The quadre bow was only inches out of reach with the single bolt still resolutely clamped on the stay. Four or five yards beyond it, the lip of the fearsome gorge and barely an arm's length away, with his hands on his knees watching over me, the dog of a man.

"I don't think so my friend," he grinned, revealing a graveyard of tombstone teeth and pushed the bow away with his boot.

"The bastard killed Reinhardt!" raged the other one, now from very close by, "So I'm going to throw him off that cliff!"

I had one chance. I had to surprise the dog in front of me or die. I raised my head and asked, as brotherly as I could, "Is that your tobacco pouch, my friend?" and nodded between his feet.

He instinctively glanced down giving me the split second that I needed. I sprang up at him, grabbed the quadre bow with one hand, smashed my other shoulder into his chin and, using all my weight, drove him across the road. I caught him completely off balance and we fairly flew towards the precipice but I had not thought of what to do if my plan worked and, as he toppled backwards, he pulled me with him. I saw the look of death in his eyes as he dragged me over but at the last moment I managed to turn my body as I fell and clung to a tiny crag in the cliff face a few feet below the edge.

I smacked into the gorge's side with a gasp as the dog let out a blood-curdling yelp all the way down. I hung on for dear life and winced from the pain already tearing through my fingers. I did not know how long I could last. Not long - a handful of seconds - and they were ticking away fast. The weight of the bow in my other hand was already ripping my arm out of its socket. Some pebbles fell on my face making me spit and gag and I looked up to see the other ugly brute glaring down at me with murderous contempt filling his eyes.

He snarled in frustration as he could still not get his hands on me to avenge his friends. But a look of retributive wickedness crossed his face and he chortled as he undid his trousers then pulled out his cock and started to piss on me. Summoning all my strength I tried to lift the quadre bow, imagining myself at the castle gymnasium completing the last in a series of demanding lifts. Come on Seb! Just do it! I got it half way but was near blinded by piss and dropped it back down. "Come on! Do or die!" I grunted and dug deep, deeper than I had ever dug before and, with one last gargantuan heave, slowly raised the tip. Finally, it was high enough and, knowing that I could only hold it for a second, I aimed as best I could and shot off my bolt. 'Zut!'

I let the bow fall back with a gasp as a look of insane horror filled the thug's face and a gut-full of blood and other bodily fluids poured down over me. I squeezed my eyes shut as the disgusting deluge continued until I heard him gurgle, "Bas... tard!" and he plummeted past me into the gorge.

I grunted and tried to control my breathing. The pain in my arms was unbearable. Something had to go: Either me or the bow. I took one last glance at the thing then faced the sky and dropped it. I could not watch it fall.

I swung my free hand up to the crag but cursed when I realised it was too small to squeeze my other hand inside. I could barely get two fingers in there which held none of my weight. There was only one thing for it. I stuck my free fingers in my mouth and whistled like there was no tomorrow then hung there in agony, hoping beyond hope to hear the familiar clip clop of Petrova's hooves. But there was nothing. Nothing but the wind.

"Thunder and lightning!" I bellowed into the chasm.

I had ten seconds left maybe less. I took one last deep breath and whistled again then roared, "Come on girl!" This one was sweeter than the rest and echoed back and forth up the gorge until it could have been heard in Ingolstadt but again, nothing.

I tried to fight the pain in my arm but it was no good, I was going to lose my grip. It was impossible not to look down and, when I glimpsed the thundering waters hundreds of feet below, my head started to spin. "Damn you stupid horse!" I screamed, "Where are you when I need you?" as her head popped over the side. "There you are my beauty!" I wheezed, "I always knew you would come! Now, kneel down and let the reins come down here please! Quick! Quick!" She shook her head and bowed and sure enough the reins came down but agonisingly dangled a few inches away from my clasping hand.

"I said blasted-well kneel down!" I gasped in pain and she

understood but took her time getting on her knees as she was so close to the edge. Finally, the reins came low enough and I seized them with both hands but poor Petrova was not ready and whinnied in panic as she took my weight.

"Steady girl!" I shouted, swinging around in the air, "Steady!" I took a deep breath as the leather creaked and she neighed and more pebbles fell down then I yelled, "Now pull. Go away! Go on girl! Yah!"

She understood and shaking with the exertion steadily lifted herself to her feet, one at a time. I was thrown into the cliff face and cried out in pain as my knuckles and knees and face smashed against the rock and slowly dragged upwards. Then with one last powerful tug, she jerked me painfully over the edge to safety. By thunder I had been saved. I gasped, deeper than I have ever gasped and lay there panting and kissing dependable terra firma and nursing my wounds. Presently, I felt a warm nose nuzzle my neck and got up on my bleeding knees to throw my arms around that beautiful horse's neck and I hugged it like it was my own mother's. I am not ashamed to say that I cried for some time afterwards with relief and for true friendship felt.

Two hours later I was thundering back into town with my new clothes torn to rags, covered with mud, blood and sweat and stinking of piss. Though elated to be alive, paradoxically I was also seething with rage. Not only because my exciting new life had been turned back into the terrifying old nightmare, but because Massenhausen, and whoever was driving the mysterious wagon, had escaped my murderous onslaught. Violence always has a profound effect on me. Sometimes I show it, sometimes I do not: but it always has a profound effect. This time it was clearly visible and, as such, none of the gay townsfolk took the trouble to say hello as I was obviously not in the mood for a chat about the weather. There was only one person I wanted to see.

I burst into Bassus' study and found him discussing something with one of his valets. Being the true friend he was he instantly dismissed the young man the moment he saw my ravaged state and approached me, asking in an appalled tone, "What on earth has happened? Have you been robbed? Tell me now."

"Someone, well lots of people actually, tried to kill me."

"Who? Why? Where? Come in and sit down."

He showed me to a seat where I explained what I could. I put it to him, in the strongest possible terms, that Massenhausen had been present and that my assailants were definitely in his charge and, as such, it was imperative what Ambrosini may know. He confessed that, when asked, the printer had claimed that his son had completed the particular job in question and that he did not remember.

"But I saw them talking to each other, sir," I beseeched, "What about rule number three? Surely, our society's rules allow us to get to the bottom of this."

"These are questions for another day, my friend because I'm afraid I have some bad news for you."

"For me, sir? More?" I gawped.

"I have another confession to make. Gretchen's bird regretfully killed a messenger pigeon this morning and, as we did not know to whom it belonged, I'm afraid we read the message. It was sent to you from Ingolstadt. Apparently your father is gravely ill and you must go to see him immediately."

He passed me a bloodstained piece of paper but I was too stunned to read it and stared at him.

"I have arranged a carriage to take you there now. Your horse can be drawn behind and all your belongings have been packed along with the university's catalogue. The driver has instructions not to stop until you arrive at your destination."

I shook my head and tried to grasp what he was saying. Was it true? He helped me up and escorted me out of his office and along the hallway, hastily explaining as he went, "I have a place in Sandersdorf, not ten miles from Ingolstadt, to which I migrate during the summer months. I will be there in a few days time." He stopped and held my shoulders, "Promise me, Sebastian, whatever happens, you will come and find us: *all* of us, there." He squeezed my arms and looked intensely into my eyes making sure that I understood as I was, no doubt, in a bit of a daze.

"Of course sir," I mumbled. It had all happened too quickly to digest and it seemed the very next moment that I was waving him goodbye from the rear window of yet another carriage as I went back on the road again.

Chapter 20

Death

I have been on some rough journeys in my life but that journey home to Tuffengarten to see my ailing father was the roughest. Perhaps because I had dreamt my eventual homecoming such a different affair: Positive, happy, full of good cheer and one more pleasant memory to savour in the future when the reality was so utterly opposite in every single way. Not only did I spend the entire time wearing myself out fretting about one thing or another; my father, my mother, me, Francesca, my child, the Illuminati, Massenhausen, my work, education, Petrova cantering behind, even Bassus' ruined book under my pillow back in Poschavio, on and on ad nauseam but, at last, the weather turned for the worse. Indeed, as soon as we left sunny Poschiavo the heavens opened and, as far as I can recall, it did not stop raining the whole way home.

My driver and I had to pull the carriage out of a hundred ditches along the way and I ruined almost all my new clothes by covering them with filth from the road or grease from the wheels. This was to say nothing of our journey through the Alps which, although we took the lower and slightly longer route, was now beset with torrid floodwaters from the melting snow making that part of the trip not only challenging and slow but utterly terrifying, especially coming down the other side as we were almost washed away on a couple of occasions by the daunting rivers pouring across the roads. Suffice to say, some two weeks later one muggy afternoon in May, battered, filthy and weary we finally rolled into Tuffengarten. I jumped down from the carriage outside my parent's house and my mother was quickly at the door to welcome me.

When I came away from her embrace I noticed that she had been crying and with some trepidation I asked, "How is father?"

She burst into tears and put her hand over her mouth, blubbering, "God has taken him now. I have said goodbye." She peered through her tears and sobbed, "And you came in a carriage but... he never saw it." She flung herself into my arms and I held her and rocked her and patted her back like a child.

Those who say that it is better to travel than to arrive have got it spot on, rough journey or not. That was that. He was dead. It had already been a bad few weeks and the shock hit me like a cannonball shot from close range. I remembered putting his stockings on his bed and him not saying goodbye. I did not fight the urge and sobbed along with my mother. It had only happened two days before I got there and so, at least, I was in time for the funeral. Though, maybe if the weather had been better, I might have had the chance to tell him something, anything before he left, at least, goodbye.

The funeral was a small affair and, after thanking the last of the mourners and bidding them farewell, I put my arm round my mother's shoulders and slowly walked her from the graveyard. After a few peaceful steps she broke the silence.

"There is something I have to tell you, Sebastian." She threw me a sideways glance and added, "But I don't want you to be angry."

I knew that I was going to be angry the moment she said this but it was her husband's funeral so I respectfully let her continue. We came to a stop and she looked at me with a strangely intense expression as though she had swallowed a bee. Now I was more frightened than angry. She let out a sudden gasp and blurted, "He owed money," then squinted up at me, "Quite a lot of money."

"How much?" I asked.

"If we sold the house there would not be enough."

"How much?" I repeated.

"If we sold five houses there would just be enough."

"How much?" She was right, I was getting angry.

"One thousand seven hundred and seventy six thalers."

"How much!" I gawked.

"He owes it to a man called Solomon," she fretted, "He employs something called compound interest... It seems usurious but he keeps coming to the house with Peter Kronenberg."

"Peter Kronenberg... from school?"

"Yes, he has grown very big and strong so when your father would argue that the interest was too much Peter would stand up and your father would falter because he feared reprisals."

"Damn it! Father told me that our family have ever owed money." She cowered but I could not further hurt her feelings and offered, "I have enough to pay. *Just* enough mind."

Curiosity immediately got the better of her and I could tell that she was going to ask from where I had got such a tidy sum, but I put her in her place. After all, was I now not the man of the house? The pawned house.

"No, you may not ask where I got it from," I warned her, "Then I won't get angry. Agreed?"

"Agreed," she sniffed.

We started walking again and, as we reach the gates she glanced at me again and asked, "I suppose you have not decided whether you will become a priest yet?"

For once I wished Danzer was by my side, if only to promptly bring this line of questioning to an end once and for all. Unfortunately, he was hundreds of miles away, probably with his head stuck in a bottle or inbetween some wench's bosoms so I wearily sighed, "I said that I would think about it, Mother and that's what I'm doing, thinking about it."

That seemed to shut her up so we walked out of the graveyard and I tried to remember which circle of Dante's Hell you were sent to if you had been nagged to death.

I headed back to Ingolstadt once again stuck in a carriage with too much time to my hands and too many things to think. My mind was awash with so many conflicting waves of emotions that I could not separate one from another as they all crashed together in a writhing, torrid sea of morbid confusion and stressful angst. In the end, my concern over the money surfaced above all others. One day ago I had been financially comfortable, now I was broke. The psychological chasm between solvency and bankruptcy was vast. My father was gone and there was nothing I could do about it, apart from regret and deny and remember and mourn. My child was not to be born for another month and that problem could be dealt with when it arrived, but the money was now. Today. I would have to collect my savings and return to Tuffengarten before the next hefty interest payment was due in two weeks time or I would not be able to cover the bill and my widowed mother would be thrown out of her house which I discovered had been worryingly used as collateral. Good grief.

Every time I considered these financial woes I rubbed my forehead with stress. It was a fortune. Everything I had. During my darkest hours rattling through the night I even contemplated selling my wonderful timepiece though I knew that I could not sell a gift and part of our society's honoured heritage. Of course, I would rather die than sell Petrova, it would have been like selling my best friend. Going through my other possessions I suddenly remembered the Professor's confiscated riches in the bowels of the castle and obviously these transformed my calculations.

For was I not somehow entitled to this money? I was a most trusted member of our organisation and there was much more than I needed, or anyone else for that matter. Indeed, I only required a tiny fraction. Surely, upon discovering my dire straits Van Halestrom would offer me the money as a matter of course. Thus removing my need to ask or, heaven forbid, having to earn it all back, as I had done before, the hard way.

I relaxed somewhat at this but, as was my way, continued to rack my brains for contingency plans and, as I neared Ingolstadt, I had another burst of inspiration. I decided that I would copy the Professor's design of the quadre bow and sell it to my father's old customers. Brilliant! Might make a tidy profit into the bargain. After all, it was certainly a revolutionary weapon. You could always tell that by the look on its victim's faces. I found my writing box amongst my things and attempted to draw the weapon from memory but after a while it occurred to me that I could not remember the clever system of wheels and pulleys well enough though I tried many times. *[24]

I dismounted the coach outside Ingolstadt University and ordered the driver to wait then strode through the gates to find the Professor. A lot had happened since I was last there and there was much to talk about. I pounded on his door and, as usual, did not have to wait long for a response. "Come, Sebastian," he called in a tone suggesting that I was there for an appointment.

I opened the door to find him at his desk puffing on his pipe. His hawkish eyes scanned mine and he asked, "How is your father?"

"He is dead, sir," I stated plainly, "And has left me a debtor."

"All the planets. And your Mother? Is she coping?"

"As well as can be expected, sir but my father's debts hang over her too."

---

24. **Quadre Bow.** Amazingly, some sketches of the quadre bow came with this manuscript, some more finished than others, which I believe must be the drawings that S. Drechsler mentions and can be viewed by E Book readers.

"And you, Sebastian, how are you?"

"I'm fine, Professor. I was a little upset a few days ago but I feel that I've overcome my grief now and all is well."

He looked concerned and said, "I think you may be in shock, Sebastian. You'd better sit down."

"I'm fine, Professor. I've been sitting down for the last two weeks now and it hasn't done me any good whatsoever. So, if it's all right with you, I'll stand please." I stuck out my chin, stiffened my lip and began, "In light of my present financial circumstances, sir, I am considering manufacturing our quadre bows and selling them to my father's old customers."

He shook his head and told me point blank, "No, Sebastian, we don't divulge our society's secrets. I cannot let you do that."

"Damn it, Professor. I need the money."

"I understand..." he began.

"I know there's a fortune at the castle," I rudely interrupted, "Why can I not have some of that?"

"Because, that money, like the bow, Sebastian, belongs to our society."

"But *I* belong to our society."

"We have never formally made an agreement: A guarantee."

"You never said I had to."

"You never asked. I wanted to discuss it on the patio but..."

"But there is no one else, sir. There was Bacon, then you, then me next. I know it was never said but surely that's what was meant. Then shouldn't I be entitled to the money?"

"You are different."

"*Different*? How, sir? In what way am I different?"

"Technically, you're not eligible."

"What?" I blustered, "Why ever not?"

"You're not an orphan."

I stared at him in disbelief but he was serious.

"That's ridiculous, Professor."

"Maybe, but it's the rule."

I clenched my teeth but could not contain my frustration any longer.

"Damn it, man! I watched my father get buried not two days ago so I'm halfway there already. What should I do next to become eligible for something that I am already clearly part of; kill my own mother?"

I stormed out. I could stay there no longer. I did not say goodbye. I did not see his face before I left. I reached the carriage in the street outside but paced up and down trying to decide what to do. I had to stable Petrova and go back to my quarters round the corner to get my strongbox of money but I somehow felt my concentration drawn elsewhere. I was distracted by the sight of Willy hurrying from the gates and untying one of Van Halestrom's horses from the railings. "What's he doing here?" I muttered to myself as he scurried over the road with the horse.

"Master Drechsler. I didn't know you were due back." He seemed quite perplexed and stammered, "I... I have just seen the Professor but really... it is you that I should see."

"Why? What's wrong?" I barked.

"It's Miss Francesca, Master Drechsler. She's... not well, sir."

"We'll follow you!" I shouted then jumped back onboard the carriage as he saddled up and we set off together in some haste.

I was suspicious that events were beginning to get the better of me and that I was becoming a little unhinged but all I could do was keep calm and carry on. I suddenly realised how much I had been neglecting Francesca. I had hardly thought of her at all over the past four months and I bit my lip with shame. I plumped out my chest and brushed the dried mud off my cravat and lapels. I had done nothing wrong. Only what any normal young man would have done in the same situation. I rubbed my sweaty hands to clean off the dirt but the stains were ground in.

I pushed my head out of the window and bawled at the driver, "Can't we go any faster man?" then crashed back into the seat.

An hour later I ran through the empty corridors of the castle towards our bedchamber trying my best to keep calm though not doing very well. A maid was waiting by the open door and she curtseyed without catching my eye as I went inside.

Francesca was lying in our bed with her head up on the pillow. She looked tired with a puffy face and bags under her eyes but smiled when she saw me and held out her hands. I slipped onto the bed and swept her into my arms.

After a tender moment she sniffed, "I'm so, so sorry, Sebastian. I held her at arm's length and looked at her questioningly, "Why sorry?" She could not have known about my father.

She seemed nervous that I had to ask and cowered slightly.

"What's wrong?" I pressed, feeling that she was hiding something.

She gulped and lamented, "I... lost the child, Sebastian."

I stared at her and felt my grip tighten round her arms.

"No." I whispered. It could not be true. I looked at her belly almost expecting the swaddling child to be placed in my arms.

"How?" I asked. I was no doctor. I did not know.

"How?" she shrugged, "It's just something that happens." She sighed deeply, "But I was worried that it would."

"Why? How? ... Is it woman's intuition?"

She gulped and sniffled, "Because it's happened before."

"What?" To say this shocked me to the core was an understatement and I struggled to understand how it could have happened *before* when I was her only lover. Finally the penny dropped and I pulled myself up from the bed. Though I understood, my mind built an impervious wall that prevented me from accepting the idea. I choked and looked around for someone to help me and, like the young man I was, with my honour at stake, I could not help but ask, "Who was it?"

She could not look me in the face and, though this was perhaps not the right time, I was having a bad day, and I demanded, probably quite loudly, "Who was it?"

She peeped at me once then hid her eyes and murmured, "Danzer. Six years ago. I was very young..."

I could not bear to hear the rest. I was already striding out of the room and down the corridor.

"Sebastian!" she cried through the open door and began weeping.

It was too late for tears. I had had enough. I marched back to the carriage and luckily everyone who saw me coming had the good sense to stay out of my way. I told the driver to take me to Bassus' residence in Sandersdorf immediately and when the idiot complained that the horses were tired and needed watering, I warned him that I would knock his teeth out if he did not do it that very moment. Petrova neighed at me to calm down as I jumped back on board but I told her to shut up too and slammed the door. The carriage rattled out of the castle and back down the road with me staring dementedly from the window.

All was not well. All was not well at all. I had never been this angry in my life. Never! The fury was truly transformational. Perhaps if I had had nowhere to go, I would have gone to a tavern and got fighting drunk and ended up taking it out on some poor wretch. But the thought of seeing Bassus was the shining light in the dark and gave me a point on which to focus. Somehow, I knew that when I found him I would be free. Free from this squalid pain and shame and anger and persecution. I wanted everything he and his society could give me and I wanted it now. Right now. I wanted the privilege. I wanted the respect. I wanted the money, the carriages, the clothes, the music, the finery. I was not going to end up dead and in debt like my father after working all his life, or just plain dead helping Van Halestrom. I wanted the free and easy life and I did not care what I had to do to get it. The rest could go to blazes! I wanted to be like Bassus and, most of all, I wanted Tatyana. Yes! I wanted her. I admitted it to myself. Of course I did. Then why did I not have her?

Damn that whore Francesca! How could she even allow herself to be touched by that piece of shit! Damn tight-fisted Van Halestrom and his ridiculous rules. Damn my father and his coldness and hypocrisy. Damn my mother and her silly childish dreams and damn God for creating this mess. Yes! That's right! Damn him. Damn him most of all. Damn him and his mythical angels and his ludicrous miracles and his wanton destruction and his contradictions and damn him for making me waste my time: years and years of looking over my shoulder, or up in the sky, worrying that he could see me or that he cared, when it was all a lie. And to the seventh ring of Hell damn Danzer! I clenched my fists and kicked the carriage door. I would knock his teeth out too when I saw him, the lying, swivel-eyed, drunken bastard. The priest of a God that neither cared nor existed. The only things that existed were my feelings: My anger existed. My desire existed. My lust existed. I existed. Damn the others. I cursed that there was not a drinks cabinet in my carriage and stuck my head out of the window to scold the driver to go faster.

An early summer storm was brewing and dark clouds billowed behind rows of silver of poplar trees as we rumbled up to Sandersdorf. I had seen the majestic castle from a distance, towering above the other buildings in the town. I was not surprised. Why should I be? Everything in this man's world was larger than life and that was what I wanted: The Gentleman's life.

We pulled into the courtyard packed with thirty or forty of the most expensive and ostentatious carriages that I had ever seen. Throngs of servants, grooms, ostlers and drivers all busied themselves cleaning windows and brass work and feeding horses and going this way and that with buckets and brushes. There was obviously some sort of important gathering in the offing and I got down from the carriage amid the hubbub and gazed about.

"Sebastian!" welcomed Bassus from the steps of the keep and came over. "What excellent timing," he beamed, "I have only just arrived myself. What news my friend?"

He knew the moment he saw my eyes that it was not good and discreetly showed me inside. He led me upstairs and within two minutes had me seated on the side of a bed in an upstairs room and stood thoughtfully listening to my story. I was furious but controlled. I explained about my father then about Francesca and what had happened as even-handedly as I could but obviously found it hard to be as considerate as I might about Francesca losing the child. His eyes widened when I called her a whore, but I reined myself in and took a deep breath.

"That's all behind me now, sir," I stated when I had finished, "I have tired of my old friends and, with the passing of my father, and the imminent completion of my degree, I want to start a new life for myself but not that of a priest or a librarian working in stuffy academe. I want... I want what the society has to offer."

"I see," he nodded and rubbed his chin.

"I want it all," I said defiantly which he seemed to appreciate.

"Your timing is immaculate, my friend," he began, "As you may have guessed the society is gathering for a meeting here tonight. This was meant to take place yesterday but because our members are travelling from so far and wide they are still arriving so we are holding it later tonight. As we are now rearranging somewhat, I think there's a distinct possibility that we can incorporate your admission into the, how should I put it, higher degrees."

"Yes!" I triumphed and punched my hand. That was what I wanted to hear.

"Your enthusiasm is worthy my friend but you must learn to control your feelings, especially if we can arrange your ordination later. The properly prepared adept understands that the importance of ceremony is not physical but spiritual."

"Forgive me, sir," I cast down my eyes, "I have been through a lot recently and it is merely an indication of my will."

He gently lifted my chin with his knuckle until our eyes met and he reassured me, "Your will was never in doubt, my friend." With this he attempted to lighten the mood and clapped his hands, "Now let me get you a drink to clear your head. You'll be pleased to know we have an identical brewery here to that as in Poschiavo. You will also be pleased to know," he flicked his eyebrows and grinned, "Tatyana should be here very soon."

He left me alone and I shook my fist heavenwards then released a long tense sigh. Now, I had everything that I needed to complete my revenge. Yes! I would show them. I would show them all.

The Count soon returned with a young servant carrying a tray with two tall glasses and a large jug of beer and we shared a toast.

"To your future," he grinned and tapped his glass into mine.

"To my future," I concurred and drank deeply.

He stayed with me briefly until I had finished my first glass - approximately one minute - then left explaining that he had much to organise but asked that I stay in my quarters, as all guests were required to before the meeting took place. So I spent some time getting drunk and inspecting my tiny but fabulous rococo room which was decorated quite unlike any of the Count's residences in Poschiavo.

Once again I had a stunning view, the window ledge being low enough for me to stand upon and look out above the jumbled rooftops to the endless forest surrounding the town. Amongst the grand but strangely bizarre paintings and general bric-a-brac, including a suit of armour and several shields, there was also an old iron chair with hand clasps which stood facing the door. Bassus had told me that it was used for 'intensifying pleasure during the sexual act' and that this room was frequently used for such activities by 'special guests' of the society. I did not doubt it. There was a golden chaise longue kissing chair, gilded mirrors all over the place, including one on the ceiling above the bed and, as I discovered, even leather straps on the bedposts. I had another drink and wondered when Tatyana would get here and what I might do to her in a room such as this.

I did not have to wait long. Half an hour later, as I stood on the windowledge watching the storm clouds darken, there was a gentle tap at my door and I opened it to find her shimmering in all her glory with Bassus by her side. "Look who I have brought to see you," he beamed and she came inside lighting up the room with her presence and her glamour and her beauty. She took my hands and said in a caring but deeply sensual way, "I'm so sorry to hear of your loss."

She embraced me and I inhaled her scent and felt her voluptuous bosom pressing into me and her waist through her corset. Though it was a terrible time for me; a time of mourning and sad reflection on the passing of my father and my son, I still found an intense guilty pleasure in the touch of her body under her clothes.

She took my hands once more and looked me over, asking with a compassionate smile, "You will live, yes?"

"I will live," I repeated and she stroked my cheek then much to my delight, leant forward and kissed me softly on the lips. This arrow from Cupid's own bow was enough to instantly make me forget all my worries and feel like a completely new man.

"Come with us, Sebastian," whispered Bassus naughtily, "I want to show you around the place while there's no one around."

Tatyana grinned her approval and led me from the room by my hand as we followed him downstairs. Though I had never been to the place before I immediately felt at home. The building's bold architecture was stunning. Indeed, I considered that if I built a castle I would build one exactly the same. Maybe one day perhaps, if I served the society well I could achieve such a thing. Everything seemed possible when I was with my new friends, and the thrill of their glamorous company flooded back like déjà vu as I swept through the corridors on a wave of gloating victory. These clever, rich, talented, handsome, privileged people desired my company and I was more determined than ever to earn their respect because, through them, I knew I that could be what I had always wanted to be: a true gentleman.

We came to a grand hall lit only by the evening twilight falling through a large arched Gothic window at the far end. I stopped in the doorway upon seeing twenty or so imposing statues of all kinds, shapes, sizes and periods arranged around the room. I was seriously impressed and began respectfully walking in between the figures inspecting the frozen faces and heroic poses.

"I knew you'd like them," glowed Bassus watching me from the middle of the collection. "There are too many to display anywhere in Poschiavo. Anyway, this place suits them well don't you think? Better sense of drama." He spun on his heel, looping his cane in the over his head. "As you can see we discriminate against no creed or culture here. All religions are welcome. For each one can teach us a different lesson from the past."

He stopped next to a nightmarish carving of a man being crucified upside down in glorious white marble.

"Take this one for instance, one of my particular favourites: St Peter killed by Nero in 64AD. The flawed emperor blamed the Christian martyrs for the fire that destroyed Rome. Who'd want a religion for which you had to suffer? Don't you agree? Liberated man can do so much better eh?"

"I like this one," said Tatyana, standing by the bust of an Egyptian Pharaoh.

"Ah yes, King Akhenaten. He revolutionised Egypt in 2000 BC by worshipping the sun's rays rather than the sun itself but unfortunately, this made him a heretic. It's never been hard to fall foul of the church's dogma whichever millennia you pick."

I had been drawn to the largest statue of all and stood gazing up in awe at the huge, tormented brass figure.

"What do you think, Sebastian?" asked Bassus coming up to my side and admiring the piece himself.

"It must be a copy because the original is in Florence but it is Prometheus being feasted on by Zeus' eagle."

"You're correct on both counts, my learned friend. Poor Prometheus; all he did was try to help man by giving him the gift of fire, but the Gods never did like mortals acting on their own initiative so he was punished. Forever."

Far from finding the figures horrific, because of my spiteful mood and perhaps my loutish drunkenness, I was revelling in the depictions of brutality, as though the nightmarish poses were somehow a vent for my anger. I belched and disguised a particularly foul smelling fart as Tatyana stopped by a large, black-winged creature seated upon a throne.

"This one's my favourite of all," she called and gave me a suggestive smile. I discreetly wafted a hand behind my backside and joined her. The ungodly figure had the horned-head and cloven feet of a goat but the body of a man and was cast in coal black bronze. As I looked closer I noticed that it also had breasts.

"Ah yes: The Baphomet. Though, known by many names. Perhaps the most misunderstood and troublesome of all my statues. Trust you to pick it out, my dear."

Tatyana smiled mischievously and curtseyed.

"As you can see the pose represents the inherent duality of life." He indicated with his cane, "One hand pointing up to the heavens, the other down to our world. The sun and moon, the east and west, beauty and ugliness, the esoteric and the exoteric, the inner and outer worlds perfectly reflected in nature's androgynous balance. I give the maxim's very personification: As above, so below."

I stared at the outlandish thing for a moment and, trying to forget my hideous dream from the stagecoach, spotted that the eye sockets were hollow.

"That's right, Sebastian," said Bassus, watching my eyes, "Hollow."

"But why, sir?"

"To show that the mortal body is empty without the divine soul. Godless man is a beast and, as such, fears no divine retribution. For, to deny the soul of liberated man can find a home within the beast is to deny that, within the soul of man, dwells a beast." He smirked appreciatively at his own poetry and asked Tatyana, "And why is it your favourite, my dear?"

"Because it reminds me of Sebastian," she giggled, pointing at its groin where a huge erect penis stood pointing up at the ceiling.

"Do you recognise the likeness?" She asked and bit her lip then raised a haughty eyebrow. Though this was not the only thing that rose in the room.

"Come now, Thomas," she purred, "We must get changed for the ceremony."

"You're right as usual, my dear. Don't worry," he looked between us and smiled, "You'll both be seeing each other again soon."

"I look forward to it, Librarian. Perhaps you will have another surprise for me?" she teased and pouted with such wanton licentiousness that I had to stop myself from grabbing her right there and then. Before I could she slipped away but wobbled her bottom so pleasingly that I could not take my eyes from it.

Bassus waited till she had gone before whispering privately, "You are in luck, Sebastian. I have spoken to my colleagues and your ordination has been approved and will take place at the beginning of the meeting after the rising of the moon at half past eight." He checked his pocket watch then popped it back in his waistcoat, "Remember, my friend, this is an important affair which requires your utmost respect. Many of the society's highest membership will be in attendance. I have organised a very special ordination for you that incorporates all degrees within one ceremony, as you wished and, for which I believe you are ready. There's no introductory booklet for this ceremony, Sebastian. Adepts are expected to be prepared in all ways. Do you understand?" He looked over my filthy clothes. "With this in mind, you might like to change. I will see to it that your things are brought to your room. Now, go there and prepare yourself and I will see you at the hour of eight – prompt." His boyish smile returned and he slapped my back, grinning, "Congratulations, Sebastian. It is a great honour you are about to receive."

With this he went about his business and I returned to my room rubbing my hands with triumphant spite and lustful expectancy. I summoned back the young servant to get me another jug of beer and told him to keep them coming or he would feel the back of my hand. I changed into the suit that I had worn to the opera, guessing that Tatyana would probably not remember it as she had barely seen it for five seconds. Anyway, all my others were covered in filth after my horrendous journey from Poschiavo. I viewed my reflection in one of my many mirrors and was most pleased.

"You good looking devil," I muttered, ignoring a memory of Francesca crying in our bed with her puffy eyes. "You don't need that old piece of mutton where you're going my boy," I told myself and smoothed down my jacket as it had become creased during my travels.

I took a well earned rest in the iron chair with my glass of beer. It was curiously comfortable though the clamps got in the way a bit and tended to dirty a gentleman's cuffs. I took a long swig and imagined Tatyana sitting on my lap then had a massive fart. The beer was certainly working. I took another long swig and concentrated back on my fantasy and, after a moment, as a celebration seemed appropriate, I went to touch myself. What did I care? Anyway, who would know?

I was startled by someone turning the key in the door and I jumped up, splashing beer all over my waistcoat and shouting, "Come in! Come in! For Christ's sake. Come in!"

It was the nervous youth again this time with my gear and he bundled inside almost dropping the walking stick and causing me to rear up, "Be careful with that you oaf or I'll knock your block off!"

He put it down and scuttled out so I chased after him and kicked him up the arse to make sure he paid better attention next time. I heard him lock the door and run away, so I unpacked my things and got out my watch which I proudly arranged on my waistcoat – just so. No point in being demure now. After all, Bassus had one. So naturally I should have one too.

I carefully leant the walking stick on a cabinet next to the door then got out my feathered hat and admired myself in the mirror. I was wondering whether it was a tad too much for the ceremony, and if the rules permitted such garments, when my eyes fell on the walking stick. Stupid old thing. Why had the mad Professor given it to me in the first place? I checked my watch and the level of my beer then put my head against the door and hollered for the servant to bring me another. There was time for a couple more before my new life of luxurious splendour, deep satisfaction and moral liberation began.

Chapter 21

The Ultimate Secret

The storm finally broke and, as the first rain drops pattered on my window ledge, the hands on my watch ticked up to eight and the town's church bells softly rang out over the rooftops. Only a handful of seconds could have passed before I heard a key rattle in my door followed by a gentle tap and I straightened in the fading light.

"Prompt indeed," I murmured and emptied my glass then after checking my reflection one last time, opened the door. Bassus regarded me with his typical smile and sighed, "It is time."

I took a deep breath, pulled down my waistcoat, smoothed down my hair and followed him down the stairs. The castle was as quiet as a church on a wet Wednesday night and you could have heard a pin drop in the darkened hallways. I saw not one soul as we walked through the deserted building and murmured to myself, "Where is everybody?" I belched secretively and realised that I was probably a little bit drunk but tdid my best to conceal it. At the end of one hallway Bassus picked up a candlestick from a table and led me through an archway then down a particularly long, dark staircase up to a huge door flanked by two columns supporting an enormous stone lintel. A tiny shiver went up my spine when I saw the words, '*Gnothi seauton*' engraved in the stone. Bassus stood regarding the inscription then faced me with a cryptic expression made all the more enigmatic by the candlelight falling across his features. "You know, Sebastian, once you have entered you cannot go back?"

"Yes, sir," I said, shaking my head, "I don't want to go back."

He nodded thoughtfully and continued, "Answer truthfully, Sebastian and everything will be fine. But whatever you do, remember: don't let them get your goat. Do you understand?"

"Yes," I nodded eagerly. Though I did not completely understand, I was not nervous. He had said that before and all I had found was a room full of butchers and bakers. 'Give me everything you have,' I thought. 'After all, I have experienced a great deal.'

He composed himself and knocked distinctly three times on the door. We waited in the shadows with only the sound of the bubbling flames between us. For a moment I thought nothing was going to happen but then there was a loud clunk and the door swung back revealing a pitch black chamber. Unsure of what to do, I looked to Bassus who simply gestured ahead. So, I stuck out my chin and crossed over the threshold. He followed me inside where his candlestick illuminated two strange figures standing on either side of a small vestibule. Unlike Bahrdt and the butcher, they were wearing mysterious hooded robes covering their eyes in shadow and said nothing but stood perfectly still facing another door six feet in front of them. We stepped up to the door whereupon Bassus put down the candlestick and blindfold me then once again, knocked distinctly three times.

We waited for what seemed like an eternity until the reverberations had almost completely faded when, at last, an extremely deep and haunting voice intoned, "What do you seek?"

Another shiver went up my spine and I waited for Bassus' reply.

"I bring an adept to be brought into the light!" he called.

A second pregnant pause, even longer than the first, was finally broken when the voice dramatically boomed, "Is he prepared?"

"He is!" called out Bassus and something told me that there was no wink this time.

I heard the heavy bolts being slid back and the door steadily creak open. One of the men behind put a hand on my shoulder and walked me inside. We entered what I estimated, by the echo of the door closing behind us, was a sizeable hall. As the hand pushed me gently forward into the silence I could somehow feel a presence in the room and was certain that we were not alone. After thirty or so paces the hand bought me to a halt and I intuitively knelt on one knee.

From slightly above me I heard another voice say, "You are a third degree adept of the Society of the Craft and come before the High Council of The Thirty Third Degree seeking advancement."

At this point I had planned on whispering a private joke but my concentration was thrown off course on hearing that the society's name contained this most ominous of all Master Numbers.

"You come highly recommended by an esteemed member of the High Council but I still require the consent of my fellow Brothers before we can commence with the ordination."

There was a pause and some ruffling of robes before he called out, "Do I have the consent of the High Council of The Thirty Third Degree?" I wondered who he was asking but found out immediately as a chilling chorus of, perhaps fifty men, all solemnly replied, "Aye!"

So this was where everybody was. Though I was blindfolded I still glanced over my shoulder as it started to dawn on me that this was perhaps a much more serious affair than I had presumed. I suddenly felt very vulnerable knowing that I was being watched by so many. 'Don't mess this up Seb,' I told myself and had to concentrate to suppress a large vaporous fart.

"As in life, our society remains hidden to those who are unordained. As in life our adepts remain lost in the darkness of ignorance enlightened only as befits their degree. Brother adept, are you ready to proceed up the steps to that enlightenment?"

"Yes," I called as confidently as I could, though I already recognised the quiver of doubt in my voice. There was another ruffle and I was helped up by my elbow then pushed forward until I felt my toe touch a step which I climbed with my hand out like a blind man. For some reason, I counted the stairs as I went up, 'One, two, three, four, five, six, seven, eight, nine, ten... eleven. I tried to compose myself and went to kneel but a hand pulled me up by my armpit and the voice ordered, from much closer now, "No, adept! Our God demands no contrition. He loves you for what you *truly* are. How could the one true God despise the actions of his own creations?"

I heard some movement and a soft swish as though a curtain had fallen to the floor ahead of me and the voice carried on as if addressing the entire room, "Behold our Master architect! To advance is to be enlightened, and to be enlightene, is to advance. Adept! Do you accept that a celestial Master rules the universe?"

Realising this was the moment that I had to answer truthfully and, having considered this question a great deal, I did not have to lie. "Yes!" I called out as unselfconsciously as I could.

"Do you accept the judgemental biblical God: Adonai, is a heresy?"

Given the recent outcomes of his mercy I could not help but reply with drunken resentment, "... Yes I do."

"We worship our God without superstition as one who accepts both our light and dark selves. For, without dark there can be no light, as there can be no pleasure without pain, no love without hatred, nor beauty without ugliness. He is the embodiment of the God and Goddess within us all and it is He who brings the highest levels of realisation to the creatures of His realm. He allows us to travel to this world where only those who have shown their worthiness are given the power to experience His might and magic powers. With Him as our ritual sex partner, we manifest our lives and bring His teachings to others. To know Him is to understand Him and He must be known in the flesh."

Him? Sex partner? Flesh? I did not like the way that things were going and noticed that my hands were wet with sweat. I concealed another enormous fart, half in fear, half in flatulence but focused on my fury and my drunken will to see it through.

The voice carried on at an accelerated tempo, "Now! Into the kingdom of Eden to the embrace of Mother Nature where the tyrannical envy of Adonai ceases and where we can, despising his anger, taste the fruit of the tree of knowledge of good and evil. For this is the true ancestral home of our forefathers, where we no longer have to wait for our rewards in heaven but can take them now on earth as rightful masters of all we survey!" He was well into his stride and accelerating toward an inevitable climax, "Who is the ancient and eternal spirit of light who allows us to perceive that there is no Heaven but only Earth where we, the rational, can be Gods? Who is the spirit of man's intellectual light who guides his path to illumination? Prepare to behold the ultimate secret, adept!"

By now I was shaking in my boots and pretty certain that I did not want to know what the ultimate secret was but the voice repeated, "Who is the spirit of light, adept?"

I was pushed forward and felt my knees bang into something hard but I pulled back. I knew what the bastard wanted me to say but I still could not bring myself to do it.

"Speak the spirit's name, adept!" demanded the voice and I was pushed again but this time felt something wet touch my lips.

"Speak the Almighty's name, adept!" ordered the voice and I felt the blindfold being untied.

I panicked and tried to turn my face so I did not have to see what was coming next. but it was too late. Someone grabbed my head and held it straight as the blindfold was ripped off and my eyes burned and my teeth chattered and my heart pounded when I finally beheld the ultimate secret.

Chapter 22

Lucifer is God!

I knew it was going to be bad, but I did not know anything could be that bad. Even though I wanted to close my eyes I could not look away. Sheer horror compelled me to stare. My heart pounded, my hair stood on end and I almost swallowed my tongue in rampant, stomach-churning fear. For immediately before me, eerily cast in shadow and sitting on his throne, was the mighty Baphomet goat-headed beast from hell itself but for real this time with fur, horns, ears, gleaming eyes and the most horrid, moist, grinning lips. I was almost sick as the vile creature's stink filled my nostrils and the voice barked again, "Who is God, adept?"

I knew what I had to say and, I am not ashamed to admit, tears filled my eyes as I struggled against my will and the hand holding my head in place. What was this phantasm before me?

"Say it!"

More than anything else I wanted the nightmare to end and, though it tore my soul in half, I gasped, "Lucifer."

"Who is God, adept?" bellowed the robed man, whom I could now see standing over me, though his eyes were covered in shadow. "Tell us who is God, adept?" he bellowed again and the hand pushed me closer.

"Please God forgive me," I whispered and took a deep breath then held my head high and roared at the top of my voice, "Lucifer is God!"

Oh Lord. What have I become?" I whispered and shook my head in disgust but even out of the corner of my eye I could see the man's mouth bend into a smirk. "Now kiss His lips!"

I was going to anyway simply to make the horror end but

the hand pushed me into the abomination's face and kept me there for three revolting seconds before releasing me. I was almost sick again and wiped my mouth with disgust then heard muttering behind me. I looked over my shoulder to find myself between two towering columns on a large stone altar at the top of a broad flight of stairs leading down to a black and white chequered floor upon which a huge solitary candelabrum burned brightly and, slowly emerging from the surrounding shadows, fifty or so hooded men.

"Now kiss His arse!" demanded my tormentor.

I whipped my head back to check that he was serious. I need not have bothered. He was deadly serious and blazed, "Kiss his arse, adept!" then pointed to the shadows at the side of the altar.

I realised that the back of Baphomet's throne was made inaccessible by a long black curtain so I looked to where the man was pointing and staggered off. I groped around in the dark until I found a slit in the curtain and stepped through to the other side. Strangely, as I did, I thought that I heard laughter from the hall but continued onwards with my mind racing, 'What in Hell's name am I doing? Where am I even going?'

Something amongst the murk ahead of me brought me to a halt and I tried to make out what I was looking at. I took a few more tentative steps then realised exactly what it was. It was the pale, luminous skin of a perfectly-formed woman's rump. I took another step and all was revealed to me, in more ways than one. It was Tatyana bending over and presenting herself. I shook my head in confusion and automatically took two steps forward then faltered and took ine back. It was a nightmare and a dream come true simultaneously. A little voice in my head told me that this was what I had wanted since the first day I had seen her and there she was ready and waiting and baring all. I rubbed my chin in contemplation but jumped slightly when she asked, "Is that you, Librarian?"

"...Yes," I whispered back.

"Then, what are you waiting for?"

All this time waiting for this moment and now I did not know what to do. I truly did not know myself.

"Come on, Sebastian," she urged.

I was paralysed. This was my prize. All I had to do was take it and I could have everything I ever wanted; money, privilege, luxury, sex - everything. I had done the hard part now all I had to do was take my reward.

"Hurry," she whispered, "They'll be angry... if you do not... Come on. Hurry."

"They?" I asked.

"I don't have the time for this, Sebastian. Please come over here."

I walked over and came up behind her. She looked over her shoulder and urged, "What's wrong with you?" she hissed, "I've never known such lethargy."

That was it. I gazed at her perfect backside glistening in the dark like a beautiful full moon and I knew that I could not do it. I could kiss the very beast from Hell but I could not do this.

"I cannot do it," I said miserably.

"Don't do this, Sebastian. Come on." She wiggled about to get me in the mood.

"No. I can't." I put my hands over my eyes. I had seen enough.

"Why?" she spat.

"Because..." I only had to think about it for an instant, "I love another." I had been told to tell the truth and - rightly or wrongly- I had done so.

"I'll give you one last chance, Sebastian."

"Let me be," I said and kept my hands over my eyes. I heard someone knock something over very close by then mutter an obscenity.

"Please, Sebastian," she warned, "I do not want this to happen."

"Want what to happen?" I stupidly asked and I took away my hands to see two men coming out of the shadows with their robes hoisted around their waists and doing up their belts.

"Can I help you?" I asked in my usual polite manner though I was quite surprised to find them there in the first place: doing up their belts. I could not help but consider this anomaly until someone else tapped me on the shoulder and I turned round to see a huge fist punch me extremely hard in the face.

Chapter 23

Ignorance is Darkness

I came around lying on the floor and in total darkness. I briefly thought I was blind before realising that I had been blindfolded - again - but this time, when I tried to move I found that I had been bound and gagged as well and, so tight, that it hurt. Thunder and lightning. What was going on now? My chin felt like it had been kicked by a horse and the rest of my body like it had been thrown down a hill in a barrel. I put this down to my hangover which was of some proportion and tried to piece together everything that had happened to get me here. Where was Bassus? Surely he should be here getting me out of this mess. I panicked and went to call out for him but choked on whatever was in my mouth. Why the hell was I tied up like this? Had I not done everything they wanted? I remembered Tatyana's beautiful backside glowing in the dark and the fist hitting me in the face and then slowly recalled... shouting 'Lucifer is God!' to Baphomet on his throne. Oh dear, Sebastian. What have you gotten yourself into?

I struggled up into a seating position and, finding myself near a wall, shuffled over to it to prop myself up. I had not been waiting there long when I heard voices approaching but could not make out what they were saying. Though, whoever they were, they were definitely coming this way. My heart leapt and I told myself that it must be Bassus coming to apologise for the terrible mistake whereupon everything would be forgiven and we would all shake hands and return to the happy way we were. I held my breath as the door opened and several people entered the room. Whoever it was, one of them was carrying a candlestick because, even behind my blindfold, I could see the room become a little brighter.

I did my best to sit up straight and mumbled a muffled hello through my gag but the men paid no attention and spoke as though I were not there. "Why've you put him in here?" asked a man with a bizarre French accent. "I could have used this room instead of mine. Sally doesn't like ours one bit. Says it reminds her of a museum."

"Be quiet, Jefferson," spat a guttural voice, "I couldn't leave him where he was and you didn't have to drag the idiot on your own."

"I thought de Constanza and Bode were with you?"

"Pah. They are like paper swords."

"Please, Brothers, we haven't come here to argue," chipped in a conciliatory voice which I recognised but could not quite place.

The men began to squabble and I assumed they were members of The Council of the Thirty Third Degree but some of the names sounded strangely familiar. I had heard so many names over the past three months that I could not remember them all and I was still only half conscious. Then it hit me like a runaway stagecoach. I remembered exactly where I had heard the names before: The Book of Servants! My mind broke into a gallop. Was it Bode and de Constanza I saw doing up their trousers? No! It could not be! Perhaps there were two men both with the same names? Don't be stupid Seb. My heart turned to stone as my stuttering consciousness put everything together and I realised. No! The Council of The Thirty Third Degree... are... the... the... Illuminati!

My hair stood on end and I clenched my teeth so tight that I thought they would shatter. I was in the very heart of the beast and tied up like a pheasant on a plate.

A fourth and very familiar voice adjudicated over the quarrel, "Gentlemen, Gentlemen, calm yourselves and codenames please."

Holy Mother of God! It was Bassus! What was he doing here? Whatever it was, he did not seem in too much of a hurry to rescue me. My head started to spin and I began to feel seasick.

"Who cares about codenames now?" argued the rough voice. "In this room? On our own? What's the point?"

"Rules are rules, *Ajax*," replied Bassus.

I frantically tried to remember who Ajax was as he sneered, "Perhaps no one cares for your rules, *Hannibal*."

Oh my God! Bassus was Hannibal! He was 'H'! Bassus was Illuminati! Though consumed by fear, the sting of shock and the shame of betrayal still turned into red hot seething anger and I fought at my bonds to get the bastard. No longer caring for the niceties of polite society I let off a particularly rancid fart.

"Look's like he's angry," said the strange French accent, noticing me straining at my bonds. "And he stinks. Uuh!"

"Quiet, Jefferson. You'd be angry if you'd sealed your fate by refusing a free ride on a whore. Especially... that whore."

"Codenames, Ajax," reminded Bassus, "And could we refrain from using bad language please?"

"Sorry, Hannibal," spat Ajax. "Stay out of this *Pegasus.*"

"Do not disrespect me, Ajax," reared up Pegasus, "Firstly, I'm your superior and prospect to do even better in the future. Also, I've travelled for five days from Paris to get to this awful place, to be practically imprisoned, and I'm vexed enough already."

"I wasn't disrespectful," grunted Ajax.

"Why was he at the meeting at all?" demanded Jefferson.

"I thought we could use him to infiltrate a, should I say, hostile organisation," sighed Bassus wearily, "And we nearly succeeded."

"Nearly isn't good enough," griped Jefferson, "You'll need to improve your vetting process if you're in charge of recruitment here in Bavaria and providing safe passage to Switzerland."

Holy Mother of God! Bassus must have known who I was right from the start. And it was him who had been organising the whole operation to smuggle the Illuminati agents to safety in Poschiavo. I had been cluelessly sitting slap bang in the blasted middle of it all like a ridiculous fool. Damn it! How could I have been so gullible?

"But nothing's gone wrong so far," reasoned the gentle voice whom I now recognised as Mayr, the composer.

"And nothing would've gone wrong either if you'd let me kill him like I said," growled Ajax, "I would've slit the little runt's throat while he lay in your cosy bed - just like that. I knew he was trouble when I saw him at that whorehouse with that fool priest."

Bugger the Saints! Ajax was Massenhausen! The murderous fiend was not six feet away and I was as helpless as a baby. I stopped writhing about and froze as stiff as a corpse.

"You shouldn't have let him see you at Ambrosini's," complained Bassus, "We only stopped his messenger pigeons by Gretchen's watchfulness and her bird's instinct."

"I had to be there," sneered Massenhausen, "Remember? To get Brother Weishaupt's pathetic *apologist* pamphlets." *25

So that is what they were! Weishaupt was writing from exile and that stone-faced bitch and her evil bird had killed our blasted pigeons!

---

25. **Weishaupt Illuminati Apologist Writings in Exile.** After succesfully escaping the autorities in Bavaria Adam Weishaupt continued to write when in exile and continued to defend the actions of the Illuminati. He wrote several major pieces during this period, including: *A complete History of the Persecutions of the Illuminati in Bavaria* (1785) *A Picture of Illuminism* (1786) *An Apology for the Illuminati* (1786) and *An Improved System of Illuminism* (1787). We can only assume that the author saw one, or perhaps more, of these publications.

"Don't speak of Brother Spartacus in that tone, sir," snapped Jefferson, "He has helped us achieve a position of great power in my country from which we can take over the Congress and get Washington and that obstinate wretch Adams out of our way for good."

Good God! I was struggling to take it all in. Surely he must have been talking about America's George Washington and John Adams meaning only one thing: he must be... Thomas Jefferson! Could it really be true? Here? In this room? My head started spinning again as Bassus barrelled in, "You fail to understand the power of propaganda, Ajax. That's why we have the printing press in the first place; to mould the minds of the vile multitude because, as you damn-well know for I have told you a hundred times already, we can't just go around slitting everybody's throat who gets in our way!"

The men began to argue again and there were too many voices to hear. Though, the ugly truth was obvious. I had heard too much already. For their careless talk in front of me made it only too clear: I had squandered my one chance of getting out of there alive. Surely my luck had finally run out because there was no escape from this. Drowning in fear and regret as I was, somehow it was the vicious humiliation which cut the deepest. I had truly believed that Bassus was my friend. I had even wanted to be like him when, all along, he had been conspiring with Tatyana to deceive me. He, with his charm and wealth and privilege and she, with her beauty and wit and conniving ways, together luring me to my inevitable, pathetic downfall. Now he had disposed of me like an old sock and she had dealt me the fool's card in her own little game of Tarot. I imagined her laughing at me with all her pretty opera friends and sniffed. Oh, Sebastian you fool. I shook my head in disgrace and shed a lonely tear. What had I done?

Jefferson regained control of the argument but as he began to interrogate Bassus about me once more the door opened and a hush fell over them when a frail old voice with a thick Polish accent croaked, "Bring him."

"Yes, Master." They all obsequiously chorused.

Someone unceremoniously hauled me up and dragged me from the room as my mind floundered upon a sea of confusion, 'Who is this now? Who is it that can silence these very, very powerful men?' *26

---

26. **The Founding Fathers & The Illuminati.** Speculation has always existed of a connection between the Bavarian Illuminati and the fledgling Republic of the United States. Thomas Jefferson wrote in defence of Weishaupt when he was Ambassador to France living in Paris around this time and described him as an 'eager philanthropist.' Jefferson was not without other scandals and rumoured to have had a long-term affair with his slave girl Sally Hemmings. Washington did occasionally publicly criticise the Illuminati though this created more conspiracy theories than it quelled, some of which even claimed that Weishaupt replaced Washington as the gentlemen shared a passing resemblance. Speculation aside it is interesting that S. Drechsler recalls Jefferson saying that he 'prospects to do even better in the future' and he became president fourteen years later.

Chapter 24

The Heart of the Beast

I could tell that it was Massenhausen dragging me blindly along behind him through the castle's seemingly never-ending corridors by the way I kept banging my head against all the doors and walls. I also knew that he would kill me as soon as he got the chance and that, if it had been up to him, I would be dead already. But in the end, it was only a matter of time before one of them did away with me, in one horrid way or another.

He bundled me through another doorway and, I guessed by the long echoes of our footsteps, that we had returned to the ceremonial hall. Sure enough, he dragged me back up the steps to the top of the alter and threw me down. The bastard gave me a cuff round the ear for good luck but knocked my blindfold down which at least allowed me to see what was happening. I had another disgusting fart and hoped that he could smell it.

From my new vantage point at the base of one of the pillars I was surprised to see the Brothers crowding round the foot of the steps once more but, this time, in various states of undress, with some only wearing nightshirts while others stood around practically naked with nothing but blankets wrapped about them. In the bright light now falling from two rows of large chandeliers, I could also see that the fearsome Baphomet was, in actuality, merely Bassus' statue with a goat's carcass hung over it. So it was not an abomination from Hell but an illusion accomplished by a trick of the light, my own fear and a freshly slaughtered animal. Or was it a... sacrifice?'

"Good evening everyone!" welcomed the Polish voice grabbing everyone's attention and, while Bassus, Massenhausen and Jefferson watched from the rear of the altar, a frail, old man with a tiny square moustache dressed in nothing but a bizarre fur hat and a bed sheet over his shoulder like a toga, held out his skinny arms to the crowd. Beside him a grey-bearded Kabbalist priest in long black and gold ornate robes nodded at a large open book in his hands and, past his spindly legs on his far side, I could see a strange little girl in a black dress with dark plaited hair who could not have been more than fourteen years old. I was surprised again when the crowd milling around the bottom of the steps all reverently bowed to the odd little man and his entourage whilst most dutifully chanted, "Master!" Who was he? He regarded his disciples benevolently, nodding this way and that before asking, in his oily Polish accent, "I trust everyone has enjoyed themselves?"

A round of hooting and dirty laughter confirmed his assumptions. The Brothers had obviously been favouring pleasure over business and, by the way they slapped each other's backs or looked sheepishly about it suddenly struck me that the entire meeting was, in fact, an excuse for an orgy. My suspicions were vindicated when the little man continued greasily, "Brother Hannibal always arranges the best meetings. Does he not? Where all our sensual needs are satisfied; like ancient Shangri-La." He chuckled and stroked the hair of the girl standing in his shadow with questionable relish. "Sorry for this unwelcome interruption, but as you all know our meeting was supposed to take place yesterday and I would like to apologise for inconveniencing those who have travelled from afar. I was held up by," he glanced at the girl, "Unforeseen circumstances. But, as we all know, good things come to those who wait. Heh?"

"The dates are wrong. No good will come of it," babbled the nodding priest next to him without taking his eyes from his book. "Holy Gematria ordains it. Blood was spilled on the twelfth. Not the eleventh. The twelfth is no good. No good at all. Not good at..."

"Later, Khan," interrupted the old man, "I told you, God will provide." He muttered something under his breath in Polish then put his hands together, faced his congregation and portentously began, "Our agents continue our work in all corners of the world. Here in Europe and also in Asia, our provocateurs have started a war between Russia and Turkey from which we should derive a considerable extension of our influence. In England we make great strides in finance as we do across the great Northern Ocean in America too." He swept up a bony finger and pointed it behind him at Jefferson then continued, "Where our Brotherhood stands on the threshold of securing that entire continent into our hands for perpetuity."

"But what about right here in Bavaria, Jacob?" called out a portly Brother in his nightshirt, "I live in fear of persecution from the authorities and their backers in the Church. They hound us everywhere from dawn to dusk. There is no end to it."

"Fear not the Church, my friend," dismissed the old man with a wave of his grey hand. "I have taken it upon myself to infiltrate the very heart of the Vatican itself and I know, for a fact, because of those in the highest places whom I have under my control, that it is simply a matter of time before that great institution also falls into our hands."

"But we don't have time, Frank" complained a bald Brother holding a blanket around his loins, "We are being pursued now. Today. Our houses, our positions, our lives are at stake."

There was a flurry of support for these concerns with some similar complaints being shouted out and Bassus diplomatically tempered the growing discord, calling over the brother's heads, "Please, Gentlemen, please. And codenames always. Please."

But he was too late and my mind was already whirring like a lathe, 'Jacob Frank? Jacob Frank? Frank? Yes! I was sure that I had heard the name at the beginning of The Book of Servants, which meant that he must be Illuminati of the highest order.

Whoever he was, he was highly agitated with the dissenters and a fire burned in his eyes as he shouted, "Then move house, Tiberius!" He twitched his tiny moustache before ranting, "Is the Brotherhood not more important than your pathetic livelihood? Is not our glorious mission: The Great Work, the single-minded ambition of our entire Order throughout the aeons to secretly initiate the great tribes of the world to our sect, more important than your measly '*position*'?"

He glared out over the sullen crowd as though he were a retributive ship's captain and they his mutinous crew. "What would you be without me? Eh? Nothing! Nothing at all! All the money I have squandered on you, the riches, the wealth. You could not survive without me!"

Jefferson piped up, "Are we not a council of equals, sir, in the true republic tradition with no one leader?"

Frank turned on him, literally, even having to grab his sheet to stop it from falling down as he nagged in his old spiteful voice, "It is *I* who have been chosen by our holy bloodlines to lead, not *you*, Pegasus! Never forget it. Why do you think you address me as Master and not the other way round? While you falsely cry liberty, fraternity and egality it is my connections with the great houses of Europe who dictate the shape of the world that are key to our inevitable triumph rather than your frivolous democracies and you know it!"

Jefferson hung his head at this volley but Frank was not finished and delivered him another withering salvo, "Was it not me who gave you the money for your farm? Where else would you have got such a tidy sum? Eh? And tell me was it not me who helped to keep your regrettable affair with your slave girl a secret?"

Massenhausen chuckled at Jefferson's dressing-down but Frank noticed him guffawing and gave him a piece of the same treatment. "You are no different, Ajax! Was it not I who filled the coffers of our treasury when you and Spartacus had not one penny between you because you had embezzled the lot to pay for your gambling, whoring and drinking with your ruffian friends?"

Now it was Massenhausen's turn to hang his head as Frank turned on the crowd in the same ruthless manner, "I say to you all, if there is one of you who has not received a payment of monies from me, in some way, then let me know now! Come! I am waiting!" He furiously scanned the crowd but it appeared that he was right and everyone was in his debt as there were no dissenters whatsoever or, at least, none who had the courage to speak up.

"I thought as much," he gloated and added with deriding scorn, "Why, it is only Brother Hannibal here who seems to possess the financial acumen to actually support himself without my constant intervention!" He stood there taking deep breaths and scowling and I thought that he was spent but he threw his skinny arms back in the air and cried out, "Now let us give praise!"

Now the entire congregation including Bassus and the others on the altar, though interestingly, I noticed, not the young girl and the nodding Kabbalist priest, all knelt and bowed their heads as one. At the same time Frank's toga fell down exposing his tiny, crumpled manhood wilting in a grey bird's nest of pubic hair. One of the Brothers ran up the steps and awkwardly attempted to replace the sheet but Frank did not care and carried on as naked as Adam, "We exalt Thee, Oh mighty Lucifer, and your eternal light which guides us from atop our sacred temple! As we reverse all that is holy to be unholy we become the left hand of God to bring about your final coming and prophesied rule of the world. Bless Thee for my past incarnation, Sabbati Tzvi and our bloodlines to lead our glorious Order in triumph over the servile multitudes!"

"Bless Thee Master!" chanted the congregation.

Frank seemed satisfied by this unanimous contrition and the fire blazed in his eyes once more as he beseeched, "Now I command you all to indulge yourselves, as only you can!"

The Brothers cheered up upon hearing this put as an official command and, with prayers seemingly over, broke ranks and dispersed. Frank finally accepted his sheet from his waiting admirer and called out over the growing hubbub "Remember, Brothers; Redemption through sin! Redemption through sin!"

This ominous encouragement brought a spontaneous cheer from the departing men with some putting their arms around each other and some, perhaps it was Bode and de Constanza, even publicly kissing. My thoughts were writhing like a barrel of snakes and, consumed with fear as I was, when Frank and the others came over, I released another massive fearful fart to show it. He twitched his square moustache and rearranged his toga then looked down on me with supreme disdain and croaked, "Who is he?" [27]

"His name is Sebastian Drechsler, Master," answered Bassus, "A poor naive fool whom I tried to help but, it would appear, flew a little too close to the light."

Frank regarded me with disgust and asked, "Drechsler? Was it not he who caused all the problems in Ingolstadt?"

"And killed Kolmer," chipped in mouthy Massenhausen.

---

27. **Bavarian Illuminati & Jakob Frank.** Jakob Frank was a religious leader and mystic who frequented the Royal Courts of Europe and claimed to be the reincarnation of the self-proclaimed Messiah Sabbati Tvzi 1626-1676. The Polish religious authorities excommunicated Frank because his many transgressions, which were reputed to have included; incest, rape and murder - his form of worship involving neo-carpocratian 'redemption through sin' or purification through transgression - were too much even set against the standards of behaviour tolerated in the church in those days. His connections to the Illuminati were never proven.

"I see," grunted Frank and glared at me as though Kolmer had been his only son.

"Kill him," he said coldly and marched off without batting an eyelid followed by the nodding priest and the young girl who stopped briefly in front of me to giggle before skipping away.

When they had gone Massenhausen smiled and declared, "I will do it," which caused me to fart wildly.

Bassus pointed his finger right in his face and warned him, "As long as you don't slit his throat," which I thought decent of him.

Massenhausen grimaced and hissed through clenched teeth, "All right."

"Promise?" said Bassus, "One Brother to another?"

"On my oath," growled Massenhausen.

Bassus seemed suddenly inspired and suggested, "Why not use the opportunity to do what we did with that nosey little shit in Poschiavo. Remember? The *sacrifice*?"

I immediately revised my opinion of him.

"You mean... ?" asked Massenhausen and grinned excitedly.

"Yes. Isaac is taking it tonight." Bassus flicked his eyebrows, "Go and find him. He's in the groom's shed behind the stables."

Massenhausen seemed content with whatever horrendous act they had in store for me and Bassus observed, in his characteristic fashion, "Abracadabra. I create what I speak." He glanced at some stragglers leaving the hall and mentioned, "Now I have to, how should I say, take care of something that I left - half cocked?"

He went to commit whatever debauchery he had in mind but stopped to look at my blinking, terrified eyes and cheerily said, "Shame you didn't fit in, old fellow. I suppose our little society isn't for everyone." He smiled his boyish smile one last time and joked, "Maybe next time eh? Goodbye, Sebastian."

And with that, the bastard left. I fought against my bonds and shouted a barrage of muffled insults into my gag but, of course, he did not hear them. Massenhausen yanked me to my feet and dragged me back down the steps and through the maze of corridors making sure to bang my head into as many inanimate objects on the way as possible. As he paraded me through the house I could hear all manner of shouts and wails coming from the rooms and tried not to imagine the depraved scenes taking place. Going down one particularly dark hallway I was troubled to see, through an open door, some iron cages and trembled to think of their perverse purpose.

More importantly, I dreaded to think what they had done to this poor unknown soul in Poschiavo because it was what lay in wait for me. As hard as I fought it, I could not help but go through the many horrifying possibilities; a rack, a guillotine, a torture chair, hanging, a bed of nails, even a red poker and all while farting profusely. What horror would it be?

However long I had tried to work it out I never would have guessed. But then, no one in their right mind could have ever guessed, because no one in their right mind could have ever thought of killing someone in such an utterly insane and supremely depraved manner because its despicable cruelty and vile maliciousness was so absolutely and completely beyond all known comprehension in each and every way.

Chapter 25

Abandon Hope All Ye Who Enter Here

Eventually, we came round a shadowy corner where Massenhausen threw me against a wall and marched off, calling out, "Isaac? Are you there? I have a proposition for you."

While he talked with someone in muffled tones I became aware of a distinct whimpering from somewhere close by and scrabbled round to see who or what, was making the noise. When I beheld what I witnessed next I knew that I would never be able to forget it. For there in the darkness, outstretched upon an inverted cross propped against the wall, was Canon Danzer horrifically crucified upside down like poor St Peter. I had seen a lot that day but the sight of this obscene spectacle was truly horrendous and I was shocked to the core. I turned away at first but had to peek back in morbid fascination. He was not nailed to the thing but the tethers binding his wrists and ankles had cut deeply into his flesh and he was bleeding heavily. The blood from his ankles was trickling down over his chest and his open shirt and had splashed across his face. He mumbled feverishly from behind a blindfold in grief-stricken agony and, as he shifted about trying to relieve his pain, a handful of coins fell from the pocket of his grubby breeches onto the floor and rolled away. They certainly kept their threats of capital punishments I thought to myself and the hairs on the back of my neck stood up when I recalled the poor bastard's prophetic Tarot reading.

Without warning Massenhausen grabbed my ear and painfully lifted me up causing me to kick a boot out at him.

"Take that you bastard!" I raged into my gag. "I'm not going out without a fight!" But he pulled my head down and stuffed his knee into my face, knocking the living daylights out of me. He manhandled me inside the next room and threw me back to the floor. At least I no longer had to watch Danzer's terrible fate unfolding but now prepared to discover my own.

A slight man with dark olive skin, but obviously of some social standing, as he was wearing a smart white shirt and breeches, examined me and recomended, "We'll have to remove his bonds so he'll need to be unconscious." He sized me up and estimated, "Otherwise he won't fit." He turned to Massenhausen and shrugged, "We could drug him? Do you have any opium? I don't have my medicines with me."

Massenhausen impatiently shook his head and before I could work out what in Heaven's name they were talking about, he pulled his fist back once more and smashed it into my face.

I had not known if I would ever wake up again. I could have been killed right there and then and never have opened my eyes. So when I did it was with much trepidation because I was so scared to discover the macabre fate to which I had been condemned. But in the end it was so dark that all I could make out were two faint holes in front of me and, try as I might, such was my disorientation, I still could not tell where I was. I knew only one thing: I was in the most dreadful peril.

Behind my re-tightened gag I explored my mouth with my tongue and discovered Massenhausen's latest assault had loosened more teeth. I also felt strangely nauseous which I put down to the fact that I was jostling from side to side as if on a horse. As I tried to get my bearings I farted with such disgusting foulness that I had to fight the compulsion to vomit. I went to move but I appeared to be jammed in a seated position and hardly able to shift my body an inch in any direction. Something was stopping me. I wondered if they had found some opium because I seemed to be paralysed. Then I realised I was actually inside something. Something unyielding. As my vision slowly adjusted to the gloom I focused ahead and it seemed that, through the eyeholes, I could see some dark material. So where was I?

Inside some sort of.... sarcophagus? No! Surely it could not be? I started to panic and succumb to claustrophobia but when I heard voices talking only a few feet in front of me, though I was possessed by an all-encompassing fear, I desperately tried to listen for any clue as to my deadly predicament.

"All I know is it can't be right, Herr Long."

"It doesn't matter whether you think it's right or wrong, Dreyfuss. You're paid to drive the cart, not think."

"I'm not saying I won't drive the cart. No, sir. I'll drive the cart all night if you like. Looks like I'm gonna have to anyway to get back from Vohburg. All I'm saying is, I know it ain't right."

"Vohburg?" I choked. It was a small port on the Danube.

"You tell 'im, Dreyfuss," said someone else, "I've a mind to get off here in the middle of nowhere 'cos I hates being near the thing so much."

"Feel free to get off wherever you like. I only need Dreyfuss here to drive."

"All I'm saying..."

"I know what you're saying, sir!" snapped Long, "But if we just drive there, find the Lucius, unload and leave then everything will be well. Surely, I don't have to remind you again that we're in a hurry. After Vohburg our cargo sails tonight on a ship bound for the Americas. So, let's have no more talk about whether it's right or wrong or anything else. Thank you very much!"

Long's outburst resolved the disputation and an uneasy silence fell over them. Though I had heard enough. My knees started to shake and my heart to pound for I knew that it was me, or more precisely, what I was inside that they were talking about. The awful truth crushed me like a vice and I started to lose my mind. I tried to control myself but it was no good and no one heard me scream into my gag when I finally realised that I was trapped inside The Statue of Baphomet!

In the dark my eyes frantically shot from side to side behind the grinning goat's face. So this was to be my coffin - my doom? Who could have ever imagined such a cruel fate? That bastard Bassus. That was who. The depraved monster. He had sentenced me to death inside this revolting mausoleum. I could almost hear him laughing for I had poetically become the living soul inside the beast. I tried to rock the statue but it was so heavy that I could not move it at all. It was no good. There was no escape. None!

The cart jolted over a pothole knocking my head against the walls of my prison. The toing and froing of the wagon was playing havoc with my flatulence and another burning, rancid blast tore from my backside filling the casket with the foulest stench. I was going to suffocate on my own gas inside my own coffin, in which someone else had already been murdered. Thunder and lightning! I tried to kick out or punch or resist in anyway but it was useless. I imagined my mother weeping by the side of my grave alongside my father's but realised it could never happen because no one would ever find me. Tears filled my eyes and I sobbed helplessly into my gag.

In time, over my blubbing, I began to hear the rumble of other carts and the general sounds of a town steadily growing louder and I presumed that we had reached Vohburg. I had been through so much and was so tired, frightened, unhinged, and generally wretched that I could not think straight and, worst of all because of my desperation, had all but given up hope. Deprived of any visual distractions, I was left alone with the harrowing memories of my downfall which destroyed any remaining resolve that I may have possessed. Suffice to say, that I was a total panicking, blubbering mess with tears streaming down my face when the wagon finally came to a rest and I felt a lurch as someone dismounted.

"Stay here. And don't talk to anyone," ordered Long. "I'm going to find the captain of the Lucius but I'll be back soon."

I farted again as I heard him walk off, though whether it was due to rampant fear or flatulence, I could no longer tell.

"Phowar! Stinks round 'ere don't it?" winced one of the voices.

"It's the docks ain't it? Always stinks round the docks."

"I don't like it anyways," said the first lowering his voice.

"What, the smell?" asked the other.

"No stupid, that thing in the back. It ain't right. You could tell by the faces of that lot at the castle that they're up to no good."

"Cook says half of 'em are in that Illuminati. See. It's illegal what we're doing."

I farted again filling the statue with another cloud of rancid gas.

"Phowar! It's that smell again. Know what? I reckon it's coming from the... thing."

"Well it stinks don't it? Like this place."

I felt one of them get up to investigate. Of course! This was my chance to get them to break me out.

"I reckon I should take a look just in case," said the voice coming closer.

Yes! Yes! I silently pleaded but the other warned, "No. I don't want to see it. Seen it once, that was enough for me. You should be careful. Master Long told you to leave it alone or else he would not pay. Got to be on the boat in a minute anyways."

"Suppose you're right," said the other and the cart swayed as he moved back to his seat.

'No! Damn it! No! I roared into the gag and, necessity being the mother of invention, I summoned my guts to attention and squeezed with all my might to produce a fart of such magnitude that it would have demolished the Coliseum. Fortunately, it was not silent either and, using some nifty anal control, I managed to create a rich sound which resonated the brass sarcophagus like a French horn.

"Sweet Mother Mary! What's that? D'you hear it?" asked the first voice then recoiled, "Phowar! I'll wager you can smell it."

"It ain't right. It ain't right at all," jabbered his friend, becoming noticeably alarmed.

"Well, I don't care what that high-talking Long says, I'm gonna take a look."

"Come on!" I shouted into my gag and felt him inch back up the wagon. I bit my lip with hair-raising anticipation and, after a slow swish the canvas slipped away and I saw them both staring open-mouthed at me with the riverbank and the boats and potential freedom behind them. The man sitting in the driver's box gripped the back of the seat and pointed an accusatory finger at my eyes, wailing, "It's alive! The thing's alive! Look at its eyes! I'm off!" And, true to his word, he jumped down from the wagon and ran away, shouting, "It ain't no good! It ain't no good at all!"

Thankfully, his friend was made of sterner stuff and stood watching my wild blinking eyes as I begged God, or fate, or his own sensibilities, 'Please! Please! Please! Don't run away. Don't be scared. I'm not a beast from Hell. I'm just a foolish student who should be in his rooms writing his dissertation.' After a few seconds he hesitantly leant forward trying to decide whether I was man or beast.

"What are you then?" he half murmured to himself.

I seized my chance to tell him by means of what limited vocabulary I had at my disposal and once again squeezed for Bavaria to produce a resounding and, most definitely, human fart. As a means of a hello this crude but effective communication worked like a charm and he gasped in realisation and quickly found the catches on the side of the statue and unfastened them. After overcoming his initial shock upon finding me, he threw open the door and dragged me out.

"What in Heaven's name's going on?" he flustered as he helped me down from the wagon and removed my gag.

I slumped to the ground unable to move my legs after my confined incarceration but managed to wheeze, "Thank you. Thank you so much. You've saved my life." I wiped my face and hissed, "Now go! Leave now. Before he comes back."

He stared at me for a moment then glanced about and scratched his head before heeding my advice and hurriedly jumping back on his wagon. He did not even bother replacing the canvas but stirred his horse and I watched as the ghoulish winged Baphomet clattered off up the riverbank incongruously sitting upon its throne on the back of the cart.

I was alive. Now all I had to do was run away. I looked up and down the riverbank and went to stand but to my horror my legs folded under me. I pushed myself up again and held my weight on my arms which were fine but, my legs felt as though they were someone else's and simply would not obey my commands. I checked if my saviour was still in sight but as I looked ahead the cart disappeared round a distant corner. I cursed myself for recklessly sending him away and not staying on the wagon. Idiot! I urgently began rubbing my legs to bring them back to life but, as I did, I heard Long calling out, "Dreyfuss! I have found our boat! It's up this way!"

Shit! He was coming back. I compelled my legs with an angry whisper, "Come on! Come on!"

I could not die like this because my blasted legs would not work. I went to push myself up as Long called out again, "Dreyfuss!"

Shit! Shit! Shit! I managed to stand - just - but only staggered a measly few yards before I immediately fell down behind a wagon.

"Dreyfuss!" fumed Long, obviously getting agitated and from underneath the wagon I could see his white breeches striding towards me not twenty yards away. I looked around and saw an inn up the riverbank with a few sailors and merchants sitting outside. I had to get over there. I hauled myself up on the wagon's wheel, took a deep breath and wobbled off, anxiously glancing over my shoulder. For a few seconds I thought that I was going to make it but I lost my balance after only a few steps as my knees gave way and I fell flat on my face in a huge puddle covering myself in filth.

"Dreyfuss!" fairly screamed Long from much closer now and with me still fifty yards from the sanctuary of the inn.

I spat the mud from my mouth, pulled myself from the slime and floundered up the street. A crew of passing sailors gave me a wide berth, obviously thinking that I was a drunk or a tramp or both. I considered begging the next man who came along for help as he looked kinder but when he saw me coming he crossed the street.

"Come on Seb. You can do it!" I implored myself as I lurched along covered in shit and looking like Quasimodo. Exhausting my very last ounce of strength, I finally dragged myself to the safety of the inn and squatted down on my haunches behind a couple of sailors seated at a table who were too busy drinking tankards of beer to notice me. Good God. Somehow I had escaped. For now, at least, but without a clue what to do next. I glanced about, panting and half crazed. Who on God's green Earth could help me now?

"Hello, Sebastian," chuckled an all-too familiar voice from behind me but somehow the shock stopped me from turning around to discover what I already knew to be true. *28

---

28. **The Statue of Baphomet.** Hyman Isaac Long was an American physician who emigrated from Jamaica to New York where he was influential in
the development of Masonic organisations and also further afield in Virginia and South Carolina. In 1805, when he was travelling in Europe, border
guards found a Statue of Baphomet in his luggage and the story caused so
much international furore that eventually Long was summoned by the Pope
to the Vatican to explain. Effigies of this winged androgynous occult figure
are now usually derived from Eliphas Levi's drawings (Circa 1856) and are
seated and usually cast in Bronze. The character has enjoyed a recent surge in
popularity. In 2015 The Satanic Temple organisation commissioned a bronze
that was subsequently displayed at the Arkansas and Oklahoma state buildings in protest at the erection of a Ten Commandments Monument. After
the Ten Commandments Monument was shelved, the Satanic Temple successfully sued Netflix for using the character in the TV show: *The Chilling
Adventurers of Sabrina.*

Chapter 26

Will Wonders Never Cease?

"C'mon, Sebastian. I did say hello," cajoled the friendly voice. I took a deep breath and turned about and, though he had done it so many blasted times before, I was still shocked to the bone to see Professor Van Halestrom calmly sitting at a table in the company of two frothing tankards of beer.

"You!" was all I could utter and stared between him and the drinks.

"Correct, my friend," he smiled, "By the way you're looking at those tankards I reckon you could do with a drink. Come on, sit down." He patted the bench next to him.

I scowled at him in disbelief as he was so utterly unbelievable. Not altogether forgetting my ongoing woes, of which he seemed oblivious, I glanced back up the riverbank and saw Long pacing up and down and asking the other wagon drivers where his wagon and driver had gone. I cowered down only to hear Van Halestrom quip, "I wouldn't worry about him. Does he have a gun?"

I screwed my face up at him clearly conveying, 'How the blazes would I know?'

"I'll wager it is not as big as mine," he said and promptly produced a double-barrelled flintlock pistol from under his cloak which he plonked on the table.

I glanced around nervously upon seeing such a sizeable firearm in such a public place and sat down beside him.

"How are you?" he asked, checking my eyes.

I had not yet fully recovered from the shock of being alive and, in my bewildered state, was only capable of searching his face for any clue as to what in Hell's name he was doing there.

"You're alive I see," he smiled, reading my mind as usual, and took the froth off his tankard with a hearty slurp. "Ah. Its good. Try it."

The beautiful truth finally sank in. I was safe. I shook my head in disbelief once more and, after one more profoundly huge gasp, I grabbed the tankard and guzzled thirstily.

"That's right. Go on," encouraged Van Halestrom and watched me gulp it down. When I had drunk half of it I paused to catch my breath and he asked, "So, what have you to tell me, eh?"

I banged down the tankard, wiped my mouth and started from the top of an enormous list, the first and most pertinent being, "What in God's name are you doing here?"

"Ah yes. Bit of a surprise I expect. I overheard Massenhausen and Long divulging your destination so I came here and got this spot so I could come to your aid when required - as it were." He nodded over to the boats lining the river bank and, low and behold, moored right beside the inn, lay a large black barge named Lucius. He smiled, "Though, as I saw, you had the forthrightness to extricate yourself so I did not have to leave the drinks." He nodded at the sailors next to us and winked, "I bet this place is full of crooks."

I glared at him. What was he talking about? My mind worked like a spinning jenny trying to unravel his tangled tale.

"How... did you overhear Massenhausen and Long?"

"I was there, at Sandersdorf castle. Well, in the stables."

"Why? Why were you there, at Sandersdorf Castle in the stables?"

"Because I knew you were there."

"How? How did you know I was there?"

"I had Willy follow you. I told him that if you went to a tavern and got into a fight he should leave you alone but if you went to Sandersdorf he should tell me. I'd a hunch you'd go there."

I swigged some more beer in the vain hope that it would help me understand but it did not work at all and I demanded, "Why? Why did you have a hunch that I would go there?"

"Call it intuition if you will. You were upset."

I had suffered enough of his obfuscation already and I had only been there a minute. I had also known him long enough to know when he was keeping something from me. Finally, with everything piling up inside me like a logjam blocking a flooding river there was too much pressure and, in the end, the damn burst.

"Damn it, Man! Bassus is one of them. He's 'H'! *He*'s Hannibal! He knew who I was right from the start. Poschavio's the centre of it all. He lied to me, betrayed me, tricked me. They made me do things I did not want to. They filled my head with numbers; fives and sixes and elevens: elevens, elevens, elevens. He lured me there, to Sandersdorf to try to initiate me into their ghastly *religion*, into the Order, into the damnable Illuminati for Christ's sake, then he, Bassus, he tried to kill me! They all tried to kill me!"

He shook his head and laughed unsympathetically, "Yes. I thought he would do that."

I glared at him chortling to himself and could not help but howl, "What the hell do you mean, 'You thought he would do that'?"

He took another swig then told me straight, "Because he once tried to do it to me."

It had been a long hard day's night already. I was too angry to understand all the ramifications of what he said at once without losing my temper and I punched him in the face.

"Ow!" he moaned, rubbing his beard and wincing, "You've a good punch, my friend."

I glared at him as the pieces of the puzzle began to fit together.

"So... you sent me to Poschiavo knowing Bassus was Hannibal? And that it was the hideaway for the escaping Illuminati agents?"

He thought about it for a moment and shrugged, "Well, yes."

That was enough. I went to hit him again but the wily old bird caught my fist in his powerful grip and said, "Once is enough, Sebastian. I get the message. You're angry. Remember, you have a good punch and I have but an old face."

He smiled and gently let my hand go. I snatched it back and demanded, "But why?"

"I knew Bassus would ensure no harm came to you..."

I howled again but he held up his hand and continued his defence, "In *Poschiavo*."

I gave him the chance to explain and fidgeted with my tankard.

"Anyway," he surveyed me with an all-seeing eye, "You enjoyed yourself did you not?"

I rolled my eyes in consternation but when I thought about it I was not so sure and conceded, "Well..."

"Let me see. I wager you appreciated your fine lodgings and, of course, the library. Your work was congenial. You read a lot, soaked up the local culture, relaxed, heard some music, sampled the fashions, met some interesting people. Eh? Yes? Considered your dissertation and learned a lot about yourself? Am I right?"

Damn him and his insight. It was all true. I could not even argue with the clever sod as he finished, "Well, wasn't all bad then was it? More like an extended vacation," he winked and said inscrutably, "Culture is a powerful thing eh, my friend?"

He watched my expression as if he actually *was* reading me like a book. Curse his damnable intuition. But he was not even done yet and quipped, "Music is so seductive is it not?"

I shook my head in stupefaction. It was as though he had been watching my every move from behind the blasted harpsichord or the top of my damnable wardrobe. I hoped to God he had not and recalled my bedtime reading.

"I thought so," he laughed, scaring me out of my remaining wits and I wriggled on the bench trying to avoid his searching eyes. He continued in a more serious vain, "Because you had to know, Sebastian. You had to know how easy it is to fall into their clutches. You had to see others succumb to their will in front of your face. You had to know *yourself* - in the flesh. Of course, I had my suspicions about Poschiavo, and the printing press, and the people who were coming and going but much more importantly, I had to know about *you*. And now I truly believe I do." He took a drink then wiped the froth from his beard. "I've known Bassus since we were at university together. He's always been a, well you know him; a lying, conniving, eccentric, over-privileged, murderous, sex mad, Luciferian, maniac. A very charming one at that, but a maniac all the same. He tried to get me to do all that 'Lucifer is God' bit too. Of course, I ran away like you. Though, perhaps I got a little further," he smiled, "That was a long time ago though, when we were only students and we never spoke again."

It seemed that, once again, I had been an unwitting pawn in his game of chess and, everyone else's for that matter. Nevertheless, things were slowly becoming clearer and I recalled the beginning of my adventure.

"So, it was Danzer who tore out the missing page because his name was on it."

"Well done, Sebastian. Hence his determination to retrieve the book and his subsequent relief in succeeding."

"He must have removed it the moment he got his hands on it at the brothel?"

"Probably, his inclusion in the list would also explain why he's so well informed about their plans eh? Because he's been there, listening to them." His eyes narrowed and he asked, "How is he?"

"Not good. Not good at all," I shook my head and gulped, "They have crucified him... upside down. He wasn't dead. Not a few hours ago anyway. They... they seem to be able to make him do anything they want. As though he were..."

"Mesmerised," he anticipated, "Well he is. In more ways than one. He's under their spell. His copious drinking and wenching don't help." He sighed deeply, "He knew he was playing with fire by playing one side against another. Let us hope for his safe deliverance."

Recalling my own pride and foolishness it struck me how much I had in common with Danzer and how, if things had been only a little different, it would have been me back there on that cross instead of him. I suffered a very resounding and deep pang of humility and hung my head, woefully lamenting, "I failed you, Professor."

"How so, my friend?" he enquired.

"How could I have failed you more, sir? I tried to join the Illuminati for Heaven's sake."

"I'm afraid that you may have failed the initiation," he joked.

"There was a woman, Professor." I said, after a pregnant pause.

"There frequently is." He raised an eyebrow, "And?"

"And nothing, sir," I shook my head and sighed, "I guess that in the end, I did not know myself."

"And now?"

I recalled Bassus' many elephant pictures and his beautiful handwriting along with my other countless mistakes and absurd naivety and hung my head with a depressed sigh, "And now...

I do."

"Sebastian Drechsler," he said, putting his hand on my shoulder and leaning in close, "You seem to be under the impression that you have failed at something. On the contrary, my boy, you have won. You have won both the battle over yourself and those creatures back there. As far as I can see you were a young man put under incredible pressure, placed in an impossible position who still did not crack. I'd give you a blasted medal if I had one," he beamed and slapped my back, "But you'll have to make do with a drink instead."

I faced him.

"They're all back there you know? Massenhausen, Bassus. The Marquis de Constanza and Bode - they are definitely there."

"I know," he said casually and took another swig.

I was confounded to hear this but carried on, "For pity's sake, even Thomas blasted Jefferson is there."

"I know," he noted in between gulps," I saw his carriage."

I raised my own eyebrow and told him, "And Frank. Jacob Frank, he is there."

He slowly wiped the froth from his nose and sniffed, "I didn't know that."

"Then why aren't you there?" I blurted as he finished his drink.

He banged his tankard on the table, picked up his flintlock, stood up and looked down his beaky nose at me. "Sebastian, our organisation has but two field operatives. Me and you. Forgive me if I'm wrong, but I thought it expedient to come here first and make sure you didn't end up on a ship bound for the Americas trapped inside a statue."

He had a point and I nodded respectfully.

"This is what we've been waiting for, Sebastian. This is our chance to get them all together. This could be the end for them."

He was deadly serious but I quickly ran through the long list of injuries I had been subjected to during the last few hectic hours and hazarded, "Are we prepared for such a mission, sir?".

He furrowed his brow before unclasping his cloak and opening it out. Strapped about his body was, what I estimated to be, every weapon from his secret armoury, except for perhaps his small canon, including; a pair of crossed bandoliers, at least three flintlock pistols, two large bombs, one cutlass, a sabre, numerous knives and even an axe, all polished and glinting in the faint light. I made sure none of the regulars had seen him as he assured me, "There's more on my horse."

He refastened his cloak and figured, "Half of them will be in bed, the other half will be running around in their underwear. I have already alerted Ingolstadt's sheriff who is meeting us there with reinforcements. This is it. We have them all in one place."

I baulked at the thought of returning to the castle, even with the Professor, copious weapons and the authorities by my side.

"Ah ha," he noted, looking up into the night sky, "I see our friends are out again."

He was right. The winter triangle was still shining in the heavens.

"I think I've had enough of triangles and triumvirates, Professor."

"There is one with which you are perhaps unfamiliar. You know the Greeks used the horseman as a depiction of the soul? The rider is logos, or logic, the horse, pathos, or spirit but importantly the bridle is ethos or ethics. Do you see?" His eyes twinkled like the stars above and he finished, "It's not what you have, it's what you do with it that counts."

He was right as usual. At that particular moment it was as stirring a speech as I could have imagined and I felt a profound wave of conscience crash over me. But he was not done yet.

"Speaking of horses," he said, looking toward the rear of the inn and asking, "How goes it?" He put his fingers in his mouth and effortlessly impersonated my special whistle to Petrova which had taken me years to perfect. Along with the Professor's own horse, the perfect sight for my sore eyes appeared from round the side of the inn and swayed up to the table neighing to ask where I had been. Goodness gracious me. It was Petrova. Here. Saddled up and ready to go.

"You see?" he said, collecting the reins of his own steed, "Education is a two way thing, like any good conversation."

How he managed to achieve this miracle I did not know but I was simply overjoyed and sprang up to hug my beauty.

"Yes. I found her at the stables in Sandersdorf while I was sniffing around. Bassus may be a bastard but he knows how to look after a horse. Though, it would appear, not how to stop one from being stolen."

I petted her for all she was worth. Likewise she was as happy to see me, making me all the more aware of how much I missed her.

Van Halestrom watched our tender reunion and said at this most poignant moment, "I can't begin to say how sad I feel about your child. I'm afraid, these things happen far too often. It must seem that it's only happened to you but it's unfortunately the lot of the many. Though I can happily report Francesca is recovering well and missing you too."

Another piece of my own puzzle fell into place upon hearing his kind words and I felt something in my soul removed by the catharsis.

"On the subject of elevens," he carried on in his own indubitable way, "An interesting example of the mystic relationship between the symbolic five and six is that it is said when you have come of age or mastered yourself, your five senses transcend their individual aspects and combine to make a sixth: intuition."

His horse whinnied but he steadied the animal with its bridle as the idea filtered into my subconscious where it settled, fermenting for a second until it suddenly exploded into a fire that blazed in my mind and consumed my very being. The bear traps, the tiny bloodstained shoe next to the tree, the cages, my young servants not returning, the night hunts...

"The children!" I bawled, "They have the children there. We must save them!"

Chapter 27

Call to Arms

"Well done, lad. That's the spirit!" gasped the Professor and mounted his own horse, "You'll find a new quadre bow in its holster where your old one used to be. I like to be prepared for all eventualities."

"What about Long?" I yelled, remembering my abductor as I pulled myself up onto Petrova.

"We have bigger fish to fry!" he called. "The sheriff and his men will be at Sandersdorf by dawn!"

I looked to the lightning eastern sky and told him, "I want to get there first!" I reared Petrova up, startling many people about the inn and we quickly galloped off.

I may have been battered black and blue, covered in filth, desperately in need of some new clothes and smelling like a French toilet but I was raring for action and as ready for a fight with those son-of-a-bitch Illuminati fiends as I ever had been.

We thundered through the dark countryside and, riding our horses out of their skins, completed the ten miles or so back to Sandersdorf in well less than an hour. As the Professor had predicted, when we approached the castle through the deserted streets in the early morning light, we came across Ingolstadt's sheriff waiting with a dozen armed men and two covered prison wagons outside the gatehouse. Beyond the gates I could see scores of carriages still filling the courtyard and only a couple of guards talking to the drivers.

"We have them, Professor! There're many still here!"

We rode up to the sheriff and the Professor called out, "You'll need more wagons and more men!"

"They're on the way, Herr Professor!" cried the reliable man.

"Good! Have you tried to gain entry?" asked Van Halestrom.

"The gatekeeper isn't happy, Herr Professor. He claims there are many important diplomats here and says he doesn't want us to cause a scene."

"Cause a scene?" I spat, "Has anyone left since your arrival?"

"One carriage, sir. A foreign diplomat with a strange accent bound for Paris accompanied by a young pregnant coloured girl."

"Thunder and lightning, Professor! It must've been Jefferson!"

I dismounted as the cocky gatekeeper appeared at the gatehouse doorway. He slapped his long stick into his palm and warned us, "I've already told the sheriff, I've got a list of names here and you're not on it. You're not coming in."

We were in a hurry and I had no time for this fool. I strode over to him as he arrogantly swaggered around with his stick and head butted the mouthy idiot to the floor where he stayed writhing in deserved misery.

"Come on!" I roared and jumped back up on Petrova as the sheriff's men stormed the gatehouse.

"Good man!" cried Van Halestrom and galloped after me through the opening gate. Another guard foolishly attempted to block our way as we rode past and I booted him in the face. I thundered into the courtyard and jumped down from the saddle as Van Halestrom and the sheriff's men flooded in behind me. A few drivers and footmen stood around not knowing what to do while a handful of them scattered, but one clever little bastard of a groom flew in through the main door and slammed it shut. I grabbed my bow and ran up to the door yanking at the handle and shouting, "It's locked!"

The Professor was by my side in a flash and produced a long wooden spike and a hammer from under his cloak. "Sometimes this works, sometimes it doesn't!" he declared.

The sheriff's men crowded round while he whacked the spike into the large keyhole, flipped over the hammer which had a toothed-loop on the end of the handle, slotted it over the spike then cranked the hammer clockwise once, 'Click.' As if by magic, the door swung open.

"Ta-da!" he exclaimed and ran inside unstrapping his bow from his shoulder. The rest of us charged in behind and spread out into the central hallway as the sounds of pandemonium echoed throughout the house. I could hear the groom raising the alarm somewhere down the central corridor and shouting voices coming from everywhere. A servant appeared from a door at the bottom of the sweeping staircases and dropped a tray of crockery then put his hands over his face.

"Forget the servants! We want the Council big wigs!" ordered Van Halestrom as a couple of faces in nightshirts peeked round the top of the stairs but disappeared before I could get a shot off.

"Up there, Professor!" I pointed the bow to show him.

He bounded up the stairs with one of the sheriff's men and cried, "I'll go upstairs! You take two of the men downstairs!"

I gestured at a couple of the men to follow me and we sprinted down the central corridor. I knew who I wanted: Bassus. I was not scared of him. And with my loaded bow and my rage on the boil, I felt like I could cut the head off the Medusa while staring her right in the eyes. I swung my bow at a maid screaming in a doorway as we ran past and kept my eyes peeled for real targets. They sprang wide open when I saw Massenhausen at the bottom of the corridor dragging two terrified blonde children up to a door.

"Come on!" I bellowed and sprinted like my very life depended on it. He saw the three of us bearing down on him and hastily unlocked the door then slipped behind it with his captives. I slid up to the door and grabbed the handle the very second the key turned in the lock. Damn it! There was nothing else for it. I pulled my shoulder back and smashed it into the door and almost broke my arm in the process. I cradled my shoulder in pain and cursed at the top of my voice but when I heard the sound of snivelling coming from an open door on the other side of the corridor I burst into the room.

The last twenty four hours had been beset by harrowing visions, some of which still haunt me today, and that one especially. I clenched my teeth and shook my head in horror to find six dirty-faced children imprisoned in two cages. There were three of the poor wretches in each and, as I looked amongst their bewildered expressions, I spotted one of my young helpers from Poschiavo who recognised me and pulled himself to the bars.

"You're safe now. I'll be back," I told them and after one more horrified stare, I left the room. I ordered one of the sheriff's men to stay there with them until I returned. My haste reached a new more frantic level. I knew there must be another way downstairs so I ran off deeper into the castle taking the remaining man with me and, around the next corner, I recognised where I was. After a few twists and turns, I found the room where I had last seen Danzer. Thankfully, he was no longer there and we carried on into a wine cellar at the end of which stood a door flanked by burning torches. I ran over to try the handle and was surprised when the door creaked open onto a stone staircase which descended into darkness. I grabbed one of the torches and entrusted it to my companion, instructing him, "Stay close behind so I can see what I'm aiming at. Understood?"

He nodded apprehensively and I led him down the steps with my bow at the ready. We reached the bottom and walked out onto a dirt floor as the glowing torchlight eerily lit up a low cavernous chamber hollowed out of the rock. As we advanced around a corner, worryingly losing sight of the door, I began to make out several large oblong stone blocks scattered round the floor. I took a few more steps and squinted into the darkness then realised, they were coffins. Lots and lots and lots of coffins. It was a crypt. Well it blasted-well would be if I was snooping around in it. I peered up at the ghostly stalactites as a drop of water plopped somewhere in the gloom. Where else would you expect to find Sebastian Drechsler on a Sunday morning?

I jumped upon hearing a noise up ahead and trained the bow in the same direction. Then, gesturing at the sheriff's man to stay close, I inched forward. The air was cold enough to see my breath condense in the torchlight but I strained to see anything else amongst the distorted shadows. I took another step and, hearing something move right next to me, swung the bow into the terrified faces of the pair of children. They squealed sharply and stood there shaking and hugging each other for all they were worth. I crouched down and, trying to conceal the frightening weapon, whispered, "It's all right. You're safe now." I glanced around and asked, "Which way did the nasty man go?"

Their eyes stared in terror over my shoulder and I turned to see a large open casket not a dozen feet away. They both nodded rapidly at it while keeping the same petrified expressions.

I nodded to the sheriff's man to advance but when we did the children came with us. "Stay with them," I whispered as I could see the coffin well enough. I put the bow to my chin and stalked over, all the time training the weapon on the casket and half expecting the son of a bitch to jump out of the thing at any moment. I got as close as I needed, took a deep breath and thrust the bow into - an empty coffin. Blasted children. Scared out of their wits mind. It was understandable. At that moment the sheriff's man dropped the torch throwing the cavern into darkness.

"Clumsy idiot," I muttered and sprang back over to him then almost threw up when I found him violently shaking on the floor with his throat slit next to the spluttering torch. The terrified look on the children's faces told the story. I grabbed the torch but had to support the bow with one hand which rendered me practically useless in a fight.

"Come here!" I hissed. They needed no encouragement and clung to my legs like barnacles making any movement all but impossible. I shook them off and began retracing my steps round the corner to the door.

"Everything will be all right," I assured them as we shuffled along. But my heart sank like a stone thrown down a well when I heard the door close with a bang and the key twist in the lock.

"Open the door for Christ's sake!" I hollered but there was no reply only the sound of my lonely voice echoing in the darkness and the children clung back to my legs even tighter. Curses! What was I going to do? I would have to go back through the crypt and find another way out. "Follow me," I whispered and, after wriggling free once more, wound my way between the caskets desperately shining the torch into the shadows to search for another exit. We had barely taken ten paces when there was a sudden gasp from behind and I whipped my head round to find only one terrified child shaking in the torchlight.

"Damn it! I told you to stay close," I spat and nervously glanced around as the girl ran over to me with her huge eyes darting all over the place. Making things even worse the weight of the bow was becoming unbearable and I knew that I was going to have to change hands with the torch. So, after checking around again, I quickly rested the torch against a casket and exchanged the bow to my left hand. But as I lifted the torch Massenhausen horribly rose up in the coffin next to me, clutching the whimpering boy to his chest and holding a knife to his throat.

"Fancy your chances now, fool?" he gloated with pure demonic evil shining in his eyes, "I didn't think so. One move and I'll slit his throat like your friend's over there. Now drop the bow."

He had me and he knew it. I slowly knelt down and placed the bow on the ground but brought the other child close to my side.

"Oh no you don't," he grinned, "I want that one too," and glared at the terrified girl. She squeezed my arm so hard that it hurt but there was nothing that I could do. Though it broke my heart, I pulled her off and held her out before me and told her, "Everything will be fine. Trust me."

I could tell she knew that I was lying and she gripped my arm and shook her head.

"Over here!" demanded Massenhausen as the boy under his arm squealed with fear. I had to fight the urge to cry as I wrenched her little hands off my arm and pushed her towards him. She started sobbing and wringing her hands but slowly inching closer and I could only watch as the poor child helplessly wandered into the evil bastard's clutches.

Chapter 28

The Jaws of Death

"That's right, sweetie, come to Daddy," grinned Massenhausen. I could hardly bear to watch as the little girl helplessly tottered towards him and he sat upright in the coffin, clutching the other petrified child to his chest. Then, amongst the flickering torchlight, I saw a dark shape edging up behind his casket like a jaguar stalking its prey in the jungle. Yes! My heart leapt into my mouth when I realised it was the Professor. It must have been him who had closed the door and locked it to stop our quarry from escaping.

I tried to disguise my shock and waved the torch about to keep Massenhausen's attention. The girl stopped to look back at me and Massenhausen cursed as he had to momentarily take the blade from the boy's throat to lift himself from the coffin. This was my chance. I pounced over to him and plunged the torch into his face, forcing him to fall backwards and drop the knife. He screamed in agony and tried in vain to grab the flaming torch as the boy scrabbled away to the other end of the casket.

"Die, pig dog!" I roared, swivelling it in his face as the Professor jumped up behind him, putting an arm round his neck and half throttling him to death. Massenhausen choked curses and kicked his feet but could not escape the violent onslaught.

"Here! Use these," gasped the Professor and, keeping up the pressure, threw the hammer and the spike into the side of the casket with his free hand. I threw down the torch, exposing Massenhausen's horrifically scarred, smoking face then picked up the spike and placed the tip over his heart. He was not so injured that he did not know what was happening and desperately tried to grab it but Van Halestrom squeezed his neck like a vice.

His eyes bulged from their sockets as I raised the hammer then brought it down with an almighty whack.

A fountain of blood erupted from his mouth and his eyes rolled like a slaughtered animal as a large red stain spread across his heaving jacket. I thumped the spike again and, this time, felt it go right through his body which made him frantically spasm and leap about in a rampaging fit. Such were his convulsions that the Professor let him go and he died right in front of us, shaking and spitting blood and gurgling his death rattle and do not let anyone tell you different. I care not what the history books say. I saw Count Massenhausen die that day, there, in that dark place and that is that. I gazed in awe as he came to a juddering, squirming slump but there was no time for further reflection or even celebration, for the Professor instantly thrust the torch back into my hand and picked up my bow.

"Where's yours?" I said, lifting the horrified boy to the ground.

"Hidden upstairs. I used all my ammunition. There's a pitched battle going on there now. Bring the children. I'll lead the way!"

He ran off between the coffins and I shepherded the waifs along in front of me. We caught him up when he stopped to look around but before I could ask where we were going he exclaimed, "Over there!" and ran off with us chasing behind. He must have had the eyes of a bat because we came up to a door that I could hardly see from six feet away. He flung it open and ran to the top of a flight of steps where we found him holding the handle of a door, from behind which was coming the muffled crack of musket fire and the shouts of many men. He asked, "Ready?" so I herded the children around my legs, nodded to him that I understood and he yanked open the door.

He was right as ever. There was a full scale battle raging. The sheriff's men had taken cover behind a long upturned table at the base of the sweeping staircase and a handful of Council members were firing muskets from the balcony and throwing down anything else they could get their hands on. The action was taking place about thirty feet from our door, so we filed out up the corridor in the opposite direction where a group of shocked servants, cooks, gardeners, grooms and drivers were all watching from the safety of some large alcoves. I sought out the most trustworthy looking woman amongst them and thrust the children at her, saying, "My name is Sebastian Drechsler. Bring them to me when this is finished. If anything happens to them while I'm gone I will find you. Remember; Sebastian Drechsler: The Woodturner."

She sneered at me but when I was sure that she had remembered my face I ran off to join the fray. I found the Professor by the corner of the corridor a dozen yards from the sheriff's men who were all cowering behind the battered table. One of them sprang up and shot his musket at the balcony but had to duck down when a substantial volley was returned.

The Professor passed me the double barrelled flintlock pistol. "They can't reload fast enough to make a decisive charge. Where's the quiver?" I took it off and gave it him as a mighty blunderbuss rang out and blew a massive hole in the table, sending a cloud of splinters into the air and scaring the wits out of the men behind. "We don't have long," said Van Halestrom, calmly but swiftly reloading and winding the four bows tight. He was ready in a flash and delivered the plan, "I'll give you covering fire then follow you up the stairs. Ready?"

"Ready," I replied and crouched down at the corner. We waited for a pause in the firing and, as a marble statuette smashed into a million pieces on the floor right in front of us, he yelled, "Go!"

He stepped out a head of me, found a target and fired. I ran past him to the bottom of the stairs as one of the Brothers fell screaming from the balcony and thumped head first into the floor with a sickening crunch. Van Halstrom fired again and hit another who toppled backwards, clutching his face and hideously screeching. The Brothers were hiding behind the wooden balustrade and, when I had crept halfway up the stairs, one of them stuck his head round the corner aiming the blunderbuss at me. But I beat him to it and, using my first barrel, blew his chin clean off along with half the corner post.

'Zut!' Van Halestrom cleverly shot the next between the banisters who had wrongly thought that he was safe and he flailed sideways roaring in pain with blood spraying from his groin. The remaining two did not like the odds and tore off up the adjoining short staircase to the next landing. But they were not fast enough. 'Bang!' I got the last one square between his shoulders with my second barrel. He threw his hands up then went down like a felled tree as the other dived through a doorway. Then, through the gunsmoke I spotted Bassus peek round a corner of the landing before pulling his face back.

"You!" I muttered and spied the Professor on the stairs below me reloading his bow as the sheriff's men streamed past him. Reinforcements always make you feel more heroic and I was already seeing the red mist. I threw down my empty pistol and snatched a sabre from the hand of a dead Brother then bounded up the short stairway to the next landing where I had seen Bassus. I tore round the corner and down the next passage, running past what seemed like a hundred doors but somehow knew that the bastard had kept going. My gamble paid off and when I came through an archway into a circular rotunda with several exits, I found him holding Tatyana by her elbow obviously having some kind of spat.

"Ah. Hello, Sebastian. Nice to see you," he said as if meeting me in his library. He eyed my sabre, let go of Tatyana and brandished his own.

"I wish I could say the same, *sir*," I retorted and adopted my en garde pose. Not forgetting my manners altogether I politely bowed to Tatyana, "Hello, Tatyana."

"Hello, Librarian," she anxiously curtseyed.

"My name is Sebastian, My Lady," I said, swishing my weapon and limbering up.

"You know what, my friend? quipped Bassus, "I think I preferred you when you were a little more unrefined. I like you less now you insist on being so noble. It doesn't suit you at all."

As he finished one of the sheriff's men ran into the archway behind me and looked between us trying to work out what was going on.

"Oh for Christ's sake!" griped Bassus, "Can't I get any privacy in my own home." He pulled a flintlock pistol from inside his jacket and casually blew a hole straight through the young man's forehead, decorating the wall of the rotunda in a gruesome splatter of blood and brains.

Thunder and lightning! Charming but deadly. He dropped the smoking gun as if it were a snotty hankerchief and winced, "Guns are so vulgar. Don't you think?"

He composed himself and advanced in classic duelling style; fist poised on hip, sabre up straight. I launched forward and engaged him with three sweeping cuts which he parried with ease.

"I'm not scared of you!" I grunted.

"I can see," he noted with a conceited grin then came at me with a flurry of blows that beat me back against the wall. I barely managed to parry the last and struggled to hold his blade inches from my neck as he leaned in close and whispered, "Perhaps you should be."

He was stronger than I thought but I was a dirty little bastard who had learnt to fight in a muddy village playground not a privileged fencing school and I spat in his face. He did not appreciate that at all and pulled back, furiously wiping himself then we started to fight properly.

He was good but Van Halestrom had taught me well. Though he was able to use his strength and superior weight to push me back, I spun and turned and parried faster than he could lash out and, after another titanic clash of blows, he retreated to catch his breath.

"Very good, Herr Drechsler," he panted. "You obviously have a good teacher. I think I recognise the style. A certain Professor of Ingolstadt I think?"

"You don't know him like I do," I uttured, cold as ice and leapt at him clashing my blade against his.

"I thought I recognised that watch," he grunted and came back at me with five swipes aimed at my head then a dirty low one hunting for my ankles. I jumped but only cleared the blade by a whisker, causing Tatyana to gasp with her hand over her mouth.

Confusingly, I could not tell whose side she was on and she stayed crouched in no man's land. I dodged another swipe but Bassus saw me momentarily catch her eye and, seizing his chance, cleverly flicked the sabre from my hand to send it clattering across the floor towards her.

"Oh dear, Herr Drechsler. That *is* a pity. Seems you've lost - Again." His eyes gleamed in triumph as he slowly approached to administer the coup de grâce but to my surprise Tatyana slid the weapon back to me.

Bassus glared at her and, in his measured tone, observed, "That was stupid, darling. I really wish you wouldn't do things like that."

"I was only trying to make things fair, my sweet," she smiled unconvincingly, "You always said you liked a good fair fight."

He frowned as I picked up the sword and prepared to take him on. He chimed his blade into mine but I pushed him off and delivered a bevy of powerful blows to force him back. We circled each other, panting and wiping the sweat from our brows as the shouts and clashes of heavy fighting came ever nearer. Suddenly, a group of sword-swinging men burst into the rotunda and Bassus and I were forced apart amidst a melee of flashing blades and wrestling bodies. I bobbed and weaved this way and that, but two of the sheriff's men fiercely engaged him so I looked around for Tatyana and saw her heels disappear into one of the archways.

I dodged another sweeping sword and raced after her but immediately came up to a pair of arches and had no idea which way she had gone. While I haplessly looked between them I spied the young servant huddled against the wall who had been bringing me my beers earlier. I thought he was going to run away or tell me to get lost but instead he helpfully gestured left with his eyes. "Thanks," I gasped and taking his advice, ran through the arch and up some stairs then quickly realised that I was heading straight towards my old room. Would she? I wondered as I rounded the corner and sprang up the short stairwell to my door and burst inside.

She was gazing into the sunrise from the open window and I took a step towards her but she turned round and scowled at my sabre. "Could you please put that down now. _I_ am hardly a threat."

She smiled and held me with her bewitching eyes. I went to argue but she swept over and placed a finger on my lips, softly scolding, "Do you know how much trouble you have got me into?"

"I..."

She pressed harder and gently pushed me backwards.

"Not many men refuse me, Sebastian. I wonder, what makes you so different? Tell me, because..." I felt the back of my knees bump into the iron chair. "I think I like it," she said and brushed her rosy lips across mine. I smelt her sweet perfume as she pressed her body into mine and gently pushed me down into the seat. My sabre clanged to the floor as she straddled me exactly as I had fantasised and I closed my eyes and went to push my lips into hers. But instead I heard the clamp close on my left hand and opened them just in time to see her shut the other one over my right. Damn it!

She dusted her hands and stood up smiling, "That's better. You made me nervous running around with that nasty thing."

Thunder and lightning! How the Hell did that happen? I had come here with enough weaponry to destroy the castle but thirty seconds in this vixen's company and I was helplessly clamped to a chair like an idiot.

"Why did you do it, Sebastian?" she sighed, "Everything could have been so different."

"Because, My Lady, there's a difference between right and wrong." I struggled in the chair and for an end to my sentence, "... And... I don't want to live a life that's wrong."

"Good Lord, Librarian. You think too much." Her forehead furrowed as footsteps came running up the stairs and she warned, "Let's hope you don't get what you want."

"You..."

"Be quiet, Librarian and remember, let me do the talking."

Before I could say anything Bassus flung open the door and came in glancing between us then closed it behind him. He was injured, sweating and, with his sabre covered in blood, finally looking a little ruffled but kept his cool and jauntily observed, "I would tell you two love birds to get a room but it seems you already have."

"I've managed to find our friend somewhere safe to sit down so he can't hurt anyone."

I fought against the clamps as he tossed his sabre on the bed and noted, "Well done, darling. Unfortunately, I feel..." He was interrupted by a large explosion that made the walls shudder and which was immediately followed by a powerful volley of gunfire. After the various aftershocks had faded he sighed, "... The game is up."

She stepped up to him and straightened his cravat, reassuring, "But with your connections and, of course, your seamless charm, I'm sure you'll be able to negotiate your way out of any unpleasantness."

"Yes, my sweet. It's true. But regretfully, I feel that, this time, I cannot save everyone. So, rather like a big, fat cat jumping from a sinking ship, I have to show a rather, how should I put it, unchivalrous attitude toward my companions?" He raised his eyebrows surprisingly high and pushed her backwards towards the open window.

"Careful, darling, that could be dangerous," she said, glancing over her shoulder and appearing to lose her cool.

"Sorry, my sweet," he said, putting his arm round her back and hanging her over the ledge, "But as you know, all the greatest loves: Mark Antony - Cleopatra; Orpheus - Eurydice, even Romeo and Juliet, never ended well."

"You wouldn't," she gasped.

"I'm afraid I would, my dear."

"Please, Father, no!"

She begged and while I gawped in shock he sighed nonchalantly, "Goodbye, my darling," and let her go.

"No!" I roared with hopeless anguish.

He watched her fall and adjusted his cravat then pulled a disgusted expression when, presumably, she hit the ground.

"Right then, Herr Drechsler," he said, turning to face me, "Where were we? Oh yes." He produced a key from his waistcoat. "Silly me. Too much to remember as usual." He stepped over to the door and locked it then slipped the key back into his pocket and stood in front of the handle regarding me with a forlorn expression.

"There will be a special place for you in Hell, Bassus!" I raged.

"Funnily enough, I had been planning something along those lines already. As a good friend of mine once said: better to reign in Hell than to be a slave in Heaven." Pleased with his poetic remark he put his fist to his hip and struck a pose and, as was his habit, naturally looked around for his fancy cane.

My eyes fell upon my old walking stick, leaning exactly where I had left it, propped against the cabinet not two feet from his hand. 'Pick it up you smug bastard! Pick it up!' I shouted inside but the arrogant prick failed to see it. I stared at it as hard as I dared without creating too much suspicion, hoping beyond hope that he would see me. My heart leapt when he finally noticed my eyes and spotted the stick. He picked it up, even smiling, "Oh. Thank you, kind sir. A true gentleman till the bitter end."

'Yes!' Now bang it on the floor you over-privileged pervert' I secretly raged but there was another thunderous explosion from downstairs, making him lose his thread.

"You know, Herr Drechsler, I have every reason to be cross with you." He pointed the stick's brass tip in my face and I was sure that I heard the handle click as he carried on, "You realise you ruined a perfectly good opportunity to become somebody?"

I don't want to be *somebody,* you stuck up ponce. I want to be Sebastian Drechsler!"

He shook his head and sighed with a father-like obstinance,

"This childish defiance really will not do. Sadly, as I don't have the time for you to grow up sufficiently to realise the foolishness of your ways, I feel it only right to teach you a lesson right now." With this he produced a switchblade and flicked it open then stood inspecting its razor-sharp edge and absentmindedly tapping the stick on the floor.

'Go off! Go off!' I screamed inside. 'What was wrong with the blasted thing?'

"It seems such a waste of a handsome face," he smiled and then, for once, became very serious indeed and finished, "And, seeing as you are so well secured, we might as well do something about that impudent tongue of yours while we're at it."

Chapter 29

All is Fair in Love and War

The Count grinned menacingly and took a step towards me brandishing his switchblade. 'This is it, Seb! Prepare to die!' I said to myself and shrank back in the chair as someone turned a key in the lock and banged the door into his backside knocking him forward. He instinctively caught his weight on the walking stick and, pleased with his fast reactions, arrogantly flicked his eyebrows and smirked, "Abra...!"

Kaboom!'

The stick exploded, tearing off half his jacket and hurling him backwards against the cabinet in a shower of smoke and sparks.

"Take that you bastard!" I roared as the shocked servant poked his head round the door and I implored him, "Come here now! Free me!"

He ran over and quickly released the clasps. I pulled myself up and stood over Bassus as he lay on the floor moaning and nursing his smouldering wounds. I furiously dragged him over to the window ledge to throw him out. But I could not do it. Even after what he had done. If I was going to kill him, I wanted to kill him in a fair fight. Not like this. Though I was no angel either, so I crouched over the bastard and punched him in the face.

"That's for putting me in that statue!" I bellowed and hit him again. "That's for throwing her out of the window!" then again, "That's for lying to me and making me look like an idiot in front of your perverted friends!! You lying piece of shit!" Again and again I punched until I was grabbing his cravat and pulling his head up and knocking the living daylights out of him.

"Stop! Please! I beg you! I have seen too much!"

It was the young servant boy squatting by the door. He was sobbing and bleary eyed and I looked at Bassus' pummelled face and his burnt bloodstained jacket and I threw him down.

I stood up rubbing my fist but was drawn to the window by the urgent clatter of wagon wheels. I peered into the streets to see Gretchen lashing a tiny covered wagon out from the base of the castle. I watched the evil bitch bumping down the lane for a second with my mind a quiver before I twigged. Of course! It was the wagon that I had seen Massenhausen with by the bridge near Poschiavo when I found his men checking... the traps.

"Damn it!" I quickly found Bassus' key in his waistcoat pocket, made sure he had no more weapons, leapt up, pushed the servant outside and locked the door. I ran downstairs and, fortunately, straight into the sheriff coming up the other way with two of his men.

"The master of the house, the ringleader, is upstairs," I panted, "Here's the key to the room. Arrest him and get him a doctor but whatever you do, do not get into a conversation with him."

He nodded and took the key and I pelted downstairs to the front hallway. Unable to see Van Halestrom amongst the crowds of shocked servants surveying the wreckage or battle-worn officers hauling away arrested Illuminati members, I ran to the room where I had left the sheriff's man guarding the children. Upon entering I bellowed with fury when I found the young man lying face down in a puddle of blood beside the two empty cages. I crouched down and put my hand to his neck but could not feel a pulse. "Bitch!" I tore back along the smokey corridor past the bottom of the sweeping stairs and out into the courtyard. Finding Petrova exactly where I had left her, I heroically mounted her in one flying leap. She reared up as I grabbed the reins and we galloped out of the courtyard past a crowd of concerned locals who had gathered to watch the commotion.

228

"Come on, girl!" I urged as we swept through the town's narrow lanes in the same direction as Gretchen and out onto the single road travelling west. Positive that I was on her trail, I tapped my heels into Petrova's flanks and gave her her head. About a mile down the road, when I felt certain that the wagon should be in sight, I had to slide Petrova to a halt at a junction where a sign pointed '*Ingolstadt*' one way and '*Vohburg*' the other. Shit! Which way would she go? Come on, Seb! Come on Seb! Think. Think. I wheeled Petrova about intensely examining the muddy road and there, amongst the hoof prints and puddles, I spotted fresh wheel tracks heading west for Ingolstadt.

I did not need telling twice but Petrova neighed that I was right anyway. I answered, "Yes my beauty! Now we have her!" and we galloped off in a shower of mud. After only a few hundred yards my hands clenched tight round the reins when I spotted the little covered wagon wobbling along up ahead.

"Yah!" I cried and lowered myself over Petrova's neck as we closed in. The canvas was drawn at the back so I could not see her cargo but, with the road broad and flat, I eased Petrova alongside the footboard. The hag spotted me out of the corner of her eye but emotionlessly stared forward and whipped the horse to blazes. I overtook her by two lengths then swung Petrova in front of her horse, trying to force the wagon into a shallow ditch by the side of the road but the large woman wrenched at the reins and stubbornly managed to keep it on track.

I was about to try again when I was suddenly consumed by an enormous shadow and something clawed agonisingly into my shoulder like the Devil's own fingernails. I almost fell from my saddle such was the pain and had to hang onto Petrova for dear life. I flung my hand around and felt some kind of living beast attacking me! What black magic was this? For a split second I thought that it was Baphomet back from Hell to take me with him.

Then I heard a primordial screech and a storm of feathers beating over my head as the golden eagle flew out in front of me. Holy Mother of God! It was Barabbas! The huge beast sailed along ahead of us for a few seconds before soaring high into the sky then ominously turning back and, with one beat of its enormous wings, dived in at full speed with its talons extended, coming in for the kill. Now I was the one being hunted.

Chapter 30

Dominion over the Beasts

The bird had grown since I had last seen him and had become massive. He dived at incredible speed, coming in like a feathered missile with his razor-sharp talons outstretched and ready to strike. I ducked at the very last moment, avoiding its claws by inches but felt the wind off its wings tare at my jacket and ruffle my hair. Good God! It was big. And fast. And angry. The gigantic creature was also spooking Petrova and she neighed in fear and trembled as Gretchen overtook us, still blankly looking forward, but all the time furiously whipping her horse.

I ignored the wagon and scanned the sky to see the bird coming in again and braced myself for the next attack. The eagle shrieked as it dived and spread its wings but this time, remembering my proper place in the true pecking order of things, I punched the stupid squawking beast right on its blasted beak and yelled, "Fuck off!" It was not expecting that and flew off with another beat of its vast wings.

"Let's go, my beauty!" I hollered and we resumed our chase at such devastating speed that we caught the wagon back up within a matter of seconds. The road surface abruptly changed from mud to cobbles and the wagon wheels roared and Petrova's shoes clattered and I asked her for more pace, "Nearly there my girl!" We inexorably inched up to the foot board but as we pulled alongside Gretchen swerved into us, almost forcing us off the road and I had to fight to keep Petrova on her feet.

We flew into some tight bends leading to a steep humpback bridge and Gretchen slid the wagon first one way then the other round the corners but the bend before the bridge was far tighter than the rest. At last, the over laden wagon could take no more and one of the front wheels exploded in a shower of splinters.

The horse stumbled but broke its harness before it fell over and ran off leaving the wagon to crash safely into a large pile of sand used by the stonecutters for the road works.

Gretchen clambered down from the footboard and awkwardly waded away through the sand. I dismounted and strode past the front of the wagon where the stunned children were watching from behind the bars of a cage and wriggled about to see what was happening. I picked up a shovel left standing in the sand and followed in her footsteps. She reached the top of the pile but rolled down the other side and ended up in a heap at the bottom. I slid down after her with the shovel in my hands and came to a stop by her side as she wiped the sand from her mouth and grimaced up at me. She quickly glanced between my rage-filled eyes and the shovel then grovelled with an insincere smile, "You wouldn't hurt a lady... would you?"

That was the second, and last, time that I saw her smile. I checked that the children could not see from the wagon, pulled back the shovel and spat, "No, but you're no lady."

Then using every ounce of my strength, I stuffed the blade through her neck. That wiped the smile off the evil bitch's face and I leant on the handle until I heard her spine snap and her oozing head slid onto the shovel. After working out what she had been up to I had half a mind to hold it up to the children like a triumphant Perseus, but thought better of it. They probably knew something similar had happened anyway. I slowly pushed her head into the sand with the shovel and watched her startled, bloated expression steadily disappear under the falling grains until she was finally gone. She was no more.

I went to bury the corpse but had a better idea. I put my hand across my brow and searched the sky. There, silently circling above us, I spotted Barabbas's dark silhouette against the breaking clouds.

I threw down the shovel then searched her clothes and quickly found a set of keys on her belt, before wading back up the sand pile and sliding down the other side much to the delight of the children who cheered with joy to see me coming instead of her. I jumped onto the footplate and unlocked the cage as they eagerly clung to the bars and beamed like it was Christmas. They were obviously still shaken but a lot, lot happier now they were saved and, one by one, I helped the poor waifs down from the wagon.

Petrova quickly worked out what I had planned and neighed upon seeing me walk up with six children. But she was as strong as she was clever and I had every faith in her. Five minutes later, after a bit of squeezing, we slowly swayed away from the wrecked wagon with three of the little mites in front of me and three behind.

I watched Barabbas patiently circling overhead while the children, who had cheered up no end at their newfound circumstances, happily patted Petrova's shoulders and stroked her mane. This was convenient as I did not want them to see what I hoped would happen next and aided their distractions by singing nursery rhymes very, very badly indeed.

We must have been almost a mile away because Barabbas was practically out of sight when I saw him suddenly drop like a stone. He did not come back up again and I concluded that he was eating his fill. And that there could be no more fitting end to a life, such as that evil woman's, of which I could think. Good riddance.

We soon returned to Sandersdorf where we found the crowd outside the castle had swollen to a bustling, gossiping throng of maybe a hundred souls or more. The stunned townsfolk looked on in amazement as the sheriff's men, and scores of other officials, escorted the last of the bedraggled Illuminati members into the awaiting prison wagons.

The poor castle itself looked as though a bomb had hit it and I considered, with a twisted smirk, that it had. The front door was smashed in, several windows on the ground floor were blown out and a trail of black smoke curled from the upstairs rooms. Everywhere I looked bewildered servants scratched their heads in consternation or picked up their masters' abandoned belongings. Indeed, it looked as though a small war had been fought and I wagered that the Professor must have spent his entire arsenal, and perhaps more, during the battle.

The maid whom I had left looking after the children elbowed her way through the crowd tugging the startled infants behind her and half flung them at me before regarding the other six sliding down from Petrova with an exasperated stare. She shook her head and stormed off in a huff leaving the happily reunited friends hugging and kissing one another and generally overjoyed to be safe and sound.

The Professor strode out from the broken front door into the courtyard with the sheriff and the young servant boy who had freed me earlier following in his wake. They pushed their way through the cordon of shocked onlookers and gathered next to me, Petrova and the group of children.

Van Halestrom looked amongst my new family and observed, "Why, Sebastian, you have enough children to start your own school."

"Yes," I ruefully admitted, "I'm not altogether sure what I'm going to do with them all."

"Whatever it is, my friend, I'm sure it will be immeasurably better than the future they would have had to endure if not for your bravery and determination. Well done, lad." He proudly put his hands on his hips and smiled, "You will be pleased to hear that we have made many more arrests than even I believed possible. Is that not right, Sheriff?"

"Twenty nine in all, and eight dead, Herr Professor. Plus a cart full of documents and papers and other incriminating evidence."

"I'm afraid Frank got away, Sebastian, and some of the others too. But you'll be pleased to know that we found Danzer alive, just about and," he nodded with a smile befitting a job well done and finished, "I reckon, we pretty much got the rest of them."

I was overjoyed to hear this and particularly pleased at the news about Danzer. Though I had wanted to beat the mad old Canon's head in only a few hours ago, I did not want him to die.

The children had been discussing something in a huddle with the young servant holding court in the middle. Being the oldest he seemed to take charge and took something off one of the younger ones. He looked over at me and approached holding it out in his hand, saying humbly, "We think you lost this, sir."

I was staggered to see in his dirty palm my precious silver timepiece. I stared at him in disbelief and foolishly patted down my waistcoat. With all the day's adventures I had not even noticed it was gone. And they had found it. He might have been young but he was not stupid and must have known how much it was worth. I was profoundly moved by this supremely honest act, especially after the way I had bullied him, it was an extraordinarily decent thing to do.

The Professor was also duly impressed and, instead of scolding me, as I should have rightfully expected for losing something of such great value and fraternal importance, laughed uproariously at the situation.

"Ha, ha. A finer thing I have never seen. Yes indeed! Why is it only the innocent who know how to behave? It seems, Sebastian, that you have gained some admirers. Ha, ha. Oh yes. Now, *that* is a thing of great value. Oh yes indeed!"

I took the timepiece from the boy and, after making doubly sure that the chain was fastened properly, slipped it back inside my waistcoat pocket and gave it a pat. I smiled at him once more with much sincerity and tousled his hair. In the circumstances, after all that I had been through, I had to stifle a tear of joy.

With the Illuminati routed, their meeting smashed to pieces, Bassus' castle half destroyed and seemingly the whole rotten membership in one prison cart or another, it was time to leave. I marched back into the courtyard and set about commandeering an appropriate vehicle for our journey home. After inspecting the row of carriages and, unable to find the one in which I had arrived, I quickly spotted another that suited my purposes. Seeing that the driver was not around, though I did not try too hard to find him and, given my mood had he been guarding it with his fists up, it would have made little difference. I jumped on the footplate, stirred the horses and drove it from the courtyard. The crowd parted to let me out and I collected the children then tied Petrova behind while the Professor finalised arrangements with the sheriff. With seemingly all matters attended to and everyone safely onboard, we trundled away from the hubbub with Van Halestrom in tow and soon found the road for Ingolstadt and the Castle Landfried. Finally, we were on our way home. *[29]

---

29. **Sandersdorf Castle Police Raid.** The raid on Count Bassus' castle in Sandersdorf Bavaria by the authorities on May 12th 1787 was the last and most high profile incident involving the Illuminati during their short history and marked the final end for the organisation in the country. There are no records of arrests, possibly to avoid a diplomatic incident, though a large haul of incriminating literature, secret documents, membership rosters, stolen seals, code books, accounts and other recorded evidence was definitely seized and can still be viewed today. After the affair Count Bassus suffered a fall from grace of epic proportions and, though the castle was eventually returned to him after being confiscated by the authorities for this, and other 'unpatriotic' crimes, he ended up loosing much of his lands in Poschiavo over the following years as well as his family's dwindling fortune and lived the rest of his life in obscurity as a social outcast.

Chapter 31

The Long and Winding Road

At last, (maybe for the first time in years) Van Halestrom and I were no longer in a hurry and slowly plodded along, side by side, back to the castle. Him, relaxing in his saddle and me, idly driving the coach with one hand holding the reins while the children played in the back. We took the opportunity to discuss our latest adventure as there was much to talk about, both good and bad, which provided me a convenient distraction from worrying about how I was going to explain myself to Francesca upon my return.

I told the Professor about Frank and exactly what I had seen: the Kabbalist priest, his young female companion and his strange mention of the bizarre Sabbati Tzvi. The Professor needed no encouragement to share his thoughts on the individual and, it seemed, could have derided the vicious bastard all day.

"Pah. Frank is a murderous, self-aggrandising lunatic and supposed *mystic* of the highest order, whose crazed self-belief and parlour conjury has duped many in the Royal Courts of Europe where he now holds much influence."

I could not imagine the unappealing little shit having the wherewithal to charm anyone, especially European Royalty and wondered why he had not conjured his sheet back on.

"The priest is a man called Khan whose ancestors have advised the Order for centuries in accordance with their Gematric traditions, especially on the matter of dates for whatever devilry they are up to. I know for a fact that many of them will even believe the reason they were vanquished, at all, was because the meeting's date didn't possess the correct numerology." He looked at me darkly and continued, "The girl is his daughter, Eve. She is twelve years old."

He stirred in his saddle and sighed, "Tzvi. Now there was a world class idiot. He was the original lunatic from whom Frank claims he is reincarnated and who shared his perverted interpretation of the Kabbalah which attempts to invert Moses' Ten Commandments in such a ridiculous fashion that I cannot even bring myself to mention." He shook his head, "It's pure evil in its most repellent form. The fools claim to be the left hand of God, descended from Cain and hastening their evil Messiah's prophetic return with blasphemy. What utter tripe. The truth is that they are merely perverts who have contrived their own despicable belief for the single reason that it condones their disgusting behaviour. No more, no less." *30

I remembered reading the similar medieval interpretation of Kabbalah in Bassus' library and wondered why so many supposedly enlightened men had become willing adepts.

"It seems to me, sir, that rather than being an assembly of like-minded hermetic libertarians or butchers and tailors coming together to share new ideas and all that hokum, the Order is nothing more than... well, a whorehouse and a protection racket."

"That's it, my lad. Just like ancient Rome. Sex and money have always been the most efficient ways of compromising men and, therefore, 'doing business' so I expect this state of affairs to continue into the foreseeable future. When it comes to sex, the usual method is to introduce a level of debauchery normally

---

30. **Sabbati Tvzi Dark Cults.** Strangely little is popularly known about this extremely important 17th century character. At his height Sabbati Tvzi had up to a million followers, unheard of in those days and the cleric appointed himself the messiah on the 18th June 1666 – a lot of sixes. Finally his luck ran out in Turkey when he was caught by the local sultan who commanded him to take back his messianic claim or be tortured to death whereupon Sabbati promptly converted to Islam and his adoption of the religion is thought to be the progenitor of the Young Turk movement (Sabbatean Frankism) responsible for the Armenian genocide in 1919.

forbidden during the throes of a carnal act then *bang* the snare snaps shut. Shame and the prospect of arrest and denunciation are powerful motivators. Hence all the swivelling eyes because, put simply, they're all compromised one way or another. I concede that Bassus is a good liar, one of the best, but generally none of them can look a man straight in the face. The truth is the whole Illuminati is just one festering pyramid of swivel-eyed perverts. Why do you think they have so many *secrets?*"

My recollection of Bode and Constanza appearing from the shadows doing up their belts took on a new light and I wondered what would have happened had I satisfied my desires.

He chuckled as he rode along next to me, "And you smashed it all to pieces. Ha! How I wish I could see Frank's face now. What a picture, what a picture indeed." His expression lit up like a summer's morning. "I've got it. We'll get Bacon to paint a portrait of him, as he looks today and hang it on the wall back at the castle? What about that eh? The pathetic tyrant's useless without all these deluded aristocrat followers running round doing his bidding. Now the idiot won't even be able to wipe his backside on his own." He laughed so contagiously that I could not help but join in.

We clopped up the road appreciating the beautiful countryside and after a while he spied me out of the corner of his eye and asked, "So, my boy, after all your adventures, what level do you think you are at now?"

I shook my head and sighed, "Please don't think me rude, Professor, but I'm simply glad to be alive and in all honesty, I no longer care."

As we had been talking in the same relaxed fashion for some time - nearly three years - I felt it permissable to dismiss our society's own structure of personal development so flippantly.

He smiled shrewdly and said, "You know what that means - do you not?"

For once I was blissfully apathetic and cared no more for more secrets and, unusually content with the status quo, watched a butterfly flutter-by with a satisfied shrug.

"Remember what you used to ask me? Almost every day?" he chuckled. "Come on, Sebastian? What was it?"

I only had to consider this for a moment before I remembered perpetually pestering him on the subject. "Ah yes, Professor. How could I forget? When will I know at what level I am?"

"That's right," he exclaimed and raised a finger, "And what did I always reply?" At last I understood. After all this time. I no longer cared therefore... "That's right, Sebastian," he said, now reading me like the cover of a book, "When you no longer have to ask then you have arrived. Ha, ha! And it's about time," he laughed, "Which, in turn, means there is nothing more I can teach you," he waggled his head, "Well, perhaps a bit here and there. But you're on your way now. Oh yes. You have come of age, my boy. And, as such - you are now a man. They might have a different word for it in the library at Poschiavo, or in some other ancient texts and sacred books: 'The Third Eye,' or 'The Eye of Elohim,' or 'The Eye of Horus,' or the eye of 'this' or the eye of 'that' but confound it, it might as well be 'My Grandmother's Eye.'"

I sniggered at his easy talking but he was not done and continued in the same eccentric but insightful manner.

"All they mean, all of them, is the same thing: Spiritual transcendence. And all that really means is - you understand. Not only others but, crucially, yourself. Everything about you: The good *and* the bad. You see?" He circled his hand over his head, "Also the world around you. Beyond that the universe and you *yourself*, as a universe. As above so below." He nodded then wrinkled his forehead, "It means you understand that organised religion of divine revelation is ridiculous but that, despite presenting a good argument, atheism eventually suffers from exactly the same suffocating dogmatism and, in the end, well... it becomes a religion in itself." He seemed to momentarily tie himself in a knot but waved his hand, flustering, "Look, none of that matters right now. The only spiritual *truth* is that the universe is a miracle. A true, living, wonderful, magical, mysterious, miracle and our mission, if we choose to accept it, is both to understand and tame it for the good of all. Anybody who argues with that is a total and utter blasted nitwit."

He smiled to himself and composed his thoughts then concluded with his finger aloft like a Magician on a Tarot card, "Now, you are no longer the portico of the temple, you are inside. You have become the esoteric, transcended from your own exoteric, or outer self, to your own *Holy of Holies*. You now understand why you were purposefully given misleading interpretations by those who initiated you, but, in turn, you know why you gave misleading interpretations to those who you initiated into *your* world; your mother, your father, your friends, your enemies and, I'm sure, at times, even me too. You see, lad? All are elementally the same. We, me, you, the Illuminati, even our own society, we are all our own 'Temple.' We all have our levels to ascend to become our own divine masters. We all aim to become our own sacrosanct 'Holy of Holies.' This is the ultimate truth the elite wish to keep from man, perpetually suspending him in the darkness of spiritual adolescence on his base level so they can shine their eye of enlightenment from the top of their unholy pyramid and rule over us all. That is why we fight them. So that man can be what he was born to be: Free and independent." *[31]

---

31. **U.S. President John F. Kennedy's 1963 'The Secret Societies Speech.'** Coincidentally, on April 27th 1963 President John F. Kennedy made a famously revealing speech to the American Newspaper Press Association which strangely echoes a similar sentiment to that recollected by S. Drechsler and is available for E Book readers by clicking the links.

It was one of the best speeches that I ever heard him make and I hope I have done him justice by recalling it accurately so you can benefit from it now, as I still do to this day.

In good time we returned to the castle and rumbled through the gates. I had foolishly intended to hide the carriage full of children from Francesca until I had time to properly explain myself and work out a plan, but when we pulled into the courtyard she was already waiting by the door at the top of the steps holding a shawl about her shoulders. My fears about seeing her were completely mislaid, as had been many of my other fears. Somehow, we did not need to say anything to one another, both of us instinctively knowing that, such was the depth of our lov it would overcome any tribulations that came our way and I took much, much pleasure in finally, but gently, holding her close to me once again. She was exactly as I had left her: perfect.

After some time had passed she said, "You can let me go if you want."

"I know," I said softly, "But I don't want to let you go again."

"Ooh," she cooed, nestling deeper into my embrace and making herself more comfortable. Presently, she sighed at the children playing around the carriage and observed, "It seems that we have lost one child only to have found several others."

I sighed deeply myself, having also been thinking a great deal about what I was going to do with them.

"But we can try again you know?" she smiled up at me, "To have our own."

"I've been looking forward to trying for some time, my dove," I admitted with a smile of my own and stroked her beautiful hair.

She looked deep into my eyes with much true love and finished, "There is always time, my darling. There is always time."

Chapter 32

Chip Off the Old Block

Two days later I rode Petrova into Tuffengarten with my small strongbox tied to her rump. She neighed with relief when I pulled it down and I thanked her before lugging it inside the house. It was all there. Everything I had. I sat waiting by the door for two days as my mother nervously cleaned around me and cooked and slept and cleaned again.

In the afternoon of the second day a black coach pulled up outside and I watched from the window as Peter Kronenberg got out and held the door for his master Solomon Sachs. The wizened moneylender shuffled up the garden path in his dark robes with his loafing servant in tow and I got up and opened the door. They were a little shocked to see me instead of my timid mother or my gout-ridden father and old Solomon recoiled slightly while Peter slowly worked out who I was and smiled to himself. I watched him remember the 'The Woodturner' from school but those days were long gone.

"I have your money," I said and dragged the box to the door then shoved it outside with my boot. "It's all there."

Solomon gestured to Peter who slid the box behind his master where he opened it and started to count the coins very, very slowly. Arithmetic had never been his best subject.

"He doesn't need to count it. It's all there."

"Unfortunately, young man," gloated Solomon behind his unruly grey beard, "There is another payment due." He produced a little red book from under his robes and leafed through calculating, "Let me see, let me see. Ah yes. One hundred and nineteen thalers precisely." He saw my tense expression and assured, "I have the contract of the loan if you want to see it."

"That won't be necessary," I said, putting my hand in my pocket and pulling out my purse.

I had thought that I had enough but as I counted out my last remaining coins he smirked, "Oh dear, young man. I think you are one thaler short."

Upon hearing this, my mother ran into the kitchen where I heard her open her special jar in which she kept a little money aside for a rainy day and she returned holding out a coin.

I thanked her and held it out to Solomon and said, "When I have given you this, sir I don't want to see your face again, or hear that you've been plying your usurious trade in this place. Do you understand?"

"What I do is all perfectly legal, sir," he implored, keeping his old deep set eyes fixed on mine and pityfully raising his palms.

"I don't care if its legal or not. I never want to see you again. Do you understand?"

Perhaps I stepped forward at this moment and, mistakenly thinking that I was threatening his master, Peter jumped up and aggressively pushed me back. But we were no longer at school. I jabbed him in his Adam's apple, as I had been trained to when wishing to incapacitate but not kill, and he fell on his back. While he lay there clutching his throat and gasping for air, I trod on his right hand to make him gasp a little more and to ensure that he could not use it in his master's service for some time. I grabbed Solomon by the collar then pulled his withered face to mine and forcefully repeated, "Once more, old man. Now I have given you this, *sir* I don't want to see your face again, or hear you've been plying your usurious trace in this place. Do-you-understand?"

He nodded frantically this time and I held the coin up to his face and ordered him, "Open your mouth."

He shook his head so I squeezed the collar of his robes until he choked and his stuck out his tongue. I placed the coin on it and said, "Now swallow."

He shook his head again but I put my hand over his mouth and his nose and, after a shuddering gulp during which his eyes told a painful story, he finally got his dues.

I poked my finger into his chest and defiantly told him, "This family will never owe money again. Now go!" I watched him like a hawk as he helped his driver drag the chest and the still incapacitated Peter back through the mud onto the coach and, after throwing me several apprehensive looks, they left. I waited until they had gone and escorted my mother inside. It was over for us in Tuffengarten.

Two weeks later, the gun smithy was sold along with the house to the ever-helpful Count Friedrich and she moved to a little cottage on the outskirts of Ingolstadt. Funnily enough, after that day outside our old house she never once again mentioned me becoming a priest.

Sometimes it does no good to hold onto the past and let sentimental attachments prevent you from enjoying the promise of a brand new day.

Chapter 33

By Royal Decree

After the momentous events at Sandersdorf Castle, things truly changed. Such was the debacle that for the next few months there was nothing in the newspapers *but* the story of our raid and I almost got bored of hearing about my own heroism, the Illuminati's ultimate demise and the extremely public fall from grace of its disgraced membership. Count Bassus had his estate in Sandersdorf confiscated and soon after that, as the news spread, it became impossible for him to live in Poschiavo. We heard a story circulating that Massenhausen had defied police captivity and was hiding in Regensburg but the Professor and I knew better. According to all reports Danzer made a full recovery but when we were told that he had found refuge as a confessional priest in a nunnery, I worried for the safety, and sanity, of the poor nuns locked inside the place with the crazy mad-eyed rascal. *[32]

Summer arrived in all its splendour and the weather matched everyone's high spirits at the castle. In July, Francesca and I moved out to pleasant lodgings in Ingolstadt, though my sweet was confounded to be living somewhere smaller than a palace and took great efforts to constantly remind me of the fact.

I successfully took the viva on my dissertation, choosing as my subject; 'The Literary Traditions of Hermetic Philosophy.' After politely refusing Bacon's best efforts to write one for me,

---

32. **Illuminati Agent Canon Jakob Danzer.** Jakob Danzer (1743-1796) was a catholic moral theologian. The farmer's son became lecturer on pastoral theology at Salzburg University in 1785 where he wrote '*Guide to Christian Morality'*. It is unknown when he joined the Illuminati though he was definitely a member as all researched membership rosters record and was formerly removed from his educational posts when his membership was discovered.

it was all genuinely my own work so I was very proud of myself when finally, after all that time, I successfully graduated. I had done it. At many times over the past four years I had almost forgotten why I had come to Ingolstadt in the first place but it was now impossible to overlook the fact that, after much worry, concern and hard work (that even my father would have had to admire) I was now a graduate and I pondered, at some length, what I would do with my future.

I did not see much of the Professor over the summer as he was involved in the numerous court cases and compilation of evidence required to secure the all-important convictions after the raid and, Bavaria being what it has always been, the sheer amount of paperwork and forms and bureaucracy and constant hearings meant that he was seldom around. Famously, some of the documents seized at Sandersdorf were publicly exhibited in the local council buildings in Ingolstadt including a book called; *Nachtrag von wieteren Originalschriften.* Copies of which were printed and sent to all the governments of Europe and America to warn them of the Illuminati's intentions.

Many letters were written, including several by Van Halestrom, I know because I saw them, to the American consulate in Paris and the Senate back in Washington regarding Jefferson's membership of the Order. The return correspondence claimed that the necessary individuals would 'look into the matter when the chance availed itself.' I clearly remember both the Professor and Bacon complaining that in the good old days when Franklin was in the saddle things would have been a lot different with serious repercussions for Jefferson. Indeed, Bacon claimed 'His feet wouldn't have touched the ground, sir' and that 'He would have been thrown in jail like the slave-owning colonialist that he was.' Though, I now no longer had to imagine what these men were like as I had met one - in the flesh - at least they were hundreds, if not thousands of miles away.

The final nail in the coffin for the Illuminati in Bavaria came halfway through August when the authorities announced increased sentences for membership from long jail terms and confiscations of property and monies, up to the maximum penalty of death. I remember exactly the way they put it too; '*Have their lives deprived by the sword.*' I recall thinking 'Brilliant! Some other heroic mad men can go dragging themselves through the filthy countryside, and God knows what else, getting into all manner of death-defying scrapes, to kill the bastards.'

This was not the only good news. For the Professor was summoned by royal decree, no less, in the form of a huge letter adorned with the grandest seal and ribbon that I had ever seen, to attend the court of The Duke Elector of Bavaria, Charles Theodore himself to receive a special honour for his services to the state.

That was a fine day and no mistake. The four of us dressed in all our finery bundled aboard Van Halestrom's best carriage, which faithful Willy had polished for a week, and travelled to Munich where we were treated to a luxurious state affair at the Royal Palace. Myself, Bacon and Francesca, who finally felt at home surrounded in such splendour, got to see Charles Theodore decorate Van Halestrom who seemed uncharacteristically self-conscious upon receiving an enormous medal the size of one of his birota wheels.

I was quite relieved, in the end, not to have been granted a similar recognition as the whole occasion, with its pomp and ceremony and ermine and trumpets, was a tad too ostentatious even for me. Though, I have to admit, I was extremely honoured when old Theodore, who must have been almost seventy then, took time to shake our hands and conversed with us at great lengths before eventually taking his leave and benevolently assuring us, "We could not have done it without your sterling and, much appreciated, service."

It was all highly satisfying and still provides me with a glorious memory, over which I reminisce most days of my life some seventy years later. Happy memories indeed. Ah yes. Golden days. *[33]

Now, there were only a few loose ends to tie up.

---

33. **Duke of Bavaria. The Third and Final Edict Against the Illuminati.** S. Drechsler accurately records this event as the Bavarian authorities ratified the third and final edict against the Illuminati on August 16th 1787 which increased the sentence for membership to the death penalty. Charles Theodore Elector of Bavaria (1724-1799) was considered a staunch patriot and, even after the Illuminati scare, continued a merciless persecution of secret societies until his death.

Chapter 34

If I Were a Rich Man

It must have been the start of September when I next returned to Ingolstadt University to visit the Professor because I distinctly remember the trees round the faculty showing the first signs of autumn as I walked through the gates and made my way inside. I had been busy since our last meeting and had much to tell my master.

"Come in, Sebastian!" he called as I went to knock on his door and I reflected how the habit used to confound me but now simply made me smile. An hour later we were sitting in our usual chairs around his chess table after our first match in ages which, very unusually (in fact I am sure it was the first time ever), I had won.

"You've come a long way, Sebastian. I doubt you could've achieved such an emphatic victory three years ago." He turned his black king on its side and winked. "But yet, here you are."

I was not so proud to have finally beaten him that I missed his little joke which was obviously an oblique reference to our resounding triumph over the Order which had seemed, so many times, impossible. He was right though. That battle had also been fought and won. Hooray! He relit his pipe and regarded me happily and, with our game completed and a new day on the horizon, he turned his thoughts to the future.

"So tell me, young man have you decided what you plan to do with yourself?"

This was the big one, so to speak, and I had not announced my intentions to anyone as I wanted him to be the first to hear my decision. Fittingly, for an announcement of this importance, I rose from my chair and stood up straight.

"Yes, sir." I replied.

"Yes?" he grinned after a moment and prompted, "Forgive me, Sebastian, but in this case my capacity to read your thoughts is insufficient to divine what you have planned."

"Sorry, sir. I will not bore you with all the permutations that led me to my choice..."

"You're never boring, Sebastian," he mentioned.

"Please, sir, allow me to finish. Suffice to say that I will not be entering the church."

"Oh dear. Your mother will be upset."

"On the contrary, sir, I think I can now count her acquiescence on the matter as another one of my emphatic victories."

"Ha. Good news indeed. Then what's it to be eh; a courtier, a lawyer, a politician, perhaps a diplomat? Old Theodore's staff were very impressed with you. They're always on the lookout for keen urbane graduates exactly like yourself. I saw you speaking to them for hours. It seemed as though you had much in common."

"I will get to that, Professor. Though I am flattered you feel that I could succeed in all these vocations, I'm afraid I feel my future path lies elsewhere."

Now, instead of interrupting again, he sat patiently waiting which prevented me from further prevarication so, without any further ado, I sighed and finished, "So, I have decided to become a Professor... Professor."

"That's wonderful news!" He beamed with true satisfaction, "Welcome aboard," and jumped up to vigorously shake my hand. "Let me be the first to say, I feel you've made the right decision," he winked, "For I know, from much personal experience, that you have the perfect demeanour for the role. But I'm interested, tell me, what made up your mind?"

It was a pertinent question for which I wished to furnish an equally pertinent answer. I took a moment to marshal my thoughts and began, "My education has made me the man that you see before you today, sir, and now I want to help others to do the same. For, to teach properly is the best, and only, way to rid our world of its crippling social ills, by eliminating the yawning chasm between the man in the street and the powerful elites that control him. A chasm that, in turn, creates organisations like the Illuminati which, perhaps, would not even exist nor, more importantly, be able to were the masses properly educated."

"Bravo, young man. Bravo. Excellent and insightful sentiment. I couldn't have put it better myself." He nodded approvingly then watched my eyes and urged, "But you have more to tell me?"

His mind reading was back on form as I did indeed have something of great importance to tell him. However, this was the part about which I was most nervous so I wavered hesitantly, "Now, I don't want you to be angry, sir."

He pulled a face as though he had swallowed a chicken bone sideways and demurred, "When have you ever made me angry?"

I stopped to think for a moment but the old bird was right. I could not recall him ever once being angry with me which, as I recalled my behaviour throughout our countless adventures, was quite an accomplishment in itself. With this in mind, I threw caution to the wind and started, "I have taken it upon myself to look after the children from Sandersdorf Castle. This has proved to be no easy task, as I wanted to do it properly. I have housed them, in relative comfort, and hired some of Bassus' old servants to run the place, after they were without work when his estate was confiscated, and made financial provision for this household's upkeep in the form of a charitable trust. Notwithstanding, all this has not come cheaply. So, to fund it all," I gulped and half shut my eyes, "I sold the watch."

He stared at me as though he had not heard properly which gave me further opportunity to explain.

"Theodore's Minister of Foreign Affairs bought it from me. That's what you saw us discussing. He paid the proper price mind. Not a thaler less. I was lucky to have found him. He must have been one of the only men in the country who could've afforded the blasted thing."

Still the Professor continued to stare at me in unnerving silence.

"Those children are *real* orphans, sir. So I thought, wrongly or rightly that, as the watch was given from Bacon, to you and then to me, why not pass it on to the children so they can live a good life now with a proper future ahead of them like... like me. I mean, I would have lost it without them wouldn't I? They were the ones who found it... and gave it back. Maybe they could even become our societies next generation of benefactors. Who knows..?"

I trailed off as that was all I had and waited anxiously for him to explode. I was so nervous that I even flinched when he stepped towards me because I was so convinced that he was going to launch into a fit and strike me down. Instead, for the first time in our long friendship, he held me. After realising it was not a plot to kill me, I reciprocated and put my arms around him and we shared a Platonic embrace of true fellowship. While we stood there silently holding one another, for the first time since I had known him, it truly dawned on me that he *was* an orphan.

After a moment he said joyously, "It is the single most worthy thing that I have ever heard in my life. I could not be any prouder of you." After a decidedly meaningful moment he held me at arm's length and laughed, "To hell with our rules eh? You know your own mind. Ha, ha." He shook his head and beamed, "Good man. That's right! There's no one better than yourself to captain your own ship and pick the course you think best."

He seemed genuinely overcome, indeed, I had to check as I had never witnessed if before, but I was sure that I even saw a small tear in his twinkling eyes. He discreetly wiped his face and continued in the same heartfelt manner, "Ha. I knew when I first saw you at that chess club. Oh yes. It's in the eyes, lad. The eyes have it. The eyes have it."

He stood there proudly regarding me like the father I had always longed for and proved his point by slapping my shoulder almost hard enough to knock me over. Such was his unbridled joy I could not help but be moved enough to produce a sentimental tear of my own.

He composed himself and took a deep breath before carrying on, "So, by my reckoning there is but one loose end to secure. Yes? Well, we have done it, my friend. We have destroyed the Illuminati in Bavaria. Hundreds of members have been arrested, their property and wealth have been confiscated and we have their most important secrets and documents and are even displaying them in the town hall. Others are banished and languish in lands far enough away for us to be able to claim complete and absolute victory. We have achieved everything we set out to, lad. Well done."

"We, Professor?" I gave him a wry smile.

"Yes, *we*," he nodded earnestly. "Not one of us; me, you, Bacon, Francesca, or any of the scores of others who have joined the fight, could have done it alone. Nevertheless, as you know, the Order has the multiple heads of the hydra and somewhere out there they are plotting, scheming and conspiring now to bring their evil plans to fruition. You'll be happy to know that we have changed our society's rule regarding orphans, as change can be a good thing if not then we would have all been born perfect. You know what I am about to say. Sebastian, there is no one who I can trust as I can trust you and some day, I don't know where and I don't know when, but some day in the future when I call on your services, I need to know that you'll be there."

This was the most important question of all and I ran through my adventures over the past three years remembering all the toil, joy, fear, excitement, treachery, triumph, terror and victory. Inspired by his belief in me, and the fact that I had made it this far, I finally accepted myself for what I was; trustworthy, stalwart, determined, resourceful, kind, funny and, even at times, when required, brave. Now there really was no going back.

I took a deep breath and, quelling the reservations haunting the darkest corners of my mind, stuck out my hand. He smiled deeply and shook it with a grip like mighty Atlas himself. "Thank you, Sebastian. I could not be a happier man than I am at this moment."

It was official: I was an Illuminati Hunter.

I strolled out of the university doors into a beautiful late summer's evening and the faraway sounds of children playing. A hurrying student bumped into me as he rushed past and I recalled Poschiavo's gay townsfolk all saying 'Good morning' to each other and pondered if the world was ready for such a society. I smiled to myself as I guessed not, but then I did not find too much wrong with the old one. For some reason Bassus' copy of Fanny Hill popped into my mind when I had not thought about it in months. I wondered, with a distant pang of guilt, if it was still under my old pillow and ruminated how easy it had been, by applying a little freewill, to forgo something that I had seemingly not been able to do without by simply changing my circumstances.

The Professor's words echoed in my head, 'Man was born to be free and independent.' Well, I was certainly that. I sniffed at the changing seasons in the air, put my hands in my pockets, gave a little whistle and walked out the gates. It did not matter in what direction, I could go whichever way I pleased. Good Lord, it was good to be alive. I was a man – No, a gentleman, at last, and one with the prospect of a wonderful life before him. For what more could I have ever wished? Moreover, I had learned that it did not matter whether I was a gentleman or not. What mattered was whether I was a good man or not. And now I knew that, beyond any shadow of doubt, when all was measured and everything said and done, I *was* a good man and, in the end, that was all I had ever really wanted to be. *[34]

---

34. **Illuminati Hunter: The Trilogy.** Aside from the mysterious aspects of S. Drechsler's account there are also several idiosyncrasies of his texts which remain unanswered, the main one being the number of chapters. There are thirty three in Illuminati Hunter I '*Adam Weishaupt and the Eye of Horus*' and Illuminati Hunter II '*Merchant Kolmer and The Obelisk of Nempty*' which, especially in light of the subject matter, seems an unlikely coincidence whereas this, the last in the trilogy, possesses thirty four making the grand total one hundred, $(10(0))$ being the Hermetical 'God' instead of the opposite, ninety nine or $3 \times 33 = 99$ $9 + 9 = 18$, $1 + 8 = 9$ when 9 symoblises 'Fallen' or 'The Devil.' I have not altered the number of position of the chapter breaks in these original notes and, after much speculation, I am convinced that S. Drechsler was trying to communicate a positive coded message by this Gematric use of numbers. Though, now that I have explained my own thoughts on this matter, I will let you assume your own. Another aspect which has come to my attention whilst preparing the three books for release is that, with the first being about Horus the Son, the second's concentration on Sirius the Mother and this, the third, with its focus on fatherhood, the trilogy seems to represent the family trinity, also mentioned in the Winter Triangle. Maybe this is simply another coincidence about which I will let you, the reader, come to your own conclusions. When attempting to decide whether the Illuminati still exists, again you will have to draw your own conclusions. Notably, Weishaupt said, after the ousting of the organisation from Bavaria, 'The great success of the Illuminati, after the publication of their secret writings, was to persuade the whole of Germany that the Order no longer existed and that their adepts had all renounced, not only their mysteries, but as members of a secret society.'

Special thanks

As with all endeavours there are more people behind the scenes than one may imagine. This was certainly the case when creating this book and its predecessors and I would like to take this final opportunity to thank my editors, without which, this publication would not exist. You both know who you are. Thank you from the very bottom of my heart. I am sure that you understand that I could not have done it without your sterling help and dogged perseverance. I want you both to know that I feel this book is as much your achievement as it is mine and, of course, Mr Drechsler's

I would like to dedicate the Illuminati Hunter series to my beautiful son and I look forward, with much fatherly anticipation, to the day that he can read them himself so we can have a good chat about the story. Lastly, and most certainly by no means least, I would like to thank the one person who made it all happen in the beginning. Without her inspiration and love of literature I would never have started this personal adventure. So, it is to her, I give the story because it was always about you my love.

Ethan Harrison 2020

More information including forthcoming releases, reviews and other news of these paperbacks and groundbreaking 'Live' E Books can be found at the website: Illuminati Hunter.com & Illuminati Hunter II.com & @Facebook Illuminati Hunter Book

Footnote Appendix and Hypertext Addresses

1. **Adam Weishaupt & The Bavarian Illuminati.** Widely regarded as the Grandfather of modern conspiracy, Adam Weishaupt was the founder member of the Bavarian Illuminati in 1776. He was Dean of Faculty of Canon Law at influential Ingolstadt University, (the romantic setting for Mary Shelley's *Frankenstein*), but was sacked in February 1785 under new laws banning secret societies throughout Bavaria and he subsequently fled to nearby Regensburg after incriminating Illuminati documents revealing the society's plans for power were seized by the authorities when messenger Jakob Lanz was struck by lightning and killed. The Merchant Kolmer was a mysterious German merchant from Jutland who spent many years in Egypt studying and trading ancient artefacts and was commonly believed to have initiated Weishaupt into the darker hermetic mystery school religions.

https://en.wikipedia.org/wiki/Illuminati

https://en.wikipedia.org/wiki/University_of_Ingolstadt

http://www.illuminati-news.com/bavarian-illuminati.htm
,

2. **Illuminati Codenames & Secret Documents.** The Bavarian Illuminati, being a secret society, used codes and codenames for much of its correspondence and for all clandestine messages. Agents adopted codenames usually taken from Roman or Greek antiquity especially those associated with antipathy toward Rome. Illuminati leader Adam Weishaupt famously chose the codename Spartacus, the Spartan general and ex-gladiator who led the slave mutiny against Rome in 270 B.C. Inevitably, the Illuminati was compromised by the seizure of incriminating documents. Notably, in 1784, when Illuminati messenger, Jakob Lanz, was killed by a lightning strike while delivering secret papers which were then found by the authorities and in 1786, when the residence of chief government lawyer and fellow

Illuminati agent Xavier Zwack, codename Cato, was raided by police who seized many documents copies of which were later circulated by the authorities in an attempt to alert the public and other governments to the secret society's conspiracy.

https://warningilluminati.wordpress.com/an-act-of-god/

3. **Illuminati Chief Treasurer Count Anton Massenhausen 'Ajax.'** A former student of Ingolstadt University, by 1787 Count Anton Massenhausen appears on all published Illuminati membership lists and was chief treasurer from the inception of the organisation and also one of the five original members along with Weishaupt whom he met at the university. Massenhausen had operated a lottery, amongst other things, in his time and had a reputation for drinking, gambling and womanising. Though this, by all accounts, is thought to have been spread by Weishaupt, but he was also rumoured to be a 'poltroon' (coward) though if S. Drechsler recollections are reliable this would seem to be untrue.

https://es.wikipedia.org/wiki/Anton_von_Massenhausen

4. **Bavarian Illuminati Membership 1787.** The Illuminati's ranks had swelled to over three thousand by this time. Although there had been many arrests and defections the list still included; aristocrats, judges, councillors, Barons, Counts and men from every possible walk of life and position. Johann Wolfgang Goethe, the author of *Faust*, in which the tragic character sells his soul to Mephistopheles (the Devil), was famously a member and recruited in 1784. Jacob Lange's (Tamerlane) death by a lightning strike in 1785 led to Adam Weishaupt's banishment from Bavaria after authorities found incriminating documents with his body.

https://www.yumpu.com/en/document/read/2575892/10notable-members-of-the-bavarian-illuminati

5. **Illuminati & The Great Work (Hermeticism):** The Great Work is a term used in Hermeticism from which the

occult traditions descend. On a personal level Magnum Opus (Latin interpretation) means the spiritual path towards self-transcendence and attaining this most revered metaphysical state represents the culmination of the spiritual path, the attainment of self enlightenment and the rescue of the human soul from the unconscious forces that bind it. Globally applied, it could be fairly described as a utopian internationalist single state which, merely by its very nature, could only be bought into existence by revolutionary practices to accomplish a 'One World One Collective Conscience.' Or in a corporate, cultural, geopolitical sense: Globalism.

https://www.youtube.com/watch?v=QLBjvgHrKo4

6. **Illuminati Hermetic Mystery School Religion.** The Ancient Egyptians, including several other arcane religions, Greek, Roman, Assyrian, Babylonian, anthropomorphised (personified) the stars and interpreted our own sun's passage at the solstices typically as God's or God's son or, as S. Drechsler states, 'The Son of God's' reincarnation. The iconography and personages of many contemporary faiths derive from ancient celestial observations. For example: twelve signs of the zodiac, twelve apostles. Orion's three stars, the three wise men. Occult astronomical knowledge creates another level on which religions can be considered and, in this case, establishes the backbone of the occult Hermetic Mystery School Religions practised by the Illuminati. The Winter Triangle, made from the family trinity of Illuminati favourites: Horus, Isis and Osiris, can be viewed here on the Stargazer app.

https://www.youtube.com/watch?v=p_iXe-iuAVs

https://en.wikipedia.org/wiki/Winter_Triangle

7. **Hermetic Philosophy 'Know Thyself.'** The ancient Hermetic aphorism 'Know Thyself' is recorded by the Greek Writer Pausanias circa 100 B.C. to have been inscribed in the forecourt of the Temple of Apollo at Delphi in ancient Greece. The timeless maxim is considered to be the crucial philosophical

prelude before transcendence which cannot occur, without this ancient challenge being accomplished first. Adepts of the occult tradition are expected to fully come to terms with this idea before achieving illumination.

https://www.youtube.com/watch?v=zccoaL0stbM

https://en.wikipedia.org/wiki/Know_thyself

8. Illuminati Court Cases, Banishments, Confessions & Runaways. Several arrests and court cases involving the Illuminati had taken place by 1787. Notably, three professors, Cossendy, Renner and Grünburgen, (see Illuminati Hunter II) who defected from the organisation when they did not receive the 'special powers' that they had been promised, were interrogated and gave extensive and damaging confessions. Weishaupt himself fled when threatened with arrest. Once, reportedly, even hiding in a chimney to escape the authorities. After first fleeing to nearby Regensburg he later ended up being given refuge by sympathetic Duke Ernst II of the Sax-Gotha-Altenburg family which in 1825 became the Sax-Gotha-Coburg line, intriguingly direct ancestors of the United Kingdom's Royal family.

https://modernhistoryproject.org/mhp?Article=FinalWarning&C=1.2#Exposed

9. Illuminated Philosophy 'As Above So Below.' Perhaps the best known of all philosophical aphorisms 'As above so below' is associated with Hermeticism, sacred geometry and Tarot. The philosophy generally attributes a reflective quality to nature from the tiny to the universal. In the secular context, the phrase can refer to the idea that microcosm reflects macrocosm. For example; that the ills of the individual can be reflected in the ills of society at large. In Hermeticism, the phrase can be taken to mean that earthly matters reflect the operations of the astral plane and, perhaps its most commonly known usage in western religious text would be within The Lord's Prayer: 'On Earth as it is in Heaven.' A good example of the concept in a contemporary form, can be seen in fractals and the Mandelbrot Set, wherein the same patterns exists on all scales fom the largest to the infinitely small.

https://en.wikipedia.org/wiki/As_above,_so_below

https://www.youtube.com/watch?v=2_YQcYnOtRI&t=2s

10. Poschiavo. Giuseppe Ambrosini & The Printing Press.
As S. Drechsler recalls Giuseppe Ambrosini owned a popular
bookshop in Poschiavo in which a Guttenberg printing press,
an anomaly for a town of Poschiavo's size in the late 1700's,
operated and printed many important works of the day including
several criticizing the church and the pope and, interestingly, the
Italian version of Goethe's seminal work *The Sorrows of Young
Werther* (1774 revised 1778) in Italian.

https://en.wikipedia.org/wiki/Poschiavo

11. Poschiavo & Count Bassus. Thomas Maria Baron von
Bassus was born in Poschiavo in 1742 and attended Ingolstadt
University and, upon his return, was promptly made mayor of
the ancient town at the tender age of twenty six, He had inherited
huge tracts of local land and many properties from his wealthy
parents much of it in Switzerland but also Sandersdorf in Bavaria.
Bassus was a politician and philanthropist and organised many
cultural activities in the town and even procured a printing press
for the place which was unheard of in those days and this was
operated by Giuseppe Ambrosini from his bookshop which had
a reputation for selling and printing controversial works. Bassus
was regarded as having the fine manners 'befitting his experience
of German court.' The influential Count was also a close friend
of Charles Friedrich Bahrdt a 'German Unionist and Professor
of Sacred Philology at Leipzig University' and Johann Simon
Mayr the famous composer who penned over seventy operas.

https://www.geni.com/people/Thomas-Maria-de-Bassus-
Baron/6000000083228760370

https://en.wikipedia.org/wiki/Karl_Friedrich_Bahrdt

https://en.wikipedia.org/wiki/Simon_Mayr

12. The Roman Tiburtine; Sibyl. Amazingly this mysterious painting by an unknown artist still exists today in Poschiavo in the Hotel Albrici which was also owned by Count Bassus and can be viewed here by E Book readers.

https://kozinets.net/archives/41

13. Solomon's Temple & The Pillars Jachin & Boaz. Both these icons feature heavily in occult symbolism. The original name for the Masons, often associated with organisations such as the Illuminati, was the Templars after Knights of The Temple. These warrior aristocrats became wealthy during the crusades defending pilgrims to the Holy Land and were thought to have found occult secrets in the ruins of Solomon's Temple in Jerusalem which gave them great powers. The Templars were finally rounded up and burned at the stake by Pope Clement III in 1413 for heresy and Devil worship in the form of the Baphomet when Jacques De Molay was their leader. The legendary brass columns outside the Temple's entrance known as Jachin and Boaz were thought to be indestructible on Solomon's original building and are familiar in Tarot and represent opposing aspects.

https://www.youtube.com/watch?v=M8qkj3rOJ64

https://www.youtube.com/watch?v=F3nPNaHp4hY

https://tarotdontarot.blogspot.com/2013/03/the-secret-of-high-priestess-boaz-and.html

14. Sacred Geometry: The Hexagram. The most commonly known occult symbol is the union of opposing triangles 'of the upward fire or male and the downward watery female (male/female).' The hexagram represents the maxim 'As above so below,' and produces a three dimensional cube in the centre. Hermetically known as the Star of Remphan or the Seal of

Solomon (sometimes referred to as The Star of David, though, surprisingly, this has no biblical reference) it occurs in several cultures from the orient to the Middle East and also in western mysticism. The Hexagram, with its six points, six triangles and six-sided central hexagon (666) is often seen as the arcane occult symbol for Saturn and, geometrically, shows a hexagon in its centre identical to the gas cloud situated on the planet's North Pole which, mysteriously, was only first observed by man with the Voyager Probe in 1977.

https://tarotdontarot.blogspot.com/2013/03/the-secret-of-high-priestess-boaz-and.html

http://symboldictionary.net/?p=1533

https://en.wikipedia.org/wiki/Hexagram

https://en.wikipedia.org/wiki/Saturn's_hexagon

15. **De Bassus Beer.** The De Bassus name has enjoyed a long success in the brewing industry and De Bassus beer is still brewed today in Sandersdorf Bavaria.

https://www.conspiracyarchive.com/2013/11/26/de-bassus-beer-premium-illuminati-lager/

16. **The Illuminati in Music & The Opera Alcina by George F. Handel.** The opera, also known as The Sorceress is, generally, as S. Drechsler describes and availabe to E Book readers who wish to share the author's experience. The Illuminati has always been associated with music, never more so than today but rumours abound from Mozart to the Beatles and Beyonce. Whilst many maybe difficult to substantiate, and even harder to believe, there can be no question that a sinister group wishing to control the world from behind the scenes would seek to control popular musicians for their own devices.

https://www.rollingstone.com/music/music-news/beyonce-

266

and-the-illuminati-musics-most-wtf-conspiracy-theories-explained-119376/

https://www.youtube.com/watch?v=Eo8cOapF1nQ

https://en.wikipedia.org/wiki/Alcina

17. Lurian Kabbalah. Isaac Luria (1534 -1572) developed his version of Kabbalah in the sixteenth century. Luria's idea suggested that man was moving through time to eventually become God himself, lends itself to the philosophy of spiritual autonomy popular in the renaissance. Though it is not difficult to imagine how, in the wrong hands, such spiritual 'freedom' could be problematic.

https://en.wikipedia.org/wiki/Isaac_Luria

18. The Eye of Elohim - Da'ath. Da'ath (Daat) is the mystic or invisible eleventh sefirot, or point, in Kabbalah's Tree of Life and has similar qualities in western new ageism to the The Third Eye. The other ten sefirot represent God; 1 being the masculine principle and 0 the female, thus the eleventh, which is created when connections are made between the second, third, fourth and fifth sefirot, becomes transcendent to God. It is said that when Da'ath is achieved so much light is radiated that the other sefirot become indistinguishable and become 'as one.' The Eye of Elohim (or The Eye of God) is mentioned by the serpent in The Garden of Eden from the book of Genesis as it tempts Eve to eat the apple and refers to the transcending of the soul as self-realisation. The Master or Magician card in Tarot is traditionally depicted with one hand pointing up and the other down in classic 'As above, so below' pose.

https://www.youtube.com/watch?v=-oZ_bHzlEpU

https://www.youtube.com/watch?v=B64IST5E1Hs

19. Melancholia Hermetic Insights. The hidden meanings,

allegories and plethora of symbols in Durer's masterpiece of the androgynous angel Melencolia have baffled and intrigued art historians for centuries. There were thought to be four humours controlling our state of mind according to German thinker Cornelius Agrippa, Melencolia was level one and pertained to artists.

https://www.youtube.com/watch?v=z11pYvaLctY

20. **Gematria & The Occult.** Gematria originated in Assyrian Greek Babylonian culture and is the method of ascribing alpha numerical code to letters, though the technique is often adapted to ascribe meanings to pure numbers. Tarot uses a form of numerology similar to Gematria. Six, six, six is meant to signify man in his lowest beast form, hence the number of the beast, whereas seven, seven, seven signifies man exalted. John Dee the first controller of MI5 and renowned hermetic Kabbalist referred to himself as the first agent or 007. It perhaps then can be no coincidence that MI5 is the national intelligence service five representing microcosm and MI6 international intelligence when six represents the macrocosm and, of course, together, as S. Drechsler explains, they would be eleven, or the Magician in Tarot.

https://www.youtube.com/watch?v=Aw-hUD99MNE

https://www.youtube.com/watch?v=Ms5bgw10xgM&t=11

21. **Secret Societies & Initiations.** The 18th century was perhaps the zenith of the secret society with most gentlemen of means, if not all, affiliated to one group or another. The benefits of membership were not exclusive but could vary from business, political, cultural to simply social. The practice was widespread in the middle European capital states in those days and especially prevalent within student communities. Though S. Drechsler's initiation most resembles that of the Masonic tradition many societies would have observed similar rituals with similar themes. While the play of the myth of Hiram Abiff is particular

268

to Masonic initiations the three strikes of the judge's gavel is not but is said to, in some ceremonial traditions, symbolize the three nails used for the crucifixion.

https://www.youtube.com/watch?v=BvfVR9E6KVA

http://www.secretsocietieswebsite.com/masonic-rituals-initiation-entered-apprentice/

22. Illuminati & Tarot. The belief in Tarot's divinatory meanings was developed widely in the 18th century by protestant preachers and the Masons. The themes and imagery are essentially linked with Illuminati symbolism and elements of the Ancient Mystery School Religion; the tower, the pillars Jachim and Boaz and The Magician. As contemporary philosopher and Tarot historian Michael Dummet notes 'it was only in the 1780's when the practice of fortune telling with regular playing cards had been well established for at least two decades, that anyone began to use the tarot pack for cartomancy' (fortune telling).

https://www.youtube.com/watch?v=iqQ7X3iygSM

https://www.free-tarot-reading.net/free

23. Secret Society Handshakes. Secret societies have always used clandestine messaging systems for a variety of reasons: not least signalling for help and obviously to check so see whether strangers are possible initiates. There are no end of complex hand movements within this article for EBook readers. Perhaps the most well known secret hand signal is 'the hidden hand' present in photographs and portraits from Napoleon to Stalin and Marx to Churchill.

http://www.ephesians5-11.org/handshakes.htm

24. Quadre Bow. Amazingly, some original sketches of the quadre bow came with this manuscript, some more finished than others, which I believe must have been drawn by S. Drechsler and can be viewed here by E Book readers.

http://illuminatihunter.com/images/crossbow.jpg

25. Weishaupt Illuminati Apologist Writings in Exile. After succesfully escaping the autorities in Bavaria Adam Weishaupt continued to write when in exile and continued to defend the actions of the Illuminati. He wrote several major pieces during this period, including: *A complete History of the Persecutions of the Illuminati in Bavaria* (1785) *A Picture of Illuminism* (1786) *An Apology for the Illuminati* (1786) and *An Improved System of Illuminism* (1787).

https://en.wikipedia.org/wiki/Adam_Weishaupt#Activities_in_exile

26. The Founding Fathers & The Illuminati. Speculation has always existed of a connection between the Bavarian Illuminati and the fledgling Republic of the United States. Thomas Jefferson wrote in defence of Weishaupt when he was Ambassador to France living in Paris around this time and described him as an 'eager philanthropist.' Jefferson was not without other scandals and rumoured to have had an long-term affair with his slave girl Sally Hemmings. Washington did occasionally publicly criticise the Illuminati though this created more conspiracy theories than it quelled, some of which even claimed that Weishaupt replaced Washington as the gentlemen shared a passing resemblance. Speculation aside it is interesting that S. Drechsler recalls Jefferson saying that he 'prospects to do even better in the future' and he became president fourteen years later.

https://historycollection.com/conspiracy-theories-about-our-founding-fathers/

https://en.wikipedia.org/wiki/Thomas_Jefferson

27. Bavarian Illuminati & Jakob Frank. Jakob Frank was a religious leader and mystic who frequented the Royal Courts of Europe and claimed to be the reincarnation of the self-proclaimed Messiah Sabbati Tvzi 1626-1676. The Polish religious authorities excommunicated Frank because his many transgressions, which were reputed to have included; incest, rape and murder - his form of worship involving neo-carpocratian 'redemption through sin' or purification through transgression - were too much even set against the standards of behaviour tolerated in the church in those days. His connections to the Illuminati were never proven.

https://en.wikipedia.org/wiki/Jacob_Frank

28. The Statue of Baphomet. Hyman Isaac Long was an American physician who emigrated from Jamaica to New York where he was influential in the development of Masonic organisations and also further afield in Virginia and South Carolina. In 1805, when he was travelling in Europe, border guards found a Statue of Baphomet in his luggage and the story caused so much international furore that eventually Long was summoned by the Pope to the Vatican to explain. Effigies of this winged androgynous occult figure are now usually derived from Eliphas Levi's drawings (Circa 1856) and are seated and usually cast in Bronze. The character has enjoyed a recent surge in popularity. In 2015 The Satanic Temple organisation commissioned a bronze that was subsequently displayed at the Arkansas and Oklahoma state buildings in protest at the erection of a Ten Commandments Monument. After the Ten Commandments Monument was shelved, the Satanic Temple successfully sued Netflix for using the character in the TV show: *The Chilling Adventurers of Sabrina.*

https://www.youtube.com/watch?v=NrnW6-pjQa0

https://en.wikipedia.org/wiki/Hyman_Isaac_Long

https://en.wikipedia.org/wiki/Statue_of_Baphomet

https://en.wikipedia.org/wiki/%C3%89liphas_L%C3%A9vi

29. Sandersdorf Castle Police Raid. The raid on Count Bassus' castle in Sandersdorf Bavaria by the authorities on May 12th 1787 was the last and most high profile incident involving the Illuminati during their short history and marked the final end for the organisation in the country. There are no records of arrests, possibly to avoid a diplomatic incident, though a large haul of incriminating literature, secret documents, membership rosters, stolen seals, code books, accounts and other recorded evidence was definitely seized and can still be viewed today. After the affair Count Bassus suffered a fall from grace of epic proportions and, though the castle was eventually returned to him after being confiscated by the authorities for this, and other 'unpatriotic' crimes, he ended up loosing much of his lands in Poschiavo over the following years as well as his family's dwindling fortune and lived the rest of his life in obscurity as a social outcast.

https://en.wikipedia.org/wiki/Sandersdorf_Castle

https://blakalade.wordpress.com/2013/03/31/initial-membership-list-of-the-bavarian-illuminati/

30. **Sabbati Tvzi Dark Cults.** Strangely little is popularly known about this extremely important 17th century character. At his height Sabbati Tvzi had up to a million followers, unheard of in those days and the cleric appointed himself the messiah on the 18th June 1666 – a lot of sixes. Finally his luck ran out in Turkey when he was caught by the local sultan who commanded him to take back his messianic claim or be tortured to Death whereupon Sabbati promptly converted to Islam and his adoption of the religion is thought to be the progenitor of the Young Turk movement responsible for the Armenian genocide in 1919.

https://www.youtube.com/watch?v=MogAlpPCJ6E

https://en.wikipedia.org/wiki/Sabbatai_Zevi

31. **U.S. President John F. Kennedy's 1963 'The Secret Societie Speech.'** Coincidently, on April 27th 1963 President John F. Kennedy made a famously revealing speech to the American Newspaper Press Association which strangely echoes a similar sentiment to that recollected by S. Drechsler and is available for E Book readers by clicking the links.

https://www.youtube.com/watch?v=FnkdfFAqsHA

https://www.youtube.com/watch?v=tTorn43gClo

32. **Illuminati Agent Canon Jakob Danzer.** Jakob Danzer (1743-1796) was a catholic moral theologian. The farmer's son became lecturer on pastoral theology at Salzburg University in 1785 where he wrote '*Guide to Christian Morality*'. It is unknown when he joined the Illuminati though he was definitely a member as all researched membership rosters record and was formerly removed from his educational posts when his membership was discovered.

http://www.biblebelievers.org.au/illumnas.htm

https://de.wikipedia.org/wiki/Jakob_Danzer

33. **Duke of Bavaria. The Third and Final Edict Against the Illuminati.** S. Drechsler accurately records this event as the Bavarian authorities ratified the third and final edict against the Illuminati on August 16th 1787 which increased the sentence for membership to the death penalty. Charles Theodore Elector of Bavaria (1724-1799) was considered a staunch patriot and, even after the Illuminati scare, continued a merciless persecution of secret societies until his death.

https://www.nationalgeographic.com/history/history-magazine/article/profile-adam-weishaupt-illuminati-secret-society

https://en.wikipedia.org/wiki/Charles_Theodore,_Elector_of_Bavaria

34. **Illuminati Hunter: The Trilogy.** Aside from the mysterious aspects of S. Drechsler's account there are also several idiosyncrasies of his texts which remain unanswered, the main one being the numbers of chapters. There are thirty three in Illuminati Hunter 1 'Adam Weishaupt and the Eye of Horus' and Illuminati Hunter II 'Merchant Kolmer and The Obelisk of Nempty' which, especially in light of the subject matter, seems an unlikely coincidence whereas this, the last in the trilogy,

possesses thirty four making the grand total one hundred (10(0) being God) instead of the Hermetical opposite ninety nine or 3 x 33 = 99 9 + 9 = 18, 1 + 8 = 9 when 9 symoblises 'Fallen' or the Devil. I have not altered the number of position of the chapter breaks in these original notes and, after much speculation I am convinced that S. Drechsler was trying to communicate a positive coded message by this Gematric use of numbers. Though, now that I have explained my own thoughts on this matter, I will let you assume your own. Another aspect which has come to my attention whilst preparing the three books for release is that, in the end, with the first being about Horus the Son, the second's concentration on Sirius the Mother and this, the third, with its focus on fatherhood, the trilogy represents the family trinity, also mentioned in the Winter Triangle. Maybe this is simply another coincidence about which I will let you, the reader, come to your own conclusions. When attempting to decide whether the Illuminati still exists, again you will have to draw your own conclusions. Notably, Weishaupt said, after the ousting of the organisation from Bavaria, 'The great care of the Illuminati after the publication of their secret writings was to persuade the whole of Germany that their Order no longer existed, that their adepts had all renounced, not only their mysteries, but as members of a secret society.'

http://illuminatihunter.com/

BV - #0012 - 121021 - C0 - 178/108/16 - PB - 9781914195808 - Gloss Lamination